FROM BERBER STATE TO MOROCCAN EMPIRE

The Glory of Fez Under the Marīnids

FROM BERBER STATE TO MOROCCAN EMPIRE

The Glory of Fez Under the Marīnids

MAYA SHATZMILLER

Markus Wiener Publishers
Princeton

Updated edition, third printing, 2019

For information write to: Markus Wiener Publishers
231 Nassau Street, Princeton, NJ 08542
www.markuswiener.com

Library of Congress Cataloging-in-Publication Data

Names: Shatzmiller, Maya, author.
Title: From Berber state to Moroccan empire : the glory of Fez under the Marīnids / Maya Shatzmiller.
Other titles: Berbers and the Islamic state
Description: Updated and expanded second edition. | Princeton, NJ : Markus Wiener Publishers, [2019] | Includes bibliographical references and index. | Summary: "Medieval Fez was a main center of education, art, and commerce from the 13th to the 16th centuries after the Berber tribe of the Marinids seized power in Morocco and moved the capital from Marrakesh to Fez. As non-Arabs they gained legitimacy by founding medresas, religious universities. They also supported the arts and commerce, and expanded their state into an empire. It was the Golden Age of Fez. Maya Shatzmiller draws a historical panorama of this era, highlighting its movers and shakers in locations from North Africa to the Mediterranean world"— Provided by publisher.
Identifiers: LCCN 2019030804 | ISBN 9781558769519 (paperback) | ISBN 9781558769052 (hardcover)
Subjects: LCSH: Beni Marin dynasty—History. | Berbers—Morocco—History. | Morocco—History—-647-1516.
Classification: LCC DT313 .S33 2019 | DDC 964.023—dc23
LC record available at https://lccn.loc.gov/2019030804

Markus Wiener Publishers books are printed in the United States of America on acid-free paper, and meet the guidelines for permanence and durability of the Committee on Production Guidelines for Book Longevity of the Council on Library Resources.

Contents

Acknowledgements

The thought to put my work on the Berbers and the Islamic State in book form came in the aftermath to conversations I had with Professor Peter Brown on the nature of North African history, during my stay in Princeton as a Davis Centre Fellow. The reflections he offered on shared historical and historiographical concerns led me to believe that the issues I had studied as isolated topics in the context of the Maghrebi medieval history were relevant as a whole, both to the particular and the general debate. As a Fellow of the Shelby Cullom Davis Centre for Historical Research at Princeton University, 1995-1996, I also had the good fortune to benefit from discussions with colleagues and students there, who were interested in my work, and to use the holdings of the Firestone Library on the subject. Markus Wiener of Princeton kindly offered to publish the book, and guided me through the process of putting it together. My students and research assistants at the University of Western Ontario, Craig Bell, Mark Laidman and Shondra Shahin, supplied bibliographical needs and generated graphs and tables and proof reading. Steve Rumas of Western's Social Science Computer Lab helped carrying out the technical tasks. Wendy Bichard of the History Department provided final draft with great proficiency. Susan Merskey of London, Ontario, edited the text with her usual enthusiasm and skills. I am deeply grateful to all of them.

Some of the studies in this volume were written over a period of 15 years and have been published previously, others are new. The majority were initially written in French, but the issues they dealt with continue to generate studies and publications by French, Spanish, British, American and Moroccan scholars. Given the general nature of the material currently available, my main concern in making these studies available in English is to facilitate access to them for students of North African history, and of the medieval period in particular. All the studies have been throughly revised and re-written and I have incorporated the relevant new material and discussed and made revisions where necessary. Finally, I wish to thank the respective periodicals for giving permission to publish here new versions of articles which they had originally published.

Abbreviations

Bayān al-Mughrib = Ibn ʿIdhārī, *al-Bayān al-Mughrib*, part 3, ed. A. Huici Miranda (Tetuan, 1963).

Beni ʿAbd el-Wād = Aboū Zakarya Yaḥiā Ibn Khaldoun, *Histoire des Beni Abd el-Wad*, rois de Tlemcen, éd. et tr. Alfred Bel (Alger, 1903-1911), 2 vol.

Dhakhīra = *Al-Dhakhīra al-Saniyya* (le trésor magnifique), éd. Mohammed ben Cheneb, Publ. de la Faculté des Lettres d'Alger, t. LVII (Alger, 1921).

Histoire des Berbères = ʿAbd al-Raḥman Ibn Khaldūn, *Histoire des Berbères*, tr. M. Baron de Slane (Alger, 1852-1856). Nouvelle édition publiée sous la direction de Paul Casanova (Paris, 1925-1956), 4 vol.

L'historiographie mérinide = Maya Shatzmiller, *L'historiographie Mérinide. Ibn Khaldūn et ses contemporains* (Leiden, 1982).

Kitāb al-ansāb = Manuscript K1275 Bibliothèque Générale, Rabat.

Masālik al-abṣār = Ibn Fadl Allah al-ʿOmarī, *Masālik al-abṣār fī mamālik al-amṣār,* tr. Gaudefroy-Demombynes (Paris, 1927).

Miʿyār = Ahmad b. Yaḥyā Al-Wansharīsī, *Al-Miʿyār al-muʿrib wa'l-jāmiʿ al-mughrib ʿan fatāwī ʿulamā' ifrīqiya wa'l-Andalus wa'l-Maghrib,* ed. Muḥammad Ḥajjī (Beirut), 13 vol.

Musnad = Muḥammad b. Marzūq al-Tilimsānī, *al-Musnad al-ṣaḥīh al-ḥasan fī mā'athir wa-maḥāsin mawlānā abī 'l-Ḥasan*, ed. María J. Viguera (Alger, 1981), *El Musnad: hechos memorables de Abū l'ḥasan, sultan de los Benimerines*, tr. María J. Viguera (Madrid, 1977).

Qirṭās = Ibn Abī Zarʿ, *Rawḍ al-Qirtās*, ed. C. J. Tornberg (Upsala, 1843).

Rawḍat al-Nisrīn = Ibn al-Aḥmar, *Rawḍat en-Nisrīn,* éd. et tr. annotée par G. Bouali et G. Marçais (Paris, 1917).

Tres textos = *Tres textos Árabes sobre Beréberes en el Occidente Islámico*, ed. and study, Muḥammad Yaʿlà, Fuentes Arábico-Hispanas, 20 (Madrid, 1996).

Zahra = Al-Jaznā'ī, *Zahrat al-ās*, éd. et tr. annotée Alfred Bel (Alger, 1923).

Illustrations

Photos are reproduced courtesy of the Detroit Institute of Arts.

Cover: The gate to the Marīnid necropolis in Salé completed in 1339. Photo: Rod Davis.

Chapter 1. A page from the *Kitāb al-ansāb*, Mss. Rabat K1275 written in 1312.

Chapter 2. A page from an *Almohad Qur'ān*, 12th-13th centuries. Vellum, ink, opaque, 27.2x26.5. Picture courtesy of the Detroit Museum of Arts. Accession no. 1993.70

Chapter 3. A luster-painted Brasero bowl, late 15th-century Granada. Copper Lustre. Picture courtesy of the Detroit Museum of Arts. Accession no. 63.21

Chapter 4. Amulet in gold and cloisonné, 13th-14th centuries, Muslim Spain. Picture courtesy of the Walters Art Gallery, Inventory no. 44.151.I.T.93.

Chapter 5. The *al-Qarawiyyin* Mosque in Fez.

Chapter 6. Three double gold Marīnid dinars struck by the Sultan Abū ʿInān in Bijāya, Tilimsān and Sijilmāsa, claiming the title *Commander of the Believers, amīr al-mu'minīn.* Picture courtesy of the British Museum, BMC 186, 187, 193, c49a.22.

Chapter 7. The *Medresa al-ʿAṭṭārīn* in Fez built by the Sultan Abū 'l-asan while still a Crown Prince, circa. 1321.

Chapter 8. A Berber rug from the High Atlas mountains. 1.31x1.32. Picture courtesy of the Textile Museum, Washington DC.

Chapter 9. The *Medresa Bū ʿInāniyya* in Fez built by the Marīnid Sultan Abū ʿInān in 1350-1355.

Preface to the Second Edition

Since the book first appeared there has been more interest among medieval and pre-modern historians in North Africa and in Morocco. As the 1200 anniversary of the foundation of the city of Fez was celebrated in 2008, academic interest in the historical role of the Atlantic Empires, also emphasised the position of Morocco and ties to the Medieval Mediterranean. It was between the eleventh and the sixteenth century, during the latter half of the medieval period, that the country burst into the international scene, with multiple associations with Black Africa, North Africa, Southern Europe and the Middle East. For one long historical moment Morocco's trajectory placed it at the center of world order.

The questions at the center of the book, that of the Berbers' identity and their relations as individuals and groups with an Islamic state and its Arab culture, is not unique to Morocco, nor has it been the reserve of Moroccan Berbers. The Berbers, native population of North Africa, have long struggled with questions of identity in the historical Maghreb, but under the Marīnids and linked to the structural changes in Morocco, they were forcefully articulated and come to the foreground. North African Berbers resisted their conquerors and settlers to various degrees throughout history but have also absorbed elements of their new civilizations. Late Antiquity and Christianity exercised deeper impact in Eastern North Africa epitomised by St. Augustine of Hippo, than it did in the West in Morocco. It may explain the long protracted Arab conquest of North Africa that extended over the seventh and eighth centuries. Halted by the Berbers resistance, reportedly with affinities, even conversion to Judaism, under a legendary matriarch leader, the *Kahina*. Morocco provided the Berber troops who proceeded to conquer Spain, even before North Africa itself was pacified, and settled.

In early medieval Morocco, placed as it was at the edge of the Islamic Empire, acculturation was a lengthy process. The Arab conquerors themselves, always a minority, provided only a thin layer of cultural and religious agents of Arabization and Islamization to the population. Berber identity was reinforced by the new language, culture, institutions before it was challenged by them. As Arabization and Islamization deepened, local content could be expressed by the newly gained literary tools. As in Muslim Iberia, Islamic religious, economic, political institutions borrowed from the Arab Islamic East took two hundred years to take root in North Africa. Only later can they absorb and accommodate a blended unique political and institutional model.

Yet, in Morocco there were other factors as well. As underlined in the last and new chapter of the book, the Moroccan state has undergone a conversion that saw the country transformed from a small regional and decentralized state under Idrisid or Fatimid rule, into a continental Empire beginning in the eleventh century. While in the ninth and tenth centuries state power was limited to the areas neighbouring the capital Fez, the next three dynasties to rule Morocco, Almoravids, Almohads and Marīnids, transformed the country into an international powerhouse to be reckoned with. The Berbers were at the center of the structural changes that enabled the process. It began with a demographic surge that revamped and increased population levels, proceeding with renovation of religious institutions, bonding them to the ruling dynasty and enabling resurgence of the economy buoyed by the benefits from the gold trade. The customary Islamic institutions were re-examined and re-built to become more inclusive. The new geographical borders were stretched to include and incorporate tracts of Black West Africa, the neighbouring Islamic states of Eastern North Africa, and what was left of Islamic Iberia. Urbanization deepened and new cities were built. Central administrations developed and became more sophisticated.

With the arrival to power of the new Marīnid dynasty in 1250, Marrakesh, the capital of the last two hundred years, was abandoned. Situated closer to the desert environment of the Sanhāja and Masmūda tribes, supporters of the Almoravid and Almohad dynasties it was too remote from the homeland of the Zanata tribes closer to the Mediterranean. It was rightly decided that the control of the gold routes leading from Western Africa to Mediterranean Europe could still be maintained, while the rich ports of the Mediterranean deserved more attention. The dream of an empire was revived, realized and implemented with Fez adorned with new monuments as befitting an Empire's capital. Within one hundred years, the new dynasty and the country embraced their new role as North Africa's new leaders. Conquests were expanded all the way to Libya, and the Marīnid court intervened in the politics of neighbouring Europe, the Middle East and the Mediterranean. It engaged in world diplomacy, extending protection to Christians, including their own mercenaries, and patronized religious establishments in faraway lands.

These structural changes in state institutions, religious, political and economic, evolved side by side with the idea of national identity and supported its formation. The Almoravid and the Almohad states were more 'Berberized' in the sense that the administration, civil and religious, accommodated Berber language and institutions. The policies of integrating Berber speaking religious and military elites into the state's institutions, began under their rule only to be accomplished and completed under the Marīnids. What was unique now were the cultural institutions, part of the structural change in the Islamic West, that enabled Berber expression. The great minds of Islamic thought, including Ibn Khaldūn, moving in and out of Fez, bear testimony through their writings to the intensity of intellectual life there. There is no surprise that in the process of forging national identity in Morocco, the old question of the Berbers' place in it, would re-emerge. Society and state appeared to have been readied for the Berber challenge by their achievements. The trajectory of the Marīnid state is fascinating precisely because it embodies a change in an African Atlantic shore state within a unique global setting.

Introduction

There is no better way to introduce the two historical paradigms central to this book, the Berbers and the Islamic State, than by quoting from a letter to the editor which appeared in the *Times Literary Supplement*. In it Tariq Ismail protested against the depicting of the Algerian poet Kateb Yacine (1929-1989), as a "Muslim poet":

> How ironic that Yacine should have had that label attached to him, when all his intellectual life was spent in fighting the cultural imperialism of Islam and Arabic, always defending the culture and language of his Berber ancestors. He had a deep hatred of Islam, which he considered "profoundly evil".[1]

The letter was intended to remind the literary world that the poet, Kateb Yacine, one of North Africa's distinguished sons, was engaged in more than just a literary battle. In fact, only shortly before his death, Kateb Yacine reiterated his view of the political and cultural struggle of the Berbers, in a preface to a book on the Berber question in Algeria, published in Quebec:

> They want to depict us as a minority isolated within an Arab people, when in fact it is the Arabs who are a minute minority within us, but they dominate us through religion...We are a majority which quickly becomes aware now of the Arab-Islamic affliction throughout the world, in Palestine, Iraq, Iran, wherever the people are alienated, betrayed, drowned in blood in the name of race and religion. Just imagine how a huge transmitter in *Tamaziyt* (the name of the Berber language), transmitting to the peasants in the Moroccan Rif, who do not speak any other language, will change things in North Africa. Right now there is no dialogue with the Moroccan people, there are only two States which fight each other, but the people is us, not the State.[2] It is the language which is the vehicle of history...we are lost in our history.[3]

In this moving and passionate remonstrance Kateb Yacine defined the three components of the Berber question in his country as he saw it: it is historical and not only contemporary, it is neither ideological, nor religious, and the State is responsible for its existence. In other words, while admitting that in this instance war against the Berbers was waged under the banner of a new ideology, that of Islam's, Arab's or State's Nationalism, for him the formation of Berber identity was not a product of antagonism to any particular movement, whether French colonialism, Arab nationalism, or Islamic fundamentalism, but a module of the historical nature of North Africa. Only Berber society and Berber culture's definitions vis à vis Arab culture and Islamic history would prevent the "disappearance of the Berbers from their own history", which had been their lot until now. He equated the Arab-Islamic invasion with the Roman-Christian one and, as he saw it, the match was always the same; only the names of the players, religions and cultures have changed.[4] The State, not particularly Islamic or Christian, was the tool of this form of oppression, which enforced cultural hegemony through political coercion. Kateb Yacine himself was a prototype and product of the process: like many French speaking Kabyle Berbers, he was known and always identified himself by a name which carried Arab and Islamic connotations, but chose to write in the language of the colonizers.[5]

The cultural oppression of the state, which Kateb Yacine denounced with poetic eloquence, was articulated by classical historians in scholarly terms. The forced acculturation of the Berbers was for them a historical structure, one that had lasted the thousand "Braudelian" years, and the reaction to it remained an integral part of North African history for the span of numerous colonizations.[6] Marcel Bénabou, Peter Brown, W. H. C. Frend, Margurite Rachet, all agreed that the term 'resistance' was best suited for depicting the relationships of North Africa with Roman civilization, "because it expressed different manifestations of 'African particularism'."[7] Things did not change with the advent of Christianity in North Africa. 'African particularism' could be detected behind Donatism, the religious schism within the Catholic Church in North Africa, in the fourth century. What began as a theological disputation grew into a 'nucleus of social and political discontent' that could be interpreted by historians as a 'movement of protest in Roman Africa' and 'part of an impressive continuum of Berber history'.[8] In this case, as in the case of Kateb Yacine, the Berbers articulated expressions of 'secular grievance', using tools which they acquired by acculturation itself.[9] Thus resistance to the acculturation to Roman civilization was expressed by using Roman art and Christian religious symbols.

The Arab conquest of North Africa in the 8th century gave birth to a new political body on the Western Mediterranean shores, a Berber-Islamic state. Recognized by the idiosyncrasies of its state building process, this body, which continued to evolve throughout the entire medieval period, achieved viability, coherence and stability by implementing Islamic norms of community and statehood, identity and institutions.[10] The process was not a peaceful one, however. Friction between the conquerors and conquered found expression in movements, such as the *Ibāḍiyya* in 8th century Ifrīqiya or the *Bargawāṭiyya* in 10th century Morocco, which challenged the religion with sectarianism and the political dominance of the East with the creation of independent states. The rise of the great Berber dynasties to political hegemony, beginning with the Almoravids in the 11th century, and continuing with the Almohads in the 12th and the Marīnids in the 13th, enhanced the development of the Berber-Islamic state, but also witnessed Berber alienation expressed by resistance to acculturation to Arabic and Islamic norms. The drive to bring the Berber populace into the mainstream of Islamic statehood, through intensified islamization, indoctrination in Islamic theology and expansion of the judicial system, deepened the awareness of Berber particularism, and refined and defined its expression vis-à-vis the Islamic state and its institutions.

The Banū Marīn, or the Marīnids, were a confederation of Zanāta Berber tribes, partly nomads and partly settled in the areas of Northern and Western North Africa. Not a particular homogenous group, they managed to topple the Almohads and create a stable, even imperial state in Morocco and parts of eastern North Africa in the 13th-15th centuries, the third and last of the great Berber dynasties to rule Morocco. Invigorated by economic resurgence due to European demand for its abundant African gold, trade with Catalan, French and Italian cities, large manpower reserves and strong urban development, the Marīnid state attained political dominance in the Islamic west. The large, well trained and adequately equipped army, carried the Moroccan military machine in incursions into Spain and North Africa, and managed recurring moments of Marīnid hegemony over the entire Maghreb. Marīnid society equally became more complex and sophisticated than ever before. It was enriched by offering a sanctuary to fleeing Andalusians, hosting some of the fine and innovative minds of the period, among them Ibn Khaldūn, Ibn al-Khaṭīb and Ibn Marzūq.[11] It was a heterogenous and individualistic society, with a deeply mystical religious streak to it, yet no stranger to philosophy and ancient sciences. The great number of autobiographies written by contemporaries, *fahāris, mashā'ikh, barnamaj*, attest to a greater sense of the self, expressed by accounts of personal encounters, tales about teachers, lectures and tête-à-têtes.[12] These changes in society, especially the rise of individualism, accelerated and heightened the antagonism with the Islamic state. The story told here is that of the acculturation and alienation of the Berbers to the Islamic state under the Marīnids.

The book's first part, '*The Berbers' search for their place in Islamic history*', looks at the turbulent process of acculturation. Resistance was expressed from within the mainstream of Maghrebi Islam and used legitimate Islamic symbols, idioms and tools to deconstruct and reconstruct the official history of their conversion.[13] The Berbers' attempts to conform to Islamic norms were in conflict with their identity and self respect because of this history; they did not openly contest the image inflicted on them, but expressed their resistance to it by writing a new history of their conversion to Islam. Once more, resistance to Islamic norms could only be articulated through Islamic and Arabic mediums. In cultivating a myth of Arab origin and praise of the Berber race, Berber genealogists and historians could use them as legitimacy tools. The role played by the Andalusi Berbers in this process is given here its legitimate and weighty place.[14]

The strength of the Marīnid state is the second premise which underlies this book, and the focus of the second and third parts. Anthropologists like to paint a picture of a weak Maghrebi Islamic state, an outcome of the inherently fragile predicament of Maghrebi society. They propose a model of primitive and crude process of state formation, inspired by their observations of nomadic state building process in the Maghreb today. The view of a permanent 'statelessness' and deficient society resulted from assumed native destructive social patterns of nomadism and Oriental religion, namely Islam.[15] Others preferred to see in it the likeness of the state building process in poor, third world countries.[16] The medieval chroniclers, in particular Ibn Khaldūn, have also contributed to the creation of the deficiency model by pointing to Islam as the only factor which could have held the Berbers together and provide the only justification for the rise and fall of political units. Such reasoning inspired disparaging views of the Maghrebi state, and distorted the historical evidence provided by Ibn Khaldūn in the *Kitāb al-ʿibar* and the *Muqaddima*.[17] Historians, however, see a different picture and the vision of the perpetual state of chaos in North Africa found its strongest opponents among followers of Braudel's *longue durée* historical concept. According to them between the 2nd and 13th centuries there was an uninterrupted urban settlement in North Africa, and permanence of division of labour, production and elites in the cities.[18]

In the second part of this book, '*Devising an Islamic state*', the process of the Marīnid state formation and the development of its Islamic institutions, are dealt with. The Marīnids wanted to build an Islamic state, inspired by Islamic norms, run by experienced Muslims. This was not easy, however. Like the Almohads before them, the Marīnids used Islam as a tool in consensus building and unification of the tribal body by setting religious goals, and, like them, proceeded by staffing Islamic institutions with Berber speakers, defending the legitimacy of the Berber language and legitimizing the Berber speaking population in a religious context. Tensions between the central government and the quasi-autonomous towns, with their Arabized elites, forced them to bring new elements into the political and bureaucratic system, and to staff Islamic institutions not only with Berbers but the occasional *dhimmis*, coercing, manipulating, controlling, and counterbalancing their influence where and when they could.

It was not a detached and mystical religiosity which empowered the state, but the Islamic institutions. Social, religious and economic institutions survived the rise and fall of dynasties and preserved the cohesiveness of the community and gave it stability, order and endurance. The best demonstration of the strength of the Islamic institutions is their longevity and their survival in post-conquest situations, long after the Islamic state was gone, as was the case in the Crusaders and Spanish Reconquista's administrations.[19] In other instances military-cum-ideological institutions, such as the Ottoman *ghazā'*, which raised the raiding of non-Muslims to a way of life, gave power and endurance to the formation of the Ottoman state, carrying it forward for hundreds of years.[20] Institutionalized clergy efficiently regulated the relationship with the political institutions in modern Morocco.[21] The third part, '*Implementing Islamic Institutions*', aims to study the strength and power of the Islamic institutions under the Marīnids.

It analyses the evolution of three, one cultural, the religious college, *medresa*, and two social and economic ones, the *waqf*, the endowment for the public good, and the Islamic state's domain. In their Marīnid incarnation, all were responsible with varying degrees of success, for streamlining and organizing the lives of the subjects of the Islamic state, as the Marīnids were quick to realize. They repeatedly used institutional strategies, such as the introduction of colleges to train Berber speaking jurists, to wrest control from the institutional scholars, the *ʿulamāʾ*, over matters of religious legitimacy, policy and jurisprudence.

The sources used here for the study of the individual and group malaise, are in themselves and by themselves pieces of the puzzle. Language was a central issue for the Berber-Islamic state. The Almohads acknowledged the legitimacy of the Berber language by permitting its use in religious books and public Islamic ceremonies, as they did by incorporating Berber institutions into the Islamic state, thus recognizing their importance for the relationship with the Berbers.[22] But expression of resistance used the Arabic, as could be seen in manuscript Rabat K1275, to which I have referred throughout as *Kitab al-ansāb,* a response to acculturation in a new era dominated by Berber dynasties. The circumstances surrounding the compilation of this important text are still obscure, but its recent publication as three distinct texts does not obfuscate its message. Ibn Marzūq's *Musnad* is a unique account of survival when his previous world, destroyed by the Marīnid state's military prowess, was held together by the strength of the Islamic institutions which offered him a new chance. Ibn Khaldūn's chronicle *Kitāb al-ʿibar*, remains the important and detailed source of information on the medieval history of the Maghreb we have always held it to be, but its importance goes beyond sheer historical information. Ibn Khaldūn's resolution to make Berber dynasties the core of his great political history of the Maghreb is a lasting testimony to his recognition of a Berber identity within the Islamic framework, with its own society and institutions, a belief he shared with other North African and Andalusian historians.[23] Written for a historically minded society, which began experimenting with the national and local historiography, his concept of Berber centred history is the best embodiment of the history of the Maghreb as a history of the Berbers.

All in all, the view offered here of the Berbers' existence within the Islamic state's framework of the medieval Maghreb, is a new, yet not unfamiliar one, of what is unique about North African history. This book studies how the Berbers participated in the process of the state's formation in the medieval Maghreb, while at the same time resisting uniformity and conformity to cultural norms and institutions, through which acculturation was enforced. It relates this story in terms of interaction and resistance, creativity and digression, evolution and disruption, a continuous process of negotiation between the individual and society over identity and state's power. It is not only the story of what happened to an ethnic identity, expressed in particularities such as local origins, language, social structures, but also, as was the case with other ethnic group, to whom Kateb Yacine alluded, Persians, Turks, Indians, what happened to their essential characteristics with the advent of the new religion and the new state.

Historians were sceptical about whether independent Berber cultural and intellectual activity could have existed, and some even rejected the likelihood of ever finding out, even though it was spanning a long chronological period and a unique thematic journey.[24] It is easy, though, to see why a Berber contribution to the Islamic legacy was not recognized, even rejected. Since the Berbers had no written language of their own and did not leave proper literary documentation behind, it was assumed that if they made any contribution at all, it was not as Berbers, but within an Arab and Islamic cultural framework, or that they were absorbed into Arab society and culture, and participated in the high culture. Yet, historians are willing to recognize that the heretical movements which appeared in medieval North Africa represented a form of resistance to Islamic and Arabic acculturation, even though they were using symbols taken from this culture to express it. More importantly, there is a reasonable amount of evidence to challenge the view that no independent Berber intellectual and literary activity existed, and to substantiate expressions of Berber self awareness in the Arab chronicles. They provide us with numerous manifestations of "unofficial" Berber creativity, if only we care to read them correctly. Together these might have been only a few types of response, but they are the ones we can document.

1

THE BERBERS' SEARCH FOR THEIR PLACE IN ISLAMIC HISTORY

CHAPTER 1

An Unknown Source for the History of the Berbers*

A page from the *Kitāb al-ansāb*

The Islamic phase in North Africa's history opened with the Arab conquest in the 7th century, but the Berbers themselves were not immediately aware that they had become a part of this religion's universe. Nor did they learn about the larger political body they had joined after opposition to the conquest and to Islam ended, or even after the first versions of these events were written. When the official account of the history of the conquest of North Africa started circulating, it revealed to the Berbers that they did not succumb to the Arab conquest without a fight and that the initial conquest was followed by a period of Berber resistance both to Islam and to Arab political dominance. That only a series of consecutive military campaigns forced the Berbers to submit to the new religion and the new masters. As the process of Islamization and Arabization proceeded, later generations became acquainted with the historical details of their conversion and were faced with the dilemma which amounted to a conflict between their self respect as individuals and Muslims and their existence within an Islamic nation which was devoted to upholding Islamic values and Arabic culture. Berber intellectuals became more and more uneasy about that story, which was incompatible with the Islamic identity which they were asked, and were eager, to adopt. In the next three chapters we will examine a corpus of medieval chronicles in order to understand the reaction of the Berbers to the story, as well as to other cultural and political developments which inspired their drive to redefine themselves in historical terms, and using historical and historiographical tools such as content, context and structure, to analyze them.

In 1934 Évariste Lévi-Provençal published in Rabat a collection of historical fragments about the noble deeds of the Berbers, entitled *Mafākhir al-Barbar*.[1] In spite of the obvious importance of this collection, there was general ignorance at the time about the origin of the work in question, and its author. It seemed that the only detail which could be established from the

**Arabica*, 31(1983): 73-79.

text, was the date of composition, 712/1312. Twenty years later, in 1954, the same scholar published in *Arabica*, of which he was the founder and first editor, a French translation of what he called, "A new narration of the Conquest of North Africa by the Arabs", taken, he said, from another chronicle which followed the text of the *Mafākhir al-Barbar*, in a manuscript that he privately owned.[2] In 1955 he published a third manuscript, a text of three documents about the adoption of the title *amīr al-Muslimīn* by the Almoravid ruler, Yūsuf b. Tāshūfīn, which, "are found in a recent manuscript which belongs to my private collection."[3] At that point he was still unable to determine the origin of either work, their authors, relations, or the motivation behind their composition.[4] No one suspected a connection between them at the time.

It later appeared that a manuscript which contained all the fragments published by Lévi-Provençal, as well as other fragments arranged in chronological order and dealing with the Berbers, was preserved at the Bibliothèque Générale in Rabat. This manuscript, number K1275, holds 169 folios, 159 of which make up the complete text under discussion, all dealing with the history of the Berbers, from the moment of their conversion to Islam to the year 712/1312. It carries the title *Kitāb al-Ansāb li-Abī Ḥayyān*. A reading of the entire manuscript and the study of its various parts reveals that both the content and context of the compilation are exceptional vis à vis its contemporaries. More importantly, it sheds new light on the history and historiography of the Berbers.

Manuscript K1275, is a *majmūʿa*, a compilation of previously written texts, divided into three parts, each apparently an independent work, each containing an unequal number of fragments, and each having a slightly different objective while maintaining the Berbers' history as its focus.[5] The first part begins with an introduction, where the purpose and the sources of the work are laid down:

> We begin, God willing, our discourse on the genealogy of the inhabitants of the Maghreb and their history by referring to Adam and Noah, since they were the origin of all human beings. After alluding to them, we shall mention Abraham, because he is at the origin of many prophets. Then Moses and David, since they led many people out from Syria and into the Maghreb...I have written this text based on history books on one hand, and oral legacy of men, on the other, may God forgive them.[6]

The chapters in the first part are arranged in the following manner:

1. Fragments dealing with biblical characters, especially Noah and his son Ḥam, named the father of the Berbers.

2. "*Intimation of the first inhabitants of the Maghreb*", a fragment from al-Bakrī's *masālik*.

3. "*Information on the central Maghreb*".

4. "*Information on the genealogy of the first inhabitants of the Maghreb*", dealing with historians' opinions on the origin of the Berbers.

5. "*Information on the inhabitants of the Southern Maghreb,*" providing genealogies of the tribes living in the southern part of the Maghreb.

6. "*The Beginning of the Islamization of the Maghreb*", provides traditions about the enticement of the Berbers toward Islam before the conquest of the Maghreb.

7."*Information on the Maghrebi crowds who came calling on the Prophet.*"

8. "*Information on the central Maghreb and the conquest of the southern Maghreb*". (The two chapters published by Lévi-Provençal under the title, *A New Narration of the Conquest of North Africa by the Arabs*).

9. "*The creation of the land and the climates,*" provides information on the geographical conditions, including details about fixing the direction of the *qibla* in the Maghrebi mosques.[7]

The second part is composed of two large segments.[8] The first is the work published under the title *Mafākhir al-Barbar*. The second, entitled "*The early history of the Berbers and their eminence*", deals with various themes, partly mentioned before, such as the story of a delegation of Berbers who came calling upon the caliph ʿUmar seeking Islam, the campaign of ʿUqba b. Nāfiʿ in the West, the Berber tribes in al-Andalus, (all details included by Lévi-Provençal in the *Mafākhir*) the Arab origin of the mahdi Ibn Tūmart and history of the Idrisids.

The third part is composed of a few segments pertinent to the status of the land in the Maghreb, the *jizya*, head tax, and epistles written by Ibn al-ʿArabī, al-Ghazālī, Yūsuf b. Tāshufīn, al-Jāḥīz and the caliph al-Mustaẓhir.[9] The last cluster of segments deals with Ibn Hūd and the Ṣanhāja Berbers in al-Andalus.

On its own account manuscript K1275 stands out as a curious historical piece. Despite its fragmentary nature the work suggests a homogeneity which could not have been accidental. All the fragments share a thematic unity, since all address a single subject, the Berbers. A second element of unity is provided by the historiographical structure. All three parts are individual *majmūʿas* in themselves, each one a collection of fragments, with segments derived from a given number of sources which are used repeatedly in the different parts. A third element which creates a historical comprehensiveness and unites the parts of the *majmūʿa* is a concern to cover each period in chronological order. A fourth unifying ingredient are the cross-references from one part to another throughout the work.[10] The frequent allusions to ʿUbayd Allāh Ṣāliḥ b. ʿAbd al-Ḥalīm, a traditionist and historian who provided information on many subjects throughout the entire work, adds a fifth element of wholeness.[11] The content and structure of the *majmūʿa* point to an editorial effort by a single person, who remains unnamed throughout the work, but every element in it indicates that the segments were intentionally put together. Could Ibn ʿAbd al-Ḥalīm be the author or the compiler, who took such care to closely check and match its various parts?

Opinions vary about who the author might have been, nor is there any agreement about who put it together. In the newly published edition, Dr. Yaʿla upholds the existence of three separate works and three different authors. According to him two works, the *Kitāb al-Ansāb* written by Ibn ʿAbd al-Ḥalīm and the *Kitāb Mafākhir al-Barbar* by an anonymous author, date from the early 14th century and one, *Kitāb shawāhid al-gilla* by Ibn al-ʿArabī, from the 12th century.[12] M. Bencherifa maintains that the entire work is by ʿAbd al-Ḥalīm,[13] since the name of ʿUbayd Allāh appears continuously throughout the work, as a source of traditions, compiler of *ḥadīths* and a witness to events. E. Lévi-Provençal attributed the text of the *New narration*, to him, "one ʿUbayd Allāh Ṣāliḥ b. ʿAbd al-Ḥalīm," but the text of the *Mafākhir* to Ibn ʿIdhārī.[14] No new external source has come to light to confirm either theory, nor was a direct reference to any of the three works found, and all attributions are still based on the text itself. The only fact we can agree on is that ʿAbd al-Ḥalīm was a contemporary of the writing or compiling, even though he was not necessarily the one who put the whole thing together. On the other hand, the general Andalusi background of the work, including the large number of quotations from works written by Spanish authors, makes it necessary to consider at least, *pro forma*, the possibility that Abū Ḥayyān if he is indeed the one referred to in the title, was, in fact, the author or compiler. Chronologically speaking, Muḥammad b. Yūsuf Athīr al-Dīn Abū Ḥayyān could have been the author or the compiler. A grammarian and traditionist, he was born in Granada in 654/1256, left his home town in 679/1280, and died in Cairo in 745/1344.[15] Himself of Berber origin, he bore the *kunya* al-Nafzī, and centered his intellectual activity on commentary and tradition, and on biographies of famous individuals, their social groups and their history, especially those of the Maghreb.[16] Pons Boigues, the 19th century Spanish scholar, did not include work under the title of *Kitāb al-ansāb* nor *Mafākhir al-barbar,* among his compositions in the entry that he reserved for him in his biographical dictionary, yet the disciplines in which he was interested are those represented in the work. It is not impossible that Abū Ḥayyān compiled the work in the East, but at the present state of our knowledge, it is futile to speculate further without the help of an auxiliary source.

Deprived of the benefit of knowing who the compiler was, and what was his motivation for putting these different sources together, we have to turn to its historiographical modules, its content and subject to provide us with an answer.

There is much to be gained by situating the work within the historiographical context of the time. If, as the chronicler told us, it was compiled in 712/1312 in Morocco, it was done under the Marīnid ruler, Abū Sāʿīd ʿUthmān, 710/1310-731/1331, and should be considered part and parcel of the body of the Marīnid historiography. Yet, some of its attributes do not fit with what we know about other historical works of the time. For instance, there is no direct mention of the Marīnid dynasty in the text itself and the only time their name is mentioned is when ʿUbayd Allāh said in the chapter dealing with the Maghrebi genealogies that he did not see any author (presumably from among the early genealogists) mention the Banū Marīn, except for the author of *Kitāb Rujar*, al-Idrīsī, mentioned earlier in the text, namely in the 12th century.[17] The failure to attach the work to the dynasty is somewhat surprising given that contemporary authors, in particular those who were either attached to the court or hoping to gain access to it, dedicated their works to the Marīnid rulers. Yet, the omission of reference to the

Marīnids, when coupled with the special attention given to the Almohads, indicates that the *majmūʿa* belongs, in spirit as well as in content, to the post or pseudo-Almohad literary movement which continued to flourish in Morocco simultaneously to and alongside the Marīnid centered historiography.[18] It was in fact a separate branch of the historical literature, which included works such as Ibn ʿIdhārī's *Bayān al-Mughrib,* also completed in 712/1312, and the anonymous *al-Ḥulal al-mawshiyya*, written in 786/1384, which were written in the margins of the Marīnid court historiography, probably outside the Marīnid political domain, either in the Moroccan South, or outside Morocco itself. This group of works was distinguished by a continuous interest in the Almohad experience in the Maghrebi and Andalusi history, and by its role as promoters of Berber identity. Our compiler expressed his attachment to the Almohad legacy in several ways: Firstly he devoted a detailed account in the *majmūʿa* to the Almohad dynasty, from the mahdi Ibn Tūmart to the last caliph Abū Debbūs. Secondly, he reviewed the entire historical literature on the Almohads, including the most recent, the *Naẓm al-jumān* by Ibn al-Qaṭṭān composed in the middle of the 13th century.[19] Thirdly, he invoked Berber centered historical works which were written during the Almohad centuries, 12th-13th, providing building blocks for a new history of the Berbers.[20] Even the fact that the identity of the author or compiler remains unknown is a characteristic of the pseudo-Almohad literature. For reasons which we still do not fully comprehend and in great contrast to the Marīnid chronicles, almost all the historians who contributed to the pseudo-Almohad literary wave remain anonymous, whether we refer to Ibn ʿIdhārī or to the author of the *Ḥulal al-mawshiyya.*[21] Like them the author or compiler of the work did not identify himself in the work.[22] The attachment to the Almohad legacy in mid Marīnid dominion is comprehensible only from a point of view of someone who sets out to write the Berbers' history. The Almohads occupy a special place in this history: They were the first to implement Berber institutions in an Islamic garb and match them with a policy of accrediting the Berber language as equal to the Arabic, even in matters of worship. The Almohads appointed to the positions of preaching and leading the prayer, *khiṭāba* and *imāma*, only individuals who could utter their unitarian credo, the *tawḥīd,* in the Berber language. To support this policy, they managed to get a *fatwā* which vouched that anyone who could not speak Arabic could say the prayer in Berber.[23] The "Berber sensitive" policies survived and were maintained after the Almohads were no longer the masters in the Ḥafṣid state in Tunisia,[24] or in Morocco, where the Marīnids continued the practice of recruiting Berber speakers to fulfill clerical functions.[25]

The *majmūʿa* adds another dimension to the study of the Berbers in Maghrebi historiography since it shows that Ibn Khaldūn's *Kitāb al-ʿibar* was not an isolated attempt to create 'ex nihilo' a history of the Berbers, but a continuation of work began by previous authors, who were intrigued and preoccupied by the same questions. In comparison, Ibn Khaldūn's *Kitāb al-ʿibar* is an encyclopedic work which deals with the subject most comprehensively, but which stands nonetheless, on the shoulders of its predecessors with their more modest work. It shows that the *ʿIbar* was not unique, nor the first in its plan to deal with the history of the Berbers in terms of race and dynasty, and that its place is at the end of the process, not at its beginning.[26]

Beyond the historiographical examination, which is revealing in itself and by itself, the message of the work is expressed by the use of three underlying themes, of which only the first is examined in this chapter: a new history of conversion, a myth of Arab origin, and the praise of the Berber race. All were presented in terms and in the form of historical evidence, but the new history of conversion found in the *majmūʿa,* comes in the form of an alternative to the "official" history of the Berbers' conversion to Islam. The information, some as historical accounts, some in the form of *ḥadīth*s, amount to traditions which claim that conversion did not take place during and after the conquest, but prior to it, in a peaceful manner and out of genuine conviction. These *ḥadīth*s about the early conversion of the Berbers to Islam and their attachment to the Prophet, which we find abundantly told in the *Kitāb al-ansāb* were clearly not authentic but locally fabricated and the events described were badly synchronized. The first version deals with chronology:

> ...after the arrival of the Berbers in the Maghreb from Palestine, their leader, Ifriqūsh, built the city of Ifrīqiya and raided the Rūm. His entry into the Maghreb with the Berbers took place about 500 years after the death of Goliath. Since Allāh sent ʿIsa about 1000 years after David, therefore Dhū 'l-Qarnayn was before ʿIsa, and it was he who converted the Maghrebis to Islam.... (aslama ʿalā yadayhi ahl al-Maghreb).[27]

A second version of the conversion story in the *Kitāb al-ansāb* claimed that certain Berber groups arrived at the Prophet's house in Medina, while others addressed his successors, the caliphs ʿUmar and ʿUthmān, requesting to be converted to Islam.[28] A third version claimed that the Berbers' early conversion to Islam came in response to the letter sent by the Prophet, inviting the nations of the world to convert to his new religion.[29] The two latter versions are quoted from Abū Majd al-Maghīlī's *Kitāb Ansāb al-barbar wamulūkihim*.[30] A fourth version reported that conversion took place under ʿUqba b. Nāfiʿ in the most peaceful way: "...ʿUqba reported that when he arrived to the Haskūra land, he invited their chief to accept Islam. They all converted at that point, and there was no war between them...".[31] More versions composed in that vein can also be found in the *Kitāb al-ansāb*.[32] Why would any one want to fabricate such *ḥadīth*s?

To fully appreciate the significance of these *ḥadīth*s we need to accept the premise that they were provided as an answer to the problem the work has come to address, rather then being the problem itself. The problem, a social and intellectual malaise among the Berbers, and dissatisfaction with the place given to them within the Islamic and the Maghrebi history. The reason behind the fabricated *ḥadīth*s was to rewrite the history of the Berbers' conversion to Islam in the 7th century, in such a way that it would remove the stigma which tainted their historical image. The Berbers attempted to alter the story of their conversion to Islam through the manipulation of legendary and mythical information, substituting Arab conquest with a mission to the Prophet in order to create a new, or different, historical identity and to offer an option for another image, different from the one which Arabo-Islamic history gave them. Their identity as Muslims and their newly acquired culture obliged them to adopt the official version as their history, although this presented them as renegades. Arab-Islamic history, as they saw it, promoted and spread a negative image of their race and their historical behavior. The problem was that although this historical episode was forging anti-Berber sentiments, repudiating it meant repudiating Islam, since Islam and the Arabs were inseparable. "We came to you for the love of Islam and in order to convert..." say the Berbers to the caliph ʿUmar in one of these *ḥadīth*s, thus contradicting the official version of how they revolted and reneged several times. It was this intellectual malaise which was the reason behind the preoccupation with different versions of the

Berbers' conversion to Islam, as well as with "new" versions of the story of the conquest of the Maghreb, which Lévi-Provençal accepted as authentic accounts of the conquest, believing that they "were kept and circulated in the mountains of the Neffis".[33]

Like the expressions of 'African particularism' in the classical period, the foregoing information represents a separate "unofficial" history. These themes constitute the Berbers' response to the required acculturation to Islamic and Arab norms, the paradigms to which they had to conform. Together they amount to a conscientious effort to create a new historical identity for the Berbers. It forced them to confront the question of their own identity, and their place in the Islamic history. The antagonism provoked by these paradigms was enhanced by the changes in their environment, whether in their homeland North Africa, or in their adoptive land, Spain. Even though the use of Arabic language and symbols submitted Berber identity further to those of Arabs and Muslims, this was the only way in which the intellectual malaise could be expressed and articulated, by using Arabic language and Islamic identity notions.[34] Why, where and when, this problem came to the surface, what political events precipitated it, who and what helped to foster and encourage it, and by whom it was articulated, are the questions which will occupy us now, as its manifestations, the myth of the Berbers' Arab origin and the praise of the Berber race, will be explored further in the next two chapters.

CHAPTER 2

The Myth of the Berbers' Origin*

A page from an *Almohad Qur'ān*, 12th-13th centuries.

The interest of studying a myth of origin lies initially in the notion that genealogies, a literary genre which retrace the origin of races and families, preserve the traditions about the origin of a nation as it was conceived by the first generations.[1] In the case of the Berbers, however, it was much more complex and historically significant than it had first appeared to be, for in the medieval Maghreb, the myth of Arab origin, together with the new history of conversion and praise of the Berber race, became tools, articulating expressions of both embrace and disapproval of Arab and Islamic norms and cultural perceptions.[2] Contemporary sources, particularly Ibn Khaldūn, corroborate this view. In this chapter we shall reconstruct the history of the Berbers' myth of Arab origin in the medieval Islamic Maghreb, its attributes, what it consisted of, the motives, variations and transformations which occurred in it, its content and context, when and where it appeared for the first time, and why, and what affinities or connections it had to the rise of the Berber dynasties.

Every historian, modern or medieval, who is introduced to the history of North Africa through the work of Ibn Khaldūn quickly learns that the native Berbers claimed to be descended from the same stock as their Arab conquerors. In the *Kitāb al-ʿibar*, Ibn Khaldūn has a long, drawn out discussion of the traditions and historical narrations dealing with this issue, in an effort to distinguish between the false and the true in this matter. He quotes events which had taken place under obscure circumstances, in unnamed lands, and in past centuries, and speaks of legendary ancestors in unknown places; in sum, a myth of origin.[3] After examining this body of evidence, Ibn Khaldūn accepted as authentic the claim of some of the Berber tribes, of the Kutāma and the Ṣanhāja, that they did indeed have Arab ancestors, and condemned the Zanāta tribes for making a false claim to an Arab origin. Moreover, he denounced the motivation behind the latter's assertion, an abhorrence of the Berber race, which they said, was "repugnant and abject." Ibn Khaldūn,

**Revue de l'Occident Musulman et de la Méditerranée*, 35(1983): 145–56.

keen observer of his society that he was, noticed that regardless of whether such claims were historically sound or unsubstantiated, the issue itself, that is, the question of racial origin, went beyond a simple literary motive because it gained actual significance as a political and social factor for contemporaries. Indeed, Ibn Khaldūn's masters, the Marīnid rulers of 14th-century Morocco, who were Zanāta Berbers themselves, were forced to legitimize their rule and had to call upon their court panegyrists to retrieve or establish a myth of origin.

The Arabs were fond of genealogies and quite early used them in different contexts.[4] Classified as a science, *ʿilm al-nasab*, the genre was among the earliest literary expressions cultivated in the Arab-Islamic sphere. Arab genealogists shared the common stock of biblical and classical history, and their genealogies show traits and historiographical and contextual affinities with the Christian and Jewish genealogies, which include a tribe as a home unit, a choice of ancestors amongst the biblical forefathers,[5] and the fabrication of genealogies in order to praise one line above the other. Similarly, Arab genealogies were fabricated in order to safeguard social status and material advantages, to justify the usurpation of power, or to legitimize a political action. The Berbers on the other hand, did not leave a genealogy, oral traditions, neither written texts or any other cultural expressions in the Berber language attesting to the existence of a myth of origin in the Maghreb. Nonetheless, a Berber myth of origin existed well before the Arab chroniclers provided them with one.

For hundreds of years, Greek, Roman, and Byzantine historians had to explain the Berbers' presence in North Africa. They were the ones who established the Berbers' affiliation with Palestine through ancient biblical nations, which would be prominently displayed in the future. In fact the pre-Islamic information about the Palestinian origin of the inhabitants of North Africa dates back not only to Byzantine and Roman traditions but also to the Greeks and Hellenized Jews, who around the year 150 B.C., discussed the question of the migration of Jews to North Africa from the Middle East. According to these authors, the Jews arrived there together with or after the Phoenicians, referred to as Canaanites, who were themselves deported from Palestine by the conqueror Joshua b. Nun.[6] Yohanan Levy traced the elements of this tradition to a compilation entitled *Sefer Yovlim*, composed during the second century B.C.[7] L. Gernet suggested an additional link by mentioning the name of Justus of Tiberias, a Hellenized Jew, whose chronicle served as a source for the early Christian authors who wanted to explain the migration of peoples throughout the world.[8] The identification of the Phoenician settlers of Ifrīqiya with the Canaanites and other biblical tribes still persisted in Hippo at the time of Saint Augustine, the mid 5th century.[9] The inhabitants still called themselves Canaanites, though the tradition was fading as a result of the decline of Greek influences in that part of the world.[10] The Byzantine historian Prokopius, also reported this version in the mid 6th century.[11] Thus, even though the Berbers were not referred to at this stage as Philistines, or descendants of Goliath, they were clearly connected to Palestine through the identification of North African people as Canaanites. The Muslims in the East were familiar with the early biblical affiliations, and made frequent references to the biblical Canaanite lineage, but in addition they identified the Berbers as Arabs, an element strictly appropriate to Islamic history.

Based on the sources used by Ibn Khaldūn it is possible to trace and reconstruct the appearance of the myth of the Berbers' Arab origin. Two chronological periods in the development of the myth with changing locations and content, become apparent. The first phase continued from the 9th until the 12th century, the second began in the 12th century and ended in the 15th. In the first period several schools, succeeding one another in chronological order can be detected. The first, an "Eastern" one, named after the authors who lived in the Middle East, ceded its place to a second, "Andalusian" school, based in Muslim Spain. A third one, the "Ifrīqiya" school, was based in the Maghreb, completed the first phase in the chronological history of the myth of the Berbers' Arab origin.

It was the Eastern school which furnished the basic data for the creation of the myth of the Berbers' Arab origin. Its members were geographers and historians who lived during the 9th and 10th centuries in the central lands of the ʿAbbāsid empire, and who in their historical work or description of routes and lands, were confronted with the problem of the historical anonymity of the Berbers. Two questions required answers: where the Berbers came from and how they reached the Maghreb. The investigation produced three ethnic affiliations and postulated three historical events of consequence. The first, most frequently cited, proclaimed that the Berbers originated in Palestine, and fled to the Maghreb after the death of Jālūt,

Goliath, himself a member of the Arab tribe of Muḍar. Ibn Khurdadhbih (d. 250/844),[12] Ibn ʿAbd al-Ḥakam (d. 257/871),[13] and Ibn Qutayba (d. 296/907),[14] have espoused this version. The second affiliation linked the Berbers to the descendants of Ḥam, son of Noah, born in the Maghreb after his father's exile to this land, or chased to the Maghreb because of his father's curse.[15] The third affiliation gave several Berber groups, such as the Kutāma and Ṣanhāja, who were later singled out by Ibn Khaldūn as the only "true" Arabs, a Ḥimyari origin from South Yemen, whom Ifricos brought and then left in the Maghreb after he conquered it. Thus Ibn al-Kalbī (d. 204/819-820),[16] and al-Tabarī (d. 310/923) also agreed with this.[17] A fourth affiliation, least repeated, is quoted by al-Masʿūdī (d. 345/956): "...These are the remains of the Ghassānids and other tribes that have disappeared and dispersed as a result of the flood of Arim."[18] A comparison between Ibn Khaldūn's text, which deals with these affiliations, and that of the *majmūʿa,* reveals that the latter devoted more space to quoting and studying these traditions than the former, and that many additional details of the myth can be gleaned there. Thus we find the first version of the deportation to the Maghreb after the flood,[19] but only a few pages to the Goliath version,[20] even though most historians give credence to this last version.[21] To sum up, the link of the Berbers to Palestine was not new, but actually taken by the authors of the Eastern school from sources of the classical period, and accepted by general consensus as the homeland of the Berbers, from which they were chased out to Egypt, and then to the Maghreb, after the defeat and death of their leader, Goliath, sometimes by David, other times by Ifriqūsh-Ifricos. Ibn al-Kalbī (d. 204/819-820), Ibn Khurdadhbih (d. 230/844), Ibn ʿAbd al-Ḥakam (d. 257/871), Ibn Qutayba (d. 296/907), as well as al-Ṭabarī and al-Ṣūlī, all had similar versions,[22] as did Ibn Ḥawqal, who used the lost geographical work of al-Jayhānī (d. 331/943) to document it, similarly to the author of *Kitāb al-ansāb.*[23]

The genesis of the myth of the Berbers' origin in the East at this particular moment occurred because the relationship between center and periphery in the Islamic empire was changing. In order for the Arab historians who lived in the centre to write the history of the Berbers' origin, they needed to gain knowledge about the Berbers themselves and their lands, which was unavailable to them during the early years of Islamic rule. They also needed to be aware of the events unfolding in the periphery. These conditions occurred when the successive Berber revolts against Islam and the Arabs in North Africa drew attention to the area and when the geographers began to travel there and acquire information about Berbers' way of life, localities, tribal affiliations and settlement patterns. This did not take place until the 9th and 10th centuries, and slowly aroused Eastern interest in the Berbers. Only then could the question of their origins be addressed. The Eastern historians attempted to solve the problem of the Berbers' anonymity, by incorporating them into their world history, using familiar terms, retrieving traditions from Greek, Roman and Jewish historians. They affiliated the Berbers in the way that they did other groups, abiding by the rules of collective memory, incorporating them according to tribal structures and placing them in the biblical stories. These Arab historians solved the Berber question by using the same method and concept by which they had previously incorporated other groups and tribes who came into contact with Islam through the conquest. From that moment onwards, so far as they were concerned, the Berber issue was satisfactorily resolved and shelved and the Berbers were given their legitimate place within the universal Islamic history.

This was not however, the way Arabs and Berbers living in the West regarded the myth. As soon as they began to debate and discuss it, it became apparent that there, the myth's significance and meaning had changed. In Muslim Spain the *ʿilm al-nasab*, which came from the East did not include the Berbers who settled there in the 8th century. During those early years, information about the Berbers appears in chronicles, but not in the genealogical works. The increase in conversion to Islam in the next two centuries contributed to the proliferation of genealogical literature in Muslim Spain, which begin to include non-Arab genealogies. Only in the 10th century, with Aḥmad al-Rāzī, (d. 325/937), were the genealogies of both Arab and non-Arab families of al-Andalus displayed side by side in a genealogical work.[24] However, by the time the second, Andalusian, school appeared in the 10th and 11th centuries, the Arab origin given to the Berbers in the East was denied, suggesting that it had become a contested issue in a confrontation between Berbers and Arabs in al-Andalus.

Two groups of Western genealogists, divided along ethnic or racial lines appear: an Arab group of geographers, traditionalists, and historians like al-Warrāq (d. 363/973-74), Ibn Ḥazm (b. 384/994), Ibn ʿAbd al-Barr (d.

463/1070), al-Bakrī (d. 487/1094), and a Berber group of genealogists, Sabiq al-Maṭamatī,[25] Hānī b. Maṣdūr al-Kūmī, Kehlān b. Abī Luwā, Hānī b. Bakūr al-Ḍarīsī, Ayyūb b. Abū Yazīd.[26] The members of the Arab group are all known to us, thanks to other works, but the reconstitution of the Berber group, even if their names are known, is much more difficult. Ibn Ḥazm indicated several times that he had collected information from people who were versed in the study of Berber genealogy, but according to Ibn Khaldūn, Ibn Ḥazm's argument did not always correspond to the texts written by Berber geneaologists, which he himself had in front of him.[27] The compiler of the *Kitāb al-ansāb* knew who the members of this school were, and was aware of their writings, but without indicating either the locality or period of their activities. Two of them made the journey from North Africa to Spain towards the end of the 11th century. One was Ayyūb, the son of Abū Yazīd, the "man with the donkey," whose story was recorded by al-Warrāq in Cordoba. The second was Abū Muḥammad Ighnī al-Birzālī, the Ibāḍī, whom Ibn Ḥazm recorded. Both were "personalities of great piety and very knowledgable about the Berber genealogies."[28] During the years of his African revolt, Abū Yazīd entertained relationships with the Ummayad caliph al-Nāṣir, while Ayyūb, his son, first represented his father in Cordoba, and eventually became attached to the service of the caliph in the court.[29] The *ibāḍī* was linked to the Birzālīd tribe, which was allied with Abū Yazīd in North Africa, then crossed over to Spain, where it constituted a corps of Berber cavalry under al-Ḥakam II.[30] Other authors also indicate that the Berber genealogy originated during those years. Al-Bakrī echoes works by members of the Andalusian school, which like the rest of his data, was collected in Spain. Al-Idrīsī (b. 493/1100) was among the first to report the Arab origin of the Zanāta in the West.[31] The anonymous Marīnid chronicle, the *Dhakhīra al-saniyya* reiterated: "it took place during the fierce battles between Arabs and Berbers in al-Andalus in the 11th century, events known as "*al-fitna al-barbariya*," the Berber revolt."[32] The Marīnid and ʿAbd al-Wādid chroniclers who worked during the second wave of Zanāta statehood in the 13th and the 14th centuries, also referred to the myth of origin and the inclusion of the Zanāta in it, as the product of Spain,[33] and both Ibn Khaldūns quoted Al-Bakrī's findings about the Zanāta genealogy.[34] In all this the role of North Africa, the homeland of the Berbers, is minimal or non-existent.[35] The geographer Ibn Ḥawqal explained that the lack of

Maghrebi genealogists was caused by loss of Maghrebi genealogies, and he was also aware that most of his sources were Berbers living in Spain, or recent comers to Spain.

Jewish sources and Hebrew poetry from 11th century Granada would seem most unlikely sources for the Berbers' myth of origin in al-Andalus, yet it is there that we find it. No lesser author than Shmuel Hanagid (d. 1056), the Jewish vizir of Zīrīd Granada, who was a poet and community leader, repeatedly referred to the contemporary Berbers as descendants of Goliath, calling them the *Philistines*. Using the biblical expression '*Sarne Pelishtim*', the Philistine officers, which described the enemies of Samson, he alluded a number of times in his poems to his Berber lords, when riding in their company to battle their Arab Sevillian adversaries.[36] Other references to the myth appear in a Hebrew work, the *Megillat Ahimaaz*, written in Southern Italy in 1054, which discusses the Fāṭimid conquest of Egypt and Sicily, calling the Fāṭimid caliph al-Mu'izz 'King of the Yemenites.' It is clear that the reference here was not to the Arabs, who are always referred to by Jewish authors as the 'Ishmaelites,' *ha-yishmaelim*, but rather to the Kutāma Berbers, who were supporters of the Fāṭimid mission first in the Maghreb and then in Egypt. It will be remembered that the chroniclers of the East identified the Kutāma as Yemeni Arabs.[37] However, the term *Pelishtim*, Philistines, appeared one further time, never to be repeated again in Hebrew Andalusian literature, in the *Book of Tradition*, *Sefer hakabala*, a chronicle by Abraham Ibn Daud, written in Toledo in 1160.[38] Ibn Daud, a philosopher and translator of scientific works, who was familiar with Hanagid's works and was a great admirer of his, wrote his book to combat the influence of Karaite doctrines in the Jewish community. When recounting the events in Granada which resulted in the demise of Hanagid's son, Yehoseph, Ibn Daud used the biblical term *Sarne Pelishtim*, the Philistine officers, to describe the Berber chieftains, calling North Africa *Eretz Pelishtim*, the Land of the Philistines. His use of the term *Pelishtim* was not accidental, but inspired by Hanagid's verses, which he quoted throughout the entire work.[39] The fact that first Hanagid, and then Ibn Daud, identified the Zīrīd Berbers as *Sarne Pelishtim*, Philistine chieftains, is highly significant in this context, since no other Hebrew writer among the many Hebrew Andalusian poets, whether contemporary with Hanagid or living in later centuries, referred to them by that name. It is always possible that Hanagid could have acquired the idea that the Berbers originated in Palestine from the *Talmud*, which was commonly studied by the Jews in Muslim Spain and which described the arrival of the Jews in North Africa as an Hellenic myth.[40] Yet the term *Philistine officers* does not appear in the *Talmud*, and was not mentioned by earlier Hebrew writers in Muslim Spain. Hanagid acquired the usage from Arabic sources and began using it at the instigation of the Zīrīds themselves. It can only be explained by the historical circumstances of the Zīrīd rise to power in Granada as an independent *taifa* kingdom, and by Hanagid's career in their court. Its appearance indicates that it was, rather, a contemporary phrase, used in Zīrīd Granada, and commonly adopted by those attached to the Zīrīd court.

The Cordoban chronicler, Ibn Ḥayyān, described how the myth became used in Granada, when he reflected on the reason why the Zīrīd rulers took such pains to cultivate themselves: "Ḥabbūs gave himself the aura of a literary man and tried to hide his pure Berber ancestry by claiming an Ḥimyari origin... so they would not appear in any way less civilized than the Arab and hispanized kings of the Peninsula."[41] Ḥabbūs was not alone in promoting the alleged Ḥimyari origin which al-Masʿūdī and other authors from the East attributed to the Ṣanhāja, in Muslim Spain, the Afṭasids of Badajoz also claimed a Ḥimyari origin, and so did the Zīrīds in North Africa. But the Zīrīd *taifa* in Granada was the strongest and the most prominent among the 11th-century Berber *taifas* and its rulers the most arabicized among them. The *Tibyān*, written by the prince ʿAbd Allāh, the last ruler of Zīrīd Granada, displayed unusual cultural achievements by North African Berber standards. It was written in an eloquent Arabic style, with correct grammar, and enhanced by a large number of quotations from the *Qur'ān*, traditions, poetry, proverbs and literary works.[42] It even showed some knowledge of medieval scientific, astrological and astronomical works.[43]

The Zīrīds' reaction was typical. The *ʿilm al-nasab* was the traditional literary weapon, in al-Andalus and elsewhere, where claims for political power were made, and by which new converts to Islam could hope to achieve equality with other elements in their society.[44] By denying them Arab origin, the Arabs fought off attempts by ethnic groups to share in the political, economic and social power. Ibn Ḥazm's rebuttal of the Berbers' Arab origins, demonstrates that not unlike Ibn Ḥayyān, it raised his ire and provoked him to mock it:

> Several Berber tribes would like us to believe that they come from Yemen and that they descend from Ḥimyar; others say that they are descendants of Berr, descendants of Qays; but the fallacious nature of these pretensions is obvious. The fact that Qays ever had a son named Berr is absolutely unknown by any of the geneaologists; and the Ḥimyarits never went to the Maghreb except in those lies produced by the Yemenite historians.[45]

The Arab Andalusian intellectuals, like Ibn Ḥazm, who was forced to leave Granada, could not be trusted. The Berbers needed Shmuel Hanagid's knowledge of the Arabic language and literature to confirm their Arab origin. The Jews had become associated with the palace circles and were perceived as loyal.

Berber genealogy and myth of origin did not enter the Maghreb itself and were not embraced by the local historiography before the 11th century. The Berbers did not learn about their connection to the biblical Canaanite or Philistine origins directly from Roman or Byzantine sources, but two centuries later, from Arab sources, following the conquest of the Maghreb or Spain, and exclusively through Andalusian Arabo-Islamic sources.

The third school, which flourished in Ifrīqiya, between the 11th and the 13th centuries,[46] included Ibn al-Raqīq,[47] (d. 418/1027), who in addition to a long chronicle of Ifrīqiya, also wrote a genealogy; Abū Majd al-Maghīlī,[48] author of a *Kitāb fī ansāb al-barbar*; Abū ʿAlī al-Rashīq,[49] who wrote *Mizān al-ʿamal fī ayām al-duwal*; Ibn al-Wakīl,[50] author of *Al-mughrib ʿan al-maghrib*, and Khālid b. Kharas,[51] author of a chronicle of Ifrīqiya; Ibn Ḥammādu al-Burnūsī al-Sabtī,[52] who wrote the *Kitāb al-muqtabis fī aḥbār al-maghrib wa'l-andalus*, all included a chapter describing the genealogy of the Berbers; as did Ibn Ḥammād,[53] (d.628/1230), who wrote *Al-nubadh al-muḥtaja f ī aḥbār mulūk Ṣanhāja bi-Ifrīqiya wa-Bijāya,* a chronicle which also included information about the genealogy; and Abū al-Ṣalāt,[54] (d. 1235), who wrote the *Kitāb al-dibāja fī mafākhir (var. aḥbār) Ṣanhāja,* for "al-Ḥasan sāḥib al-Mahdia." For the most part, these chronicles have been lost today, except through quotations in later works. Ibn ʿIdhārī, Ibn Khaldūn, and the author of the *Kitāb al-ansāb* devoted entire works or chapters to the myth of the Berbers' origin with one significant difference: The myth is now a part of history and appears in chronicles, not in genealogies. Only small changes occur in the content of the myth of the Berbers' origin after its initiation into the Maghreb proper. In the 12th century, an attribution of an ʿAlid origin to the Almohad ruling family appeared,[55] motivated by a growing awareness that this attribution, in the East, was powerful and legitimizing.[56]

From this moment onwards, the myth of the Berbers' origin assumed considerable momentum in Maghrebi writings. Unlike historians who wrote the history of North Africa in the Middle East during this period, such as Ibn al-Athīr (d. 630/1233),[57] or al-ʿUmarī,[58] Maghrebi chroniclers devoted much space and attention to the myth, which seemed to have become a mandatory element. However, the Berber dynasties themselves did not readily adopt it in the 13th and 14th century Maghreb. The Marīnid and the ʿAbd al-Wādid rulers went out of their way to deny such claims and even the court historians were reluctant to mention it too often.[59] Moreover, when we examine the symbols of sovereignty in North Africa, we look in vain for the biblical genealogy, or the Arab origin or even the *ʿAlid* origin. It does not for instance, appear on coins of any dynasty, including that of the Idrisids.[60] It was only at the beginning of the 16th century that the term "*sharīf*" appeared for the first time on the tombstone of the monarchs of Morocco.[61] The myth of Arab origin was not used as a popular legitimization agent, or as propaganda in the quest for political authentication in medieval North Africa. What was then, its real importance? Was it significant in any way for the Maghrebi society? The failure of the myth of the Berbers' Arab origin to gain wide acceptance or use, in spite of its position in the medieval historiography as a literary theme, can be explained by a lack of acculturation to Arab and Islamic themes among the population at large. The myth of origin entered the historical writings of the medieval Maghreb and became an essential theme, even a mandatory component, because it was part and parcel of the high culture of the Islamic west. However it could not be used as propaganda because it was never endorsed by the masses. The majority of the Berbers had no access to history books or traditions written in Arabic. These were written by an elite of Arabized and Islamized intellectuals and for them. The Maghrebi history as written in the Arab-Islamic mold differed greatly from history as it was lived and told by the majority of the Berber-speaking population. The slowness of the Arabization and Islamization process in North Africa explains the gap between the high culture of the small minority of Arabized members of society, and the majority, who were still very Berber. For them the myth of origin remained marginal and inaccessible. It remained a frozen and sterile literary motif, and was not transformed, nor adapted, to changing social and political conditions in North Africa.

In the next chapter we shall examine the third theme expressing the Berbers resistance to Arabic and Islamic acculturation, the praise of the Berber race. Then it will be possible to study the phenomena as a whole, the roots of the Berbers' resistance to acculturation, its genesis, location and the historical conditions which precipitated it.

CHAPTER 3

Acculturation and Its Aftermath: The Legacy of the Andalusian Berbers*

A luster-painted brasero bowl, late 15th-century Granada.

The third and last display of the Berbers' resistance to Arabic and Islamic acculturation comes to us in the form of praise of the Berber race, *mafākhir al-Barbar*, *mafāḍil al-Barbar* or *maḥāsin ahl al-mahgrib*. Devoted to exalting and celebrating the noble qualities of the Berbers and their land, the theme appears in the chronicles side by side with the myth of origin and the genealogies, sometimes replacing it, sometimes using it in the title of a historical work, but more often than not, as a chapter following the genealogies. Even though it became prominent and articulated in the 14th-century chronicles, the theme did appear in earlier works. The *majmūʿa Kitāb al-ansab*, which carries abundant versions of it, was probably modelled on one of the earlier works devoted to the theme, Abū ʿAbd Allāh b. Abī Majd al-Maghīlī's, *Kitāb ansab al-Barbar wa-mulūkihim,* which it uses as its principal source.[1] The same theme recurred in another work, a chronicle of the history of the Maghreb entitled *al-mughrib fī akhbār mahāsin ahl-Maghrib*, written by Ibn al-Yas'a, an exilé from Marrakech, for his benefactor, Saladin.[2] Among the early sources, the *Mafākhir al-Barbar* theme also appears prominently in the writings of the Ibāḍī community in the Tunisian south, or was greatly favoured by the Ibāḍīyya writers.[3] As early as the 11th century, the chronicle of Abū Zakariya Yaḥyā shows that it was used in this sect's historical works.[4] The chronicle, entitled *Kitāb al-sīra wakhabār al-ā'ima* began with a chapter entitled *Faḍā'il al-Barbar*, and continued with the same *ḥadīths* about the Berbers being drawn to Islam before the Arab conquest of their land, which were repeated two centuries later by the compiler of the *Kitāb al-ansāb*. The affinity shown by the Ibāḍī historians to the theme was not accidental. The rise and success of the Ibāḍiyya sect was linked to the Berbers' revolts in the 8th century, and the notion that Ibāḍi theology influenced and informed the development of Berber Islam, has been acknowledged by modern writers.[5] It has been associated with the Berbers' attempts to express their resistance and individualism in religious

* *Relaciones de la Peninsula Ibérica con el Maghreb, siglos XIII-XVI*, Actas del Coloquio, M. Garcia Arenal and M. J. Viguera eds., (Madrid, 1988): 205–36.

terms, which often resulted in a non-conformist, non-mainstream Islam.

The great chronicles of the 14th century Maghreb incorporated the praise of the Berber race into the history of the Islamic West: Ibn ʿIdhārī's 712/1312, *Bayān al-mughrib*, began with a chapter called "*Faḍl al-Maghrib*", utilizing several *ḥadīths* incorporated in the *Kitāb al-ansāb*,[6] as did Ibn Khaldūn,[7] but they had a forerunner of sorts in the form of the chronicles devoted to the praise of the Ṣanhāja Berbers alone. Following the rise of the Zīrīd Ṣanhāja dynasty in Ifrīqiya, the chronicles surveyed in chapter Two also mentioned the praise of the Ṣanhāja race. Such were al-Warrāq's chronicle and geographical work,[8] al-Raqīq's (d. 418/1027-8) genealogical history of the Berbers,[9] Abū 'l-Ṣalāt's (d. 529/1135) chronicle *Kitāb al-dibāja fī mafākhir Ṣanhāja*,[10] and Ibn Ḥammād's (d. 628/1213) *Kitāb al-nubadh al-muḥtāja fī akhbār mulūk Ṣanhāja bi-Ifrīqiya wa-Bijāya*.[11] The rise of the Ṣanhāja to political hegemony not only encouraged the praise of the Berber race but also ushered in a shift to dynastic history.[12] There are no prior surviving chronicles before those of the Ṣanhāja, so no evidence as to what contemporaries thought and wrote down about the Aghlabids, the first Arab dynasty of Ifrīqiya, 184/800-296/909,[13] but there is enough evidence to date the beginning of local dynastical historiography proper, to the Zīrīd dynasty of Ifrīqiya (324/935-555/1160). With the rise to power of the Maṣmūda and Zanāta dynasties in the 13th and 14th centuries, the praise of a particular Berber group is abandoned for that of the entire race. The change also meant that race has become a historical and historiographical criterion there, expressing the view that the political achievements in this country should be accredited to the Berbers.

Yet, the chroniclers of the Ṣanhāja Zīrīd history shared a common background, they all had roots in al-Andalus, or spent some time there: al-Warrāq was an Andalusian, so was Abū 'l-Ṣalāt, and Ibn Ḥammād, originally from Ifrīqiya, was later a qāḍī in Algeciras. The earliest dated version of the "new history" of the Berbers' conversion to Islam in the *Kitāb al-ansāb* was quoted from the chronicle of the Andalusian author Abū 'l-Ḥasan ʿAlī b. ʿUmar al-Tamīmī,[14] who wrote in 402/1011 in the city of Elvira, in the vicinity of Granada.[15] We have seen in previous chapters that the Arab genealogists who confronted the Berbers in an attempt to deny them an Arab origin, had a strong Andalusian background. Ibn Ḥazm, Ibn ʿAbd al-Barr, and al-Bakrī, all were Andalusians. The Berber genealogists who opposed them, Sābic al-Matmatī, Hānī b. Maṣdūr, Kehlān b. abī Lu'wā, Hānī b. Bakūr, and Ayyūb b. al-Yazīd, also lived in Muslim Spain.[16] What happened in 11th century al-Andalus to precipitate such intellectual activity?

Political events in 11th century al-Andalus allowed North African Berbers to play a central role there. The recruitment of Berber militia from North Africa, inaugurated by the caliph al-Ḥakam II, (d. 976), encouraged Berber immigration across the strait. Maintained by al-Manṣūr ibn Abi' ʿAmr, the caliphal majordomo, the Berber units were first employed in the campaigns against the Christians, but were later unleashed against the inhabitants of the cities, especially against those of Cordoba.[17] As the crisis in the Cordoba caliphate deepened, the circumstances surrounding the crumbling of the central authority allowed the Berbers to convert their military force into political domination, and permitted the establishment of Berber *taifas* in al-Andalus. Each ethnic group, Arabs, Ibero-Romans, Berbers, Jews, Slavs, had tried to manipulate and improve their place within the Andalusian social and economic order, with only limited success.[18] With the advent of the *taifa* system, the 11th century was politically speaking the "ethnic" century par excellence. The political game had changed, the rules became more flexible, even though the negative attitude towards ethnicity remained. The *taifa* rulers identified themselves and rallied their troops in terms of their ethnic identity and waged war on each other in ethnic terms. An anti-Berber coalition was formed against Granada, the new Berber *taifa*, and when its leader, al-Muʿtamid, the Arab Sevillian *taifa* ruler, moved his army south-eastward, he ran his campaign under anti-Berber slogans, calling on the Arab refugees fleeing Zīrī's Granada to join his camp. Zīrī vowed to exterminate the Arabs from his dominions and an ethnic cleansing effort was under way.[19]

This, together with the crisis in the Cordoba Caliphate and the Berber participation in the massacres which followed it, served as catalysts in the wave of Berberophobia which swept al-Andalus in the 11th century. Muslim authors from the East did not express Berber hatred. Apart from one comment by Ibn al-Kalbī, no pre-11th century genealogist appeared to have had a negative view of the Berbers, but Ibn Ḥayyān and ʿAbd Allāh b. Zīrī were candid about the strong anti-Berber feelings around them. Thus ʿAbd Allāh: "The opposition to the Berbers was prompted by the hostility to the fact that they established themselves in this district and by the hate of the race".[20] The Berbers coming from the Maghreb, who were not accustomed to this atmosphere, must have sensed it even more. ʿAbd Allāh reports in the *Tibyān* that the Andalusian hostility towards the Berbers was the reason why Zīrī who reigned in Granada between 403-10/1013-19, abandoned it and returned to the Maghreb.[21] Berber hatred also drove the *Zanāta* and *Ṣanhāja*, traditional enemies in the Maghreb, to become allies in Muslim Spain, and form a common front.[22] Other ethnic communities experienced a similar social infirmity as the Berbers at different times, but nowhere was the stigma as strong and persistent as in the case of the Berbers, who were numerous and renewed their communities continuously. Ethnic groups expressed their opposition to Arab rejection in writings similar to the *shuʿūbiyya* literature from the East, and Ibn Ḥazm's *Jamharat ansāb al-arab* could well be seen as an Arab response to them. Unlike Iberian Slavic *shuʿūbiyya* literature, addressed to them by the Slav community, the *Sakāliba*,[23] which existed in the 9th century but melted away in the 11th, Berber *shuʿūbiyya* and the Berber problem refused to disappear.[24] Rekindled and refuelled first by the new immigrants, then by the Almoravid, Almohad and Marīnid military campaigns and invasions, Berberophobia became an ever-relevant literary theme in al-Andalus from the 11th century on.[25]

Justifying the Berber resistance to acculturation by the hostility to the Berbers in the ethnically divided Andalusian society of the 11th century, risks being seen as contradictory to the vision of a unified Andalusian nation, with Arab cultural and linguistic content and no ethnic diversity or rivalry, which some historians have advanced. This vision originated with Lévi-Provençal's *Histoire de l'Espagne Musulmane*,[26] but was also supported by recent authors such as Guichard,[27] Glick,[28] and Wasserstein.[29] One would assume that this rosy picture of national unity can only mean cultural unity, language, literature, etc., not political unity. After all, there is no denying that the central political order broke down and statehood was reconstructed on an ethnic basis and that the ethnically rifted *taifa*s' period was the prelude to the undoing of Muslim Spain.

Yet, it is precisely this view of acculturation to Islamic and Arab cultural norms in 11th-century al-Andalus among "old Berbers" which is the key to the question why the new history of the Berbers' conversion, the myth of origin and the praise of the Berber race occurred there. The longer settled, "old" Berbers, indeed achieved common Andalusian identity before the *taifa* period, before the "new" Berbers arrived, because the knowledge required for the response, could not have come from the newcomers. Berber settlement patterns in al-Andalus also favoured a more rapid acculturation. Nomadism or semi-nomadism was not high as it was in North Africa, if practised at all, and sedentarization more frequent. This also allowed for a quicker and more thorough acculturation in al-Andalus.[30] During the 11th century the intellectual and mental environment in which the "old" Berbers found themselves in al-Andalus had changed radically. As a result of political and ecological transformations, the Berbers who had previously emigrated to Spain were forced to leave their rural habitats and head for urban centres. We know about this movement because the memory of earlier Berber settlement was retained in Andalusian place names with the word 'Barbar' in them.[31] In the cities, where their social conditions deteriorated the Berbers became increasingly, a hated minority. In the words of a young Spanish historian, "Andalusian Berbers who lived in the cities "lost their onomastic idiosyncrasy but the ethnic factor emerged in the 5th/11th century and became central in social conflicts and tensions."[32] In 11th century Muslim Spain Andalusian Berbers were a minority, and, as with all minorities, were consequently under pressure to acculturate and assimilate, adopt and conform to the new norms. Unlike them, the "new" Berbers, with their fresh North African background and their military way of life would be unfamiliar with the Islamic and Arabic notions of the myth of origin and the historical conversion to Islam. The majority of North African Berbers remained Berber speaking much longer than the Andalusian Berbers did, and were also less exposed to the Arab-Islamic notions of race and religion. Moreover, they were not troubled by Andalusian denigration of them before their rise to political hegemony gave them a good reason to do so. Andalusian Berbers, the "old" Berbers, were more likely to be reminded of their Berber ethnicity in Spain, and could not have remained unaffected by the Arab denigration of the "new" Berbers for long without compromising their own social progress. Their social status within the multi ethnic society of al-Andalus was not high to begin with, but the exposure to the cultural, economic and social milieu of urban Andalusia, to Arabo-Islamic mentalities and especially to historical notions, brought home a sense of their own ethnical singularity or particularism, and reinforced their feelings of racial pride.[33] The arrival of the "new" Berber warriors from North Africa in the 11th century might have initially brought some reprieve to the humble image of the Berbers, but with the havoc they wreaked in Andalusian politics, the old Andalusian conflict returned with force. The strong military component of the new recruits upset the gentle balance within the cities as the general attitude towards the Berber communities deteriorated. This change served as the catalyst for the articulation of Berber particularism by a quest for a different historical identity and a different historical past.

An additional display of the Andalusian legacy in the development of the praise of the Berber's race had to do with the idea that a noble origin was a requirement for all those seeking or holding public political office, especially a sultan and a caliph. This notion was shared by all parties vying for political power in Islamic lands, not only in Spain, as explicitly admitted by the Zīrīd prince ʿAbd Allāh, led to the manufacturing of genealogies: "They, the people of Cordoba, put at their head a man to whom they gave the caliphal title al-Murtaḍā (ʿAbd al-Raḥman IV, d. 1018) and pretended that he was from the tribe of Quraysh, hoping to unite and bring together the population in order to support his caliphate".[34] Like the Cordobans, the Berber rulers in their attempt to secure their hold on their *taifas* and to remove the racial stigma attached to them, also advanced their quest for legitimation by promoting their Arab origin, a positive history of their conversion and praise of the Berber race. Both the Zanāta and Ṣanhāja Berbers adopted a noble genealogy, an Arab descent. The Ṣanhāja Zīrīds in Granada,[35] and the Afṭasides in Badajoz, used the Ḥimyarī connection,[36] while the revolt of the "man with the donkey" which precipitated the torrent of genealogical myths during the 11th century, helped establish the various Zanāta families: the Birzālīds in Carmona,[37] the Benni Demmer in Moron,[38] and the Banu Corra in Ronda.[39] The Berber rulers in al-Andalus, in particular the Zīrīds, did not trust Arab writers and administrators, such as Ibn Ḥazm, to spread the new propaganda. Zīrīd literary activity, like many other aspects of its history and civilization, were closely linked to Muslim Spain. Zīrīd chiefs and Zīrīd writers, religious scholars, and other intellectuals frequently crossed the Mediterranean in both directions and a continued exchange of ideas, as well as political allegiances, took place.[40] They needed to have their own intellectuals, hence the appearance of the Jews in central positions at the court, and the Berber genealogists, newcomers from North Africa. This policy was necessary to replace the Arabs who monopolized the literary tools and manipulated the intellectual and spiritual legitimacy in the world in which they shared. Although Berber tribes travelled between the Maghreb and Spain, only events taking place in their adoptive land could have triggered the resistance to acculturation. Andalusian Berbers experienced a different mental, cultural and social environment than their Maghrebi brethren, and therefore wrote a specific Berber oriented history with a particularly Berber oriented historical content.

A final historiographical body of evidence about Andalusian legacy of this question comes from a quantitative study of authors, location and themes in the writing of Berber history. For this purpose a list, presented in the Appendix, was compiled, of all sources in the *Kitāb al-ansāb*, which were used by the compiler of the *majmūʿa* and mentioning the Berbers. The list does not claim to be comprehensive but it contains fifty-two authors, a sufficient sample to provide a good general idea of who wrote the history of the Berbers, when and where. The graph plotting the rise of Berber historiography according to geographical location outlines the results.

HISTORIANS OF THE BERBERS

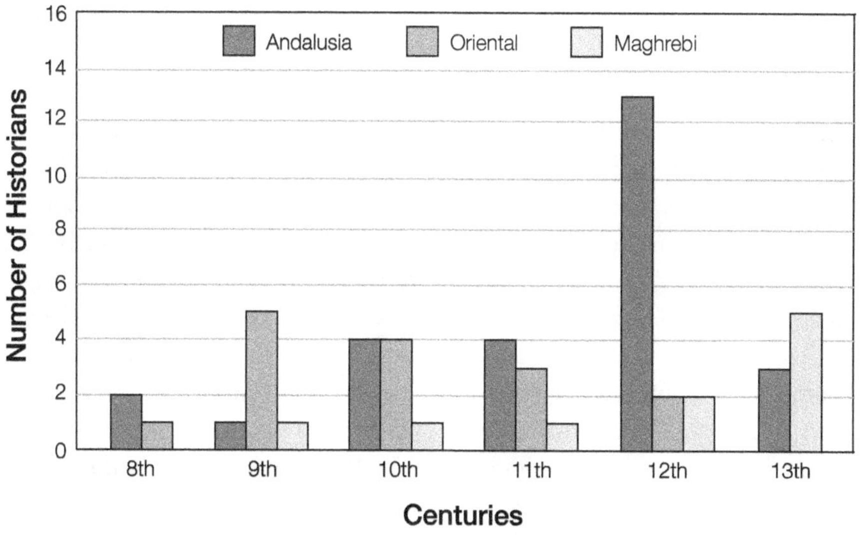

When quantified, the data of the 52 chroniclers identified shows that 26 were Andalusian, 16 Eastern and 10 Maghrebi. Of the 26 Andalusians, 2 wrote during the 8th century, 1 during the 9th, 4 during the 10th century, 4 during the 11th century, 13 wrote during the 12th century and 3 during the 13th. Among the 16 Easterners, 1 supposedly wrote in the 8th century, 5 wrote during the 9th century, 4 during the 10th century, 3 during the 11th century and 2 during the 12th. Among the 10 Maghrebis, 1 wrote in the 9th century, 1 in the 10th, 1 in the 11th, 2 in the 12th and 5 wrote during the 13th century. The numbers show that the bulk of the writing about the Berbers was centered in the East in the 9th and 10th centuries, moved to Muslim Spain and reached a peak there during the 12th, then moved to the Maghreb to peak there during the 13th. The content is also of significance. While Eastern chroniclers were cited in the early part of the *Kitāb al-ansāb*, which is devoted to the myth of origin and the Arab conquest of North Africa, the Andalusians incorporated the most significant historical theme, the history of their conversion to Islam. This shows that many features of the Maghrebi local history were inaugurated in Spain and express Andalusian historical realities and sensitivities, and that the Andalusian chronicles provided much of the framework for the Berber centred history written in the Maghreb from the 12th century onward. It shows that its genesis occurred in this part of the Islamic West, and that the earlier works on the Berbers were composed under Andalusian influences, or by Andalusians, before they were taken over by the Maghrebi chroniclers themselves.

The challenge facing the Berbers living in the Maghreb was different. For Berbers in North Africa the challenge was not Islamic or Arab normative legitimation, neither intellectual, nor literary, but one of building an Islamic state. By the time the Marīnids came aboard they were rulers in their own land and quite undisturbed by Arab denigration of the Berber race, nor by the Arabo-Islamic requirement for a noble origin. Acculturation to Islamic norms proceeded because it meant for them achieving stately coherence and wide support for their rule. For them the Islamic state identity was gained by implementing Islamic institutions, government, legal, economic, and municipal structures, which were devised in the East, imported and implemented in the West on the strength of religion. The Andalusi literary baggage resulting from the social and intellectual malaise and need for legitimation, became ultimately a part of the Maghrebi historiography, but only that. Instead, the institutions, whether inherited from a previous dynasty and implemented, or newly established, became the core of acculturation to Islamic norms and had to be adopted to the Berber-Islamic state's structures and adjusted to its subjects' conditions and needs. In the second part we shall examine how did the Berbers, rulers and ruled alike, took to this challenge.

II

DEVISING AN ISLAMIC STATE

CHAPTER 4

Rural and Urban Islam in 13th-century Morocco*

Amulet in gold and cloisonné, 13th-14th centuries, Muslim Spain.

Back on the North African shore in 13th-century Morocco the Marīnid Zanāta Berber tribes were about to launch an attack for political hegemony, but were they sufficiently acculturated to Islamic norms to have used Islam to facilitate their ascent? This question has been always answered in the negative. In fact, there is no theory which has been more readily embraced by historians of Morocco than the one which claims that, contrary to the pattern previously observed in this country, the Marīnids' rise to power was accomplished without the assistance of an ideological or religious motivation. Historians were quick to point out that there was no evidence that an Islamic religious cause existed among the Marīnid tribes when they began mobilising for the conquest of the country in the 13th century. Therefore, unlike the Almoravids' and Almohads' rise to political hegemony before them, theirs was a unique experience in the historical framework of the Medieval Maghreb.[1] The truth is that considerable confusion still reigns over the early years of the Marīnids, and we are poorly informed about the historical mechanism which transformed them into empire builders. Yet, the question of whether or not there was a religious factor behind their rise to power is not only intriguing as a historical precedent, if indeed such was the case, but also holds the key to the future developments, to the policies which the regime later devised, and to the identity it assumed as an Islamic state.

Unlike the ascent of the Almohads, which was documented from the beginning by contemporary observers, the humble beginnings of the Marīnids, a nomadic pastoral people, whose contemporaries associated their name with the quality of the wool which they produced, did not attract the chroniclers' attention.[2] They did not immediately appear as a potential political power threatening the Almohads, and the sources, which usually furnish abundant detail, provide only snippets of information about the early formative period. Ibn Abī Zarʿ and Ibn Khaldūn, the great historians

* *Studia Islamica*, LI(1979): 123–36.

of the Marīnids, did their best, repeating the small amount of information concerning the Marīnids' early years which reached them, but even this was eclipsed by the grand events which followed.[3] For that reason the discovery of the last part of Ibn ʿIdhārī's *Bayān al-Mughrib*, long thought to be lost, raised the hopes of many historians interested in the question. In his foreword to the work, which, it will be remembered, was written in 712/1312, during the height of Marīnid statehood, Ibn ʿIdhārī promised to write about the Ḥafṣids, Naṣrids, and Marīnids, "his contemporaries",[4] but the publication of this third volume proved to be a disappointment, since Ibn ʿIdhārī did not keep his promise, and the chronicle ended with the last Almohad caliph, Abū Debbūs, in 668/1269.[5] Instead, the new volume of the *Bayān* provided a detailed description of the break up and disbanding of the Almohad system, and frequently mentioned the Marīnids' involvement in it. This process provided a framework for the rise of the Marīnids, since the two realities, disbanding of the one and building up of the other, evolved side by side. Thanks to the data from the *Bayān,* and with the help of other Marīnid chronicles, especially the anonymous chronicle *al-Dhakhīra al-saniyya*, it is now possible to observe the Marīnids' rise more closely, with surprising results.[6]

The new details provided in the *Bayān* highlight a situation which was previously overlooked or rather, whose full significance was not recognized: the existence of two rival camps, the Banū Ḥamāma and the Banū ʿAskar, within the Marīnid group of tribes. An attentive reading reveals a struggle for power between the two camps, which persisted throughout the 13th and the 14th centuries, extending into the period when the unity of the Marīnid state had been taken for granted. Actually, internal dissent continued to plague the Marīnids to the end, as the Banū Waṭṭās, a branch of the Marīnid tribes, ascended against the ruling family in the 15th century.[7] One camp, the Banū ʿAskar, laid the foundations of the Marīnid political power: "The hegemony belonged to the Banū ʿAskar", said the author of the *Dhakhīra*, "and the first attacks against the Almoravids and the Almohads took place under their leadership".[8] Already during the 12th century, the ruling family achieved the formation of a solid block of Marīnid tribes, which was not in evidence earlier. Their chief, al-Mukhaḍḍab, deployed symbols of royalty and independence, banners, drums, and command of the troops. During his reign the Banū ʿAskar behaved like great lords and establishd a court where they entertained their guests and visitors with spectacles and banquets.[9] In the middle of the 12th century, however, in 540-41/1145-46 to be precise, the first battle between the Almohad army and the burgeoning Marīnid power ended in the military defeat of the Marīnids. As a result leadership of the tribes was transferred from the Banū ʿAskar to the Banū Ḥamāma, who would never again relinquish it.[10] The Banū ʿAskar detached themselves from the rest of the Marīnid tribes and formed an independent body, which the other participants in the political arena during the 12th century could not ignore.[11] The Almohads, observing the scene from their capital, recognized the new family as the only legitimate chiefs of the Marīnids: "The amīr al-mu'minin, Yaʿqūb al-Manṣūr, confirmed the authority of the amīr Maḥyū over all the Marīnid tribes," says the author of the *Dhakhīra,* describing the events of the year 590/1193,[12] and he proceeded to use the same terms to describe the reign of Maḥyū's son, ʿAbd al-Ḥaqq.[13] The existence of two rival Marīnid branches pitted against one another in the desire to attain and control the leadership during this period, explained the two seemingly contradictory phrases which the chronicler used to describe the Marīnids, one saying that 'the Marīnids did not submit themselves to a ruler', and the other, that 'they participated next to the Almohad troops in the battle of Alarcos', which took place in 1195. It was the Banū ʿAskar who, independently from the other Marīnid tribes, pursued a policy of opposition to the Almohads, and it is to them that the chronicler referred when he spoke about the 'Marīnids who will not submit to a state'. The Banū Ḥamāma were the allies of the Almohads and enjoyed their support in the contest for leadership.[14]

Things came to a head in 614-15/1217-18, when the Banū ʿAskar declared war on the Marīnids and claimed command of the clan. Assisted by the nomadic Arab tribe of the Riyāḥ, allies of the Almohads, they came close to crushing their enemies, who only managed with great difficulty to snatch victory from the jaws of defeat. The Banū Ḥamāma paid the ultimate price. Both their leader ʿAbd al-Ḥaqq and his eldest son Idrīs, perished on the battlefield.[15] For the next twenty years, until the reign of Abū Saʿīd ʿUthmān I, 637/1239, there was no further indication of independent activity from the Banū ʿAskar. Following the death of ʿAbd al-Ḥaqq they were the only Marīnids who did not renew the oath of allegiance, the *bayʿa,* to his brother Abū Maʿaref, and in defiance joined the Almohads in their fight against the ascending Marīnids.[16] In 638/1240, they appeared before the city of Meknes, demanding the proceeds of the protection fee, the *khufāra*, usually paid to the Banū Ḥamāma, as leaders of the Marīnids, for protecting the city from marauding nomads.[17] In 642/1244, the Banū ʿAskar, together with the Almohads and the ʿAbd al-Wādids, declared war against the Marīnids, a war which ended in another defeat.[18] After the succession of Abū Yūsuf to the throne, 656/1258, they appeared to have lost any hope of regaining power and control. They were given the Eastern part of Morocco as a concession, and roamed there during the next thirty or more years. Yet, at the first sign of weakness manifested by the reigning family, the Banū ʿAskar reappeared. Several revolts took place following the death of Abū Yūsuf Yaʿqūb in 685/1286, and the coronation of his son Abū Yaʿqūb. One was led by ʿUmar ibn ʿUthmān ibn Yūsuf al-ʿAskarī who entrenched himself in the castle of Fendelawa and declared war on the Sultan. Since the rest of the Banū ʿAskar decided not to follow him, the revolt had little chance of success.[19] In 709/1309, the grand *sheikh* of the Banū ʿAskar, al-Ḥasan ibn Abī Talaq conspired with the vizier Raḥḥū al-Waṭṭāsī and with Gonzalo, the commander of the Christian troops, to replace the Sultan Abū Rābiʿ Suleimān with ʿAbd al-Ḥaqq ibn ʿUthmān the grandchild of Muḥammad b. ʿAbd al-Ḥaqq, "father of *all* the branches of the royal family" says Ibn Khaldūn, thus confirming that the old flame of disunity did not die out.[20] A few years later, yet another son of the chief of the Banū ʿAskar was responsible for conspiring against the royal family. After the Sultan Abū 'l-Ḥasan named him governor of Gibraltar, he had hoped to retain this position during the reign of his son Abū ʿInān, but when his hopes were dashed he decided to revolt against his master.[21] All in all, these revolts, even though destined to failure, show that the Banū ʿAskar continued to exist as an independent body within the confederation of the Marīnid tribes, and that their chiefs never gave up hope of somehow gaining control of the Marīnid state.

What, then, was the factor which secured the Banū Ḥamāma 's hold over the leadership of the Marīnid tribes? To find this out, we need to go back to the end of the 12th century, the decisive moments of the very first struggle between the two families for control of the tribal body.

Their groups' numbers appear to have been even, and in describing the Marīnids' way of life, the sources did not disclose any distinction between the two camps, except for one thing: their religious practices differed. It was never stated whether or not the Banū ʿAskar were devout Muslims, or whether or not Islam played any role in their political or military agenda. However, this mood changed after the transfer of power: the Banū Ḥamāma were wrapped in an Islamic mantle of piety.[22] Mayḥyū led the Marīnids alongside the Almohads in the war in al-Andalus, refered to as *jihād,* a holy war; he died covered with glory as a *shahīd,* a martyr, of wounds received in the battle. His son, ʿAbd al-Ḥaqq, subsequently became a holy man, but even more importantly, he possessed the power of the *baraka*:

> He grew under the influence of the sunna and the religion, and spent his life carrying out daily exercises in piety and devotion."[23] ... He could pronounce the *baraka*, his shirt and his pants were used in all the quarters of the Zanāta people, in order to facilitate birth...when he began to fast he would not stop... he ate only permitted foods... among the Marīnids he was considered to be a scholar of repute and a ruler whom everyone obeyed and recognized. They executed his orders, fulfilled his commands and conducted all their actions according to his opinions.[24]

ʿAbd al-Ḥaqq's mantle of the *baraka* has a familiar sound and appearance. We recognize in him the person of the Moroccan popular saint, the *ṣūfī* marabout, a well-known character of popular and mystical orders, believed by his fellow tribesmen to enjoy supernatural power, and endowed with the *baraka*, practiced healing and folk medicine. An authentic and still visible figure even today, numerous anthropologists have studied and observed him. With his healing power, his "noble" family line, his *baraka* and his followers, he was observed as recently as 1970 practicing in the Zerhoun, the very same region where ʿAbd al-Ḥaqq operated in the 13th century.[25] Although maraboutism was not systematically observed before the 17th century, this passage confirms that the phenomenon actually dates from much earlier date. The Marīnids, however, were quick to utilize the power of the *baraka*, the mythical force with which the saint was endowed. During the oath of allegiance sworn to ʿAbd al-Ḥaqq, when faced with the threat of the Banū ʿAskar, they would say: "You are our *amīr,* our chief, our *sheikh*, our *baraka*,"[26] The *amīr* responded in kind: "In the name of God, we shall march now against them, with his blessing, *barakatuhu*."[27] In these terms, never before pronounced in this context, the Marīnids' transformation into an Islamic people was declared. Normally a change of leadership in the Berber political system occurred following a military defeat, but once ʿAbd al-Ḥaqq had gained saintly attributes, the rules were no longer the same. A new mechanism was introduced, which heightened the role of Islam as a political legitimization tool, one which was powerful enough to keep the leadership in the hands of the Banū Ḥamāma.[28]

The use of Islam in the Marīnid rise to power did not end there, but was displayed once more, soon afterwards, in an urban setting. ʿAbd al-Ḥaqq perished fighting his old rivals, the Banū ʿAskar, without ever mentioning the idea of dislodging the Almohads. Yet the chroniclers recorded that within three years after his passing, in 610/1213, his son and heir, the *amīr* Abū Saʿīd I, led the Marīnids, with a plan to conquer the Maghreb under the banner of Islamic reform. The new agenda was preserved in a form of an address by Abū Saʿīd to the assembly of the Marīnid chiefs, where he presented his mission:

> The Almohads," he said, "are guilty because they neglected their duty towards the Islamic community. They neglected to provide an efficient government. They forgot their obligation towards their subjects, the *raʿiyya*. This negligence is an affront to the religious law and an insult which needs to be punished. Their annihilation therefore, constitutes a mission, and the Marīnids should take up this mission to further the well being and salvation of the Muslims."[29]

Surprising as it seems coming from somebody whom we would assume to be an unsophisticated nomad chief, the message itself was neither new nor original. In fact, it was rather a common currency in this period. Similar versions of this ideological platform were noted by other contemporaries, and attributed to other leaders. The Almohad Yayḥyā b. Naṣr, a contender for the throne, used the same cause, the well being of the Islamic community, and the same terminology when imploring the inhabitants of Marrakech to swear allegiance to him. His *risāla*, epistle, which was in effect written by the secretary Abū 'l-Ḥasan al-Saraquṣṭī in 625/1227, reads as follows:

> Know that the interest of the people, *raʿiyya*, requires a guardian to protect them and to make them respect the laws of Allāh which concern them; a guardian who should work for their welfare and improve their conditions. This goal will not be properly fulfilled except by a

> sultan who will reign over you. Know that Allāh has sent you a guardian who will look after your well being while you are asleep and do what is needed to improve your position while you are sitting down.[30]

The Almohad caliph al-Mustanṣir used the same idea and terminology in another epistle, also quoted in the *Bayān*. To encourage his subjects, who faced harsh conditions during the years 616-17/1219-20, he called upon them to place their confidence in the divine providence while portraying himself as being very concerned with their suffering and to rely on him.[31] All these documents, written during roughly the same years, highlight the notion of the Islamic ruler's obligation to his subjects and to the community, because rulers were under pressure to appease the public and placate public opinion. Through these texts we learn about the existence of social forces, mostly in the cities, where such notions about the duties of the monarch were upheld.

However, the Marīnids' use of these Islamic notions is nonetheless surprising. How and when did they gain sufficient access to Islamic ideology to be able to use it properly in these political circumstances? If neither the ideas nor the terminology used by the Marīnid *amīr* were his own, one wonders how he came to adopt them. In fact it would be hard to imagine him acquiring this ideology without outside help, since there were no jurists within the Marīnid camp itself. It seems plausible therefore, to attribute the advent of this mission among the Marīnids to the closer relationship which they developed during this period with the inhabitants of the cities of the Gharb, the north and west regions of modern Morocco, and especially with the jurists of Fez and Meknes. From the beginning of the year 614/1217, the Marīnids fostered daily contacts with the cities in the neighbourhood in which they were stationed or herding. During these years, and particularly in 1219-20, political and economic conditions deteriorated rapidly, as a result of a series of calamities which caused famine and food shortages. The nomads, Arabs and Berbers, following their regular patterns, arrived from the desert, and helped themselves to the produce of the cultivated lands. They also threatened the commercial routes, attacking and pillaging the caravans.[32] The Almohads' reaction was inefficient and insufficient, and the urban population voluntarily accepted the protection offered them by the Marīnids in return for regular payments, the *khufāra*.[33] During these negotiations the *amīr* Abū Saʿīd, in his capacity as chief of the Marīnids, had the opportunity to listen to the Islamic discourse. In his many meetings with the city leaders, and with the clergymen and jurists who represented the inhabitants,[34] he learned about the Almohads' weakness and that their failure to provide effective government for their subjects constituted an affront to Islamic notions of good government. The jurists indicated to the Marīnid chief that the Almohads had not honoured their commitment to the Islamic community, and that this failure disqualified them as legitimate rulers. Under the jurists' influence, and employing their vocabulary, the Marīnid Abū Saʿīd presented this argument to his tribesmen. The religious leaders encouraged Abū Saʿīd to wrest control from the Almohads, and thus have taken an active part in political life, a role that later Marīnids would grow to regret allowing them to take. As far as Abū Saʿīd was concerned, once introduced to Islamic norms of government, he became well enough acquainted with them to endorse them as his own. He embraced the cause of the community's welfare, thereby gaining justification and legitimization for a religious agenda, which, he was told, he needed in order to depose a legitimate ruler, and garner the support of the religious milieu in the cities. But he could not have developed this agenda before his meetings with the jurists and the clergy, nor did he feel the need for one.

The change in the Marīnid camp was instantaneous. A Marīnid declaration of political independence had taken place immediately, something previously thought to have taken place as late as the year 642/1244, under the leadership of Abū Yaḥyā, the fourth *amīr* of the family of the Banū Ḥamāma. The response of the Banū Marīn was just as enthusiastic as Abū Saʿīd had hoped for. The movement of the Marīnid tribes to his camp gained momentum, "The first of the Maghrebi tribes to swear allegiance to him and place themselves under his banner were the Hawāra, then came the Tasūl, the Miknāsa, the Butūya, the Batlasa, the Kaznāya, the Banū Yartiyān, and the Ghawāta".[35] The great conquests in the region of Zerhoun, in the lands of the Auraba and Ṣanhāja, Fichtāla, Sadrāta, and others also dated from that time, as did the appointment of agents, *ḥufāẓ*, in these territories.[36] His cordial relationship with the Almohads, which had proceeded cautiously on both sides until then, began to deteriorate: "The governor of Fez," said Ibn ʿIdhārī,"the *sayyid* Ibn Ibrāhīm, put much effort into controlling the Marīnids. From the year 613, he kept honouring them but watching them closely, until the year 617, when the *amīr* Abū Saʿīd ʿUthmān took over and became the only person to decide about the exchange of messengers, the expeditions and the exchange of gifts between the Marīnids and the Almohads. That situation lasted until the end of al-Mustanṣir billāh's government in 620."[37] The year 617/1220 is significant since we know that Abū Saʿīd came to power in 614/1217, and therefore the year 617/1220 must correspond to the date of his independence declaration, not to the beginning of his reign. The author of the *Dhakhīra* confirms this by saying that in 617 Abū Saʿīd had appropriated the banners and drums, always deemed to be the symbols of independence.[38] In the annals section of his chronicle he added that in the year 617, "Abū Saʿīd controlled most of the valleys of the Maghreb, and had installed his agents there".[39] During his twenty-four year reign over the Gharb, Abū Saʿīd managed to establish himself as the real master in this region. As early as 634/1236, the Almohad caliph al-Rashīd recognized him as lieutenant by dispatching robes of honour to him. Ibn ʿIdhārī noted that Abū Saʿīd entertained a delegation of Marīnids in grand style during his journey to Fez, and gave them many presents, as an independent ruler.[40] The Marīnid camp grew sufficiently to inspire fear within the Almohad camp. Ibn Wanūdīn, the great officer of the Almohad empire, saw Abū Saʿīd as the major obstacle between himself and the realization of his own ambitions.[41] It was he who paid the *amīr*'s slave to kill his master while he slept in his tent, because he himself "*conceived the idea of becoming independent*".[42] Despite the crushing defeat inflicted on the budding Marīnid state by the Almohads in 642/1244, they were able to reorganize under the *amīr* Abū Yaḥyā, a final demonstration of Abū Saʿīd's sound political organizational skills. In the long run, Abū Saʿīd knew how to achieve a coherent, powerful political body, by infusing it with a normative Islamic sense of mission and legitimacy.

Acculturation to Islamic norms was manifested at both ends of the Marīnid Berber society. Popular sainthood at the tribal level and good government in the upper political echelons were both necessary to further their cause. Between them they inspired the devising of a Berber-Islamic state. The support of the urban religious elite, which had a more sophisticated, longer established, set of Islamic norms, was no less crucial in the formation of the Marīnid state. In order to devise an Islamic state, the Marīnids required a symbiosis of all three sets of norms and the cooperation and integration of all three social groups which identified with them. In the next two chapters we will examine how this symbiosis and integration functioned and what happened when it failed.

CHAPTER 5

Out with Jewish Courtiers, Physicians, Tax Collectors and Minters*

The *al-Qarawiyyin* Mosque in Fez.

Once established in Fez, the Marīnids discovered that providing the exemplary Islamic rule to their subjects, in the name of which they conducted their operation against the Almohads, proved to be more complicated than doing away with their predecessors. Providing good government required the recognition of the Marīnid dynasty as the legitimate sovereign in Fez before the implementation of Islamic inspired policies could be undertaken. The process involved acculturation to Islamic norms and institutions on the part of both the dynasty itself and its subjects. With acculturation, the Marīnids could hope to consolidate the state's social fabric, and bring the tribal body affiliated to them to unite better with the urban population, which remained less positive and less supportive of the regime. The way in which the Marīnids interacted with two distinct social groups, the religious urban milieu of Fez and the Jews, offers an insight into how the Islamic norms of government were tested, adopted or rebuffed under social, political and economic pressures.

The two groups were opposed to one another. The Berber-Islamic state needed the urbanites because they were better acculturated to Islamic norms and could legitimize, perform services and provide ties with the rest of the Islamic lands, even though they were not always trustworthy. The situation of the Jews was equally problematic. According to the Islamic norms they, the *ahl al-dhimma*, Jews and Christians, could not be given positions of authority over Muslims, and therefore could not be employed by the state administration. Despite this provision, medieval Islamic history is replete with examples of Jews and Christians being employed at the court, in particular in financial administration and tax collection, which gave them power over Muslims and sometimes resulted in an employee's abrupt removal, and subsequently, violence against the whole Jewish community,

* "Les Juifs de Tlemcen au XIVe siècle," *La Revue des Études Juives* CXXXVII(1978): 171-77. "An Ethnic Factor in a Medieval Social Revolution: The Role of Jewish Courtiers Under the Marīnids," *Islamic Culture and Society: Essays in Honour of Professor Aziz Ahmad* (New Delhi, 1983): 149-64.

the "enemies of Allāh".[1] Such was the case of the Jewish vizier of Granada, Yehoseph, son of Shmuel Hanagid, in the 11th century neighboring Spain, and to Jews and Christians in Mamluk 14th century Egypt, where the *fatwās* issued by jurists testify how employment of *dhimmis* violates the laws of the Qur'ān.[2]

The status of the Marīnid Jews and their relationship with the court, however, was not that unusual or different from the historical experience of other Jewish communities under Islamic rule, except that, in this context, it gave rise to a historical debate among scholars precisely because on the one hand, the Marīnid rule was deemed an auspicious period for the Jews, but on the other, it was often marred by religious, fiscal and social persecution.[3] Prominent Marīnid historians such Ibn Abī Zarʿ in his *Qirṭās,* and al-Ḥakīm in his minting manual, frequently referred to the Jews, past or present, with the phrase *laʿanahum Allāh,* "May God curse them", while mob attacks on the Jews took a high toll on lives and property, not unlike their experiences under the Almohads.[4] Yet, in an apparent contradiction, Jewish courtiers appeared in the Marīnid court on two separate occasions, almost side by side with these attacks. The Banū Roqāsa were there at the beginning of the 14th century and the Banū Batās in the middle of the 15th. On the basis of this association with the court, historians suggested that the reason for the dynasty's benevolent attitude towards the Jews lay in the existence of a large group of Judaized Berbers, dating back to antiquity, among the Zanāta and that familiarity with them induced the Marīnids, who belonged to the Zanāta family, to demonstrate a particularly benign attitude towards the Jews.[5] According to this premise, the Marīnids had come to know the Jews during their wanderings in the central and western North African plains, and therefore, in the words of David Corcos, a protagonist of this theory, they displayed "an attitude which without question goes beyond the bounds of simple tolerance" towards them.[6] This theory has many flaws, however.[7] Most of the information about the Berbers' conversion to Judaism was recent, dating from the 11th and 12th centuries, which explains the silence of Jewish and Christian sources about such an event taking place prior to the Muslim conquest. The information itself is of a legendary nature, derived from reports based on anthropological observations rather than from historical evidence. Instances of individual Jews living among Berber tribes, cases of Jews converted to Islam, willingly or by force, the existence of legends about the ten lost tribes being alive in North Africa, and the missionary work of Jewish merchants criss-crossing the Maghreb on the caravan routes, could all be factors which contributed to the circulation of rumors about Judaized Berbers. In addition, the most recent studies of the heresy among the Berghāwāta Berber tribes, which some believed to have been "a kingdom of Judaized Berbers", until its elimination in 543/1148, have shown that this was not the case.[8] On the whole, there is neither solid historical evidence, nor sufficient anthropological or ethnic basis to support the idea of Berbers' conversion to Judaism.[9]

In addition, very little information is available about the Jews in Fez before the Marīnids. According to 14th-century writers, the settlement of Jews in Fez dates back to the time of Idris II, sometime around 193/808. Initially settled near the river Aghlān, or near Bāb ḥiṣn Saʿdūn, the Jews were forced to pay the *jizya*, head tax, of thirty thousand dinar yearly.[10] Around 1100 they complained about anti-Jewish feelings in Fez, in a Geniza letter where the author spoke openly about the situation there, compared to the comfortable atmosphere in Almeria, Spain.[11] During the middle years of the 14th century there is much more evidence about the Jewish community in Fez. They were named in a *fatwā* requesting access to a water canal which went through a mosque adjacent to their quarter.[12] Their connections with Arab philosophers are illustrated in the work of Judah b. Nissim Ibn Malkah, a 14th-century Jewish philosopher in Fez,[13] who wrote a philosophical tractate in Arabic, later abridged in Hebrew, which reveals Islamic influences.[14] Yet, to answer the question of whether and why the Marīnids seemed to have been more hospitable towards the Jews than other dynasties in Morocco, we need to examine the situation within the larger frame of their relations with their Muslim subjects, especially with the religious milieu of Fez.[15]

A few events which took place during the first 100 years of Marīnid rule demonstrated that relationships between the two were bad almost from the very beginning. A first revolt against the Marīnids occurred under the first sultan, Abū Bakr, 642-57/1244-58, in 648/1250. Maybe Abū Bakr was perceptive enough to predict that this revolt would be significant for the future of the Marīnid relationship with the city, or maybe he was simply ferocious, but he did not hesitate to put to death six leaders of the revolt, among them the *qāḍī* and his son. The chroniclers who mentioned this event agreed that it was a lesson which the Fezis will remember in years to come.[16] But in spite of the severity of the punishment, another uprising occurred in 675/1276 under the second sultan Abū Yūsuf, 657-85/1258-86. This upheaval ended with the first assault on the Jews, after a Muslim girl claimed that a Jew had assailed her in his house: "Fourteen Jews had been killed by the time the news reached the *Amīr al-Muslimīn*, who came riding with his soldiers to drive the mob away from the Jewish quarters and stop the pillage. Without his intervention none of the Jews would have survived; later he publicly warned the inhabitants of the *medina*, the old quarter, that no one should bother the *dhimma* Jews, under the threat of a severe punishment. On the next day Abū Yūsuf began to build the White City, Fez Jdid, his capital".[17]

The construction of a new Marīnid capital, the new Fez, is attributed by historians to the lack of space in the old *medina* for Abū Yūsuf's large army and his growing administration.[18] Sometimes it is attributed to the urban tradition of North Africa, where rulers liked to build new capitals, but, contemporaries tended to associate it with the tension between the Marīnids and the Fezīs. In fact Abū Yūsuf actually contemplated choosing Marrakech, the Almohad capital, as his residence and is reported to have lived there for the six months following its conquest by the Marīnids, until the hostility of the locals drove him to Fez.[19] Ibn Marzūq, even though not a native Fezī, wrote in 772/1370, that Abū Yūsuf built Fez Jdid, in order to separate, *tamayyaza*, himself from the crowd of Fez.[20] Still later, another Moroccan historian, writing about the biographies of the learned men of Fez, reported that Abū Yūsuf's decision to build the city followed an argument with the *qāḍī* al-Waryaghilī, a prominent clergyman of the city.[21] The sources do not indicate whether Abū Yūsuf himself employed Jews in his administration at the time of the incident, but his son and successor, Abū Yaʿqūb, fraternized with the Jews and included them in his immediate entourage during his father's lifetime.[22] The outburst of anti-Jewish feelings during this time might well be related to the regime's association with them. Regardless of whether or not the attack on the Jews was the final straw in the strained relationship between Fez and the Marīnids, the violent attack on them convinced Abū Yūsuf that there was no hope of reaching a peaceful coexistence in Fez, and furthermore, of the need to protect the Jews. Eventually they were transferred to the new city and settled in their new quarters, which became the Jewish ghetto, the *mellāḥ*.

Why were the Fezīs so hostile towards the Marīnids? The residents of Fez considered themselves to be cultivated and refined in comparison to their new rulers, who they thought were simple and rude nomads who had seized power by brutal force. They felt that the traditional aura of Fez, the noble origin of its founder, Idris, the legendary attributes of its foundation, and its urban and religious institutions, as well as its celebrity as the capital of intellectual and religious life, conferred on them a certain pre-eminence and independence, which the new rulers did not respect. The Andalusian geographer Abū Saʿīd al-Gharnaṭī who lived in the early years of the Marīnid rule said that "the residents of Fez are well educated, learned, and intelligent; the town is a true arsenal where one finds more physicians, jurists, scholars, and nobles, *sharīfs*, than in any other city".[23] But such was not always the case. Earlier authors such as al-Muqaddasī, writing around 375/985, said that the Fezīs "were ignoramuses and slow learners, the scholars are rare amongst them, but the agitation frequent".[24] A century later, al-Bakrī gave unflattering opinions as well,[25] but clearly things have changed for the Fezīs over time, and whether or not such grounds justified rejecting the Marīnids, disapproval towards them remained a constant feeling in the capital. The revolt of the city in 648/1250,[26] and the assassination of the last Marīnid sultan and his replacement by a *sharīf* in 870/1465,[27] the two principal events which began and ended the Marīnid rule in Fez, demonstrated that this ongoing antagonism between rulers and subjects, was neither an isolated case nor historical accident. Islamic perceptions also had something to do with it. Even though Abū Yūsuf wanted and gained Islamic legitimacy by undertaking a successful campaign, a *jihād* in fact, in al-Andalus, in response to the call for help from the Muslims stranded there, his reputation was tarnished, because he collected unlawful taxes and other fiscal dues to finance it.[28] The reign of his son, Abū Yaʿqūb, 685-707/1286-1307, was not popular either with the keepers of Islamic norms. When he succeeded to the throne he cancelled the non-Qur'ānic taxes imposed by his father, but he clashed with the city's clergymen, after he fired the Qarawīyīn mosque's *imām*, who they had selected. His difficulties with his subjects increased even further towards the end of the century, when a severe drought, followed by a famine and pestilence, fell on Morocco.[29] The short reigns of each of his two successors,

707-10/1307-10, were also marked by several riots against them in the city. In 707/1307, a revolt broke out in Fez, once again on religious grounds, when the city's *mufti* ordered the public flogging of the Naṣrid ambassador to the Marīnid court, because his breath smelled of wine. The humiliated ambassador complained to the vizir, who ordered that the *mufti*'s men who had carried out the sentence be put to death. When the people of the city rose to rescue them, the Marīnid sultan Abū Rābiʿ Suleimān was forced to fire his vizir in order to appease the crowd.[30] In 718/1318 there was another popular revolt, when the body of Idris, the 8th century founder of the city, appeared in his tomb. The people gathered from all sides because of this. The authorities feared a *fitna*, revolt, and the sultan Abū Saʿīd had to use his troops in order to disperse the crowd.[31] This uprising was particularly significant because it indicated the transformation of the cult of Idris, hitherto unmentioned, into a political movement hostile towards the Marīnids, and which would later play an important role in mobilizing opposition.[32]

The clergy's opposition to the regime led to a quiet social revolution in Fez, compelling the court to turn to non-Fezīs in order to fill administrative positions such as secretaries, courtiers, poets and historians. The Jews were not the only ones to benefit from this sudden vacuum at the top, since there was no shortage of talented, educated and prominent outsiders, fleeing the advancing reconquista in Spain, who were willing to take positions in the Maghrebi administrations.[33] Prince Abū Mālik, d.671/1272, tried to have his protégés integrated into the administration while the court was residing in Marrakech, but encountered strong opposition from the local cadres, and was forced to abandon his plan. However, once settled in Fez, the Marīnids continued to replace local dignitaries with newcomers.[34] Both Abū Yūsuf and Abū Yaʿqūb already had an entourage of newcomers, who were not members of local families.[35] For example, al-Malzūzī, supervisor, *muḥtasib*, historian and poet, was a Zanāta Berber born in Meknes;[36] Ibn al-Muraḥḥal, a jurist and poet attached to the court, was a newcomer from Spain who had lived in Ceuta before coming to Fez;[37] and al-Milyānī, a tax collector and secretary was a native of Ifrīqiya, who had lived there until he was driven out, and then joined the Marīnids.[38] New jurists, Zanāta Berber *fuqahā'*, loyal to the regime, were recruited for the opening of the *medresas*, one of the new institutions the Marīnids introduced.[39] The Jews were the latest addition to these social parvenus.

The Banū Roqāsa, the first family of Jewish courtiers, appeared in the last decade of the 13th century.[40] Khalīfa b. Ḥayā b. Roqāsa was a Jewish palace attendant who enjoyed a commanding position in the Marīnid court for several years before his master Abū Yaʿqūb became sultan of Morocco. While in power, he enjoyed having all the dignitaries and army chiefs honor and obey him, but subsequently lost his position to a Muslim, ʿAbd Allāh b. Madyan. The Banū Madyan were also newcomers from the northern city of Qṣar al-kebir, who had arrived in Fez not long before ʿAbd Allāh b. Madyan challenged the Jewish Khalīfa and succeeded him.[41] The Jew was killed with most of his family.[42] His cousin, Khalīfa b. Ibrāhīm b. Roqāsa, entered the court's service not long afterwards, but only held the position for long enough to allow him to take revenge on ʿAbd Allāh b. Madyan.[43] Both Jews served as *ḥājib,* palace attendants, not viziers.[44]

By the middle of the Marīnid rule, the position of the Jews had not improved. The short stint at the court did not change their status in any meaningful way, and it continued to oscillate between mere toleration and outright banning. But the Jews' incidental association with the Marīnid state also reproduced itself in the economic sphere. Jews were recruited sporadically into the Marīnid financial administration in spite the norm which ban their employment there. Ibn ʿIdhārī mentioned that Jews were present in the city of Azemour on the Atlantic coast, which was an important trade center.[45] A Jew named Ibn Shalūkha was even custodian of the government treasury, *khāzin al-māl,* in Sijilmāsa, the desert port in the far south.[46] But the strongest Jewish presence was felt in the royal mint, in Fez and other cities. According to the head of the royal mint, *dār al-sikka*, the Jews dominated the different minting trades, in addition to being money changers, goldsmiths and silversmiths. Al-Ḥakīm, the author of a minting manual,[47] accused the Jews of sneaking into these noble occupations, whereas in the past they had been reduced to working only at menial and despicable trades, such as tanners, painters, embalmers, peddlers, porters, tailors and measurers.[48] Those Muslims who did not want to submit their children to control by non-believers, *dhimmi*s, left the trades associated with the mint altogether.[49] As a result, "the Jews, may the curse of Allāh be upon them, took over the trade in gold and silver for themselves, and therefore the taxes and income of the mint, diminished".[50] Once the Jews had taken over the goldsmith trades, al-Ḥakīm continued, they needed to obtain gold and silver and entered the money changing business, which necessitated frequent visits to the mint. The government agents, *wulāt, ʿummāl,* entrusted them with the collection of the taxes in other areas, a job which led to abuse and fraud against the Muslims.[51] Their power was revoked in 736/1335, when complaints reached the sultan Abū ʾl-Ḥasan, and he decided to put an end to this practice. After establishing the facts of the fraud, he ordered that the Jews should be removed from goldsmithery, money changing and tax collection in every region under his rule. Moreover, if they traded in the market or were making a living in one of the trades, they should also pay the applicable taxes, a duty from which they, unlike the Muslims, were currently exempted.[52] However, continued al-Ḥakīm, the Jews did not stay away for long, and the fraudulent in minting of dinars and dirhams, clipped coins, and the minting of coins outside the royal mint, resumed on their return. An order issued by Abū ʿInān, the son of Abū ʾl-Ḥasan, imposed further restrictions on their activities. No minting was allowed outside the *dār al-ḍarb* they could not purchase gold and silver before it had first been offered to the *amīn*, director of the mint, their money changing activities were supervised, and no wine could be presented to Muslims or offered for sale by them. The Jewish elders signed official documents with the court, taking responsibility in the name of their entire community for the fulfillment of these conditions.[53]

Abū ʾl-Ḥasan was the Marīnid sultan most bent on upholding Islamic norms in his government.[54] Like Abū Yūsuf he fought the Christians in al-Andalus, but fared better in his battles with his Muslim neighbors. He embarked on a policy of eliminating the Jews from the public sector in Morocco and pursued it in the cities in the central Maghreb which the Marīnids conquered. An incident which occurred in Tlemcen after it surrendered to the Marīnid troops, gave Abū ʾl-Ḥasan the opportunity to demonstrate that he upheld Islamic norms against employment of Jews by refusing to apply medication prescribed by a Jewish physician, as long as the Jew refused to convert to Islam.[55]

This confrontation took place in 738/1337, the year in which Abū ʾl-Ḥasan acquired jurisdiction over the Jewish community of Tlemcen. Arabic and Hebrew sources are mostly silent about the Jews of Tlemcen in the 14th century. After being driven out of Morocco and the Maghreb by the

Almohads, they were believed to avoid settling there but the Aragonese archives furnish plenty of evidence that this was not the case. Not only did a large community live there, but Tlemcen's Jews appear to have acted as intermediaries in the gold trade and in the export of slaves from the Sudan to Europe.[56] More information about Tlemcen's Jews comes from the relatively abundant rabbinical *responsa*, which date from the beginning of the 15th century, somewhat later than the period under consideration.[57] The *responsa* confirm that Jews from Spain and Majorca went to the Maghreb following the 1391 persecutions, settling around Alger rather than in Tlemcen. The limited number of requests for juridical consultations addressed to and from Tlemcen corroborate the existence of a small community, which can be explained by the city's precarious political situation in the 14th century. From the 13th century, when Tlemcen became the capital city of the Banū ʿAbd al-Wād, a Zanāta dynasty related to the Marīnids, the region became prey to Marīnid attacks from the west and Ḥafṣid attacks from the east.[58] Today, we do not know who the physician in question was, how long he lived in Tlemcen, and whether he gained his medical training in the Maghreb or elsewhere. However, Ibn Marzūq who seemed to have had contacts with the Jewish community in Tlemcen, was acquainted with the physician in question for many years and respected both his dexterity and knowledge. Ibn Marzūq also noted the presence of Jewish women, who were stationed at the gates to search the clothes of other women who came from the countryside to sell small items.[59] Their role was not limited to searching, however. During the siege of 707/1307, they, together with Christian women were designated as executioners of royal women who preferred to die rather than submit themselves to the Marīnids.[60]

The employment of Jewish physicians in Muslim and Christian courts was a long established tradition.[61] Abū 'l-Ḥasan's son, Abū ʿInān, requested the services of Ibrāhīm b. Zarzar, the Jewish physician in Granada, a few years later, and was greatly annoyed when the latter refused to come.[62] Abū 'l-Ḥasan built hospitals in Fez, so was, presumably, concerned with medical standards in his state, but he rejected a highly qualified Jewish physician. Faced with the disapproval resulting from his actions of removing legitimate Islamic rulers, he needed to reinforce his claim of being a pious and just ruler, carrying his ancestors' title *mujāhid*, warrior of holy war, he chose to uphold his Islamic uprightness by not employing Jews in any capacity in his administration. Abū 'l-Ḥasan's conduct in this episode is the exception which proves the rule: the dynasty had to steer a course between the requirement to acculturate and implement Islamic norms in personal and political life, and the needs of the Marīnid state.

Neither popular resistance, nor organized public manifestations of disapproval towards the Marīnid dynasty disappeared in the second half of the Marīnid rule. Rather, they became latent, only to reappear in full force in the 15th century. The second instance of the Jewish rise to power took place against a backlash of public resentment and violence, in circumstances similar to the first appearance. In the 15th century, however, the relationship between the Marīnids and their subjects deteriorated. The attacks of the Portuguese and Spanish fleets on the coastal cities aroused feelings of vulnerability and religious fanaticism, which led to resentment over the weak Marīnid response.[63] A grass roots movement was formed, with the intent of replacing the Marīnids with a Sharīfī family. The sovereign and his entourage found themselves not merely ill at ease in Fez, but living practically in isolation, alienated from the people. Leo Africanus, a Moroccan convert to Christianity living in 16th-century Italy, remarked that very few respected people, apart from the close family of the ruler and the people of the court, lived in the new Fez. This was because people feared for their reputation considered employment by the court repugnant. They would not even give their daughters in marriage to the people of the court...The result of this situation was that not a single educated and honest man would agree to maintain close relations with the rulers, eat with them at table and above all, receive a present or a grant from them.[64] These were the political and social conditions which brought the Jews, this time the Banū Batās family, back to Fez. Again the Jews were not the only people to benefit from the trend. The situation also gave Muslims, who had been disgraced and alienated for one reason or another, a chance to integrate or re-integrate themselves into the system. Ibn al-Aḥmar's reappointment as great *qāḍī* of the court, may be cited as an example of this pattern. A descendant of the Naṣrid royal family of Granada, born in 726/1325 and educated in Fez, he decided to leave the Marīnid capital in 763/1361 and join a rival branch in Marrakech. That decision quickly proved to be mistaken, as the secessionist branch disintegrated and the future Marīnid historian was disgraced and shunned. Although he returned to Fez a few years later, his defection was never forgotten and he was doomed to serve as a minor assistant in the royal chancellery, complaining bitterly about his dire situation in his writings. Around the year 803/1400, even though there was no evidence that he had had a previous judicial career or a name as a jurist, he was appointed a great *qāḍī* to the court. However, since at this time the jurists employed in the city's justice administration had become increasingly anti-Marīnid, and were leaving the court service in droves, he was called upon to fill one of the vacancies.[65] In the ensuing insurrection in 870/1465, the Jew Harūn b. Batās, and his brother Shawil (Saul) or Shamouil (Samuel) shared the fall of the Marīnids. The Marīnid association with the Jews triggered calamity for the Jewish community of Fez as well.[66] On the basis of a similar accusation to the one of 675/1276, that the Jews had insulted a *sharīfa*, a noble woman, the mob, headed by the religious leaders, attacked the Jewish quarters, killing and plundering. It is believed that a large part of the Jewish community of Fez perished, along with many other Jews in various cities in Morocco. In contrast to the 675/1276 event, neither the sultan nor his troops could or would protect them. The Fez uprising in 1465 was the final one, albeit the most important, since it put an end to the Marīnid dynasty and temporarily to the Jewish community. The references in the few Jewish chronicles state unequivocally that the 1465 attack resulted in the conversion and total annihilation of the Jewish community of Fez.[67]

When making appointments of power in the administration, the Marīnids did not favor the Jews unless they were forced to do so by lack of popular support, or better candidates. But when a Marīnid ruler enjoyed some degree of cooperation from the Fezī families and clergymen, as Abū 'l-Ḥasan did, he was only too ready to dispense with the services of the Jews. It was also evident that these appointments only increased the hostility and resentment of society at large to the Jews and the regime. As far as individual Jews were concerned, they agreed to be elevated to positions of power at the court, even though it put them and the community in jeopardy. But individual Jews were not unique in gaining positions of power without the traditional support of a cohesive social group. The Marīnid regime, because of its destructive power was a disruptive factor, changing structures, social fabric and policies, which together with the changing political realities in the area, promoted individualism. This policy was maintained not only at the court but in public institutions as well. Portrayed in the next chapter is a Muslim, the *Khaṭīb* al-Mazdaghī, whose fall from grace in the Marīnid court exposed the strength and the weakness of the regime's policy of recruitment.

CHAPTER 6

The Fall of the *Khaṭīb* Abū 'l-Faḍl Al-Mazdaghī*

Marīnid Gold
Fāris al-Mutawakkil
Type I BMC 186
c49a.22

Marīnid Gold
Fāris al-Mutawakkil
Type I BMC 187
c49a.22

Marīnid Gold
Fāris al-Mutawakkil
Type III BMC 193
c49a.22

Three double gold Marīnid dinars struck by the Sultan Abū ʿInān in Bijāya, Tilimsān and Sijilmāsa, claiming the title *Commander of the Believers, amīr al-mu'minīn.*

The friction between the Islamic norms of government and the needs and interests of the dynasty was reflected in the sporadic employment at court of elements such as Jews, and frequently pitted the Marīnids against the religious milieu of Fez. But what happened when one of their own appointees was caught in embezzlement, especially when he was a client not only of the court, but also of the religious milieu? The outcome was nothing less than sheer drama and nowhere was this conflict better displayed than in the case of the 14th century Fezī clergyman turned failed investor.

Al-Jaznā'ī, the author of the *Zahrat al-ās*, a chronicle of the city of Fez and its two principle mosques, related how Abū 'l-Faḍl al-Mazdaghī his illustrious contemporary and the celebrated preacher of the Qarawīyīn mosque, had fallen from grace.[1] Al-Mazdaghī had carried out the two important functions of *imām*, prayer leader and *khaṭīb*, preacher, in the central mosque of Fez, the Qarawīyīn mosque, since 726/1325, when, at the height of his twenty-year career, he had lost his enormous fortune by amassing debts of more than thirty-one-thousand gold dinars. This bankruptcy would have been extraordinary enough under normal circumstances, but the matter was aggravated by the fact that the loss involved deposits made by the public, orphans' inheritance money, and revenue from *waqf* endowments which he, a clergyman and a community leader of great repute, administered. When the Marīnid sultan Abū 'l-Ḥasan, 734-49/1333-48, who, at the time, was resting his troops after the siege of al-Manṣūra,[2] heard about it, he demoted al-Mazdaghī from his public functions.[3] The scandal must have been quite an event at the time since al-Jaznā'ī was not alone in reporting it. The *khatīb* Muḥammad b. Aḥmad Ibn Marzūq, another colleague and contemporary of al-Mazdaghī, was even an eye witness to the event, and left a colorful, full and detailed description.[4] Ibn Marzūq was a secretary to Abū 'l-Ḥasan at the time and met Abū 'l-Faḍl on the road to

**La Revue des Études Islamiques*, 47(1979): 239-47.

the Marīnid court at al-Manṣūra, and later participated in the resolution of the affair.[5] Although he composed the *Musnad* in 772/1370 in Tunis, where he was living in exile, his account goes beyond describing the personal misfortune of al-Mazdaghī, giving a rare insight into the Marīnid state's policies and organization. Ibn Marzūq's account is a part of the sixteenth chapter of his *Musnad*, the memoir he wrote to commemorate the noble qualities and deeds of his master, the Marīnid sultan Abū 'l-Ḥasan. In this chapter, devoted to the "timidity" of Abū 'l-Ḥasan, *fī ḥayā'ihi,* Ibn Marzūq gives several examples of events in which this character trait was displayed, the affair in question being one such occasion.

In order to set the scene for the drama, we need to familiarize ourselves with the *khaṭīb* and his career and situate him and his patrician family in the 14th-century Fezī social scenery with which our two narrators were acquainted. Abū 'l-Faḍl was a highly respected individual, well known throughout Fez. His family, the al-Mazdaghīs, had been established in the city for many years, and its members had held public office for at least a hundred years, since the 13th century. Some were judges, like Abū Jaʿfar b. Aḥmad al-Mazdaghī who served as a *qāḍī* in Fez until his death in 669/1270.[6] Several other members of the family were jurists who left *fatwās*, legal opinions, which are now preserved in *al-Miʿyār,* the Malikī collection of these legal rulings.[7] The 14th century chronicles, *al-Dhakhīra al-saniyya,*[8] *Rawḍ al-Qirṭās,*[9] and *Zahrat al-ās*,[10] confirm that Abū 'l-Faḍl himself was the fourth generation of al-Mazdaghīs to have served as *imām* in the Qarawīyīn mosque. Abū ʿAbd Allāh Muḥammad, who was appointed in the year 653/1255, was first to hold this post.[11] He was the son of the *sheikh* Abū 'l-Ḥajjāj Yūsuf al-Mazdaghī a known scholar of his time, who held another position, probably that of a teacher, in the mosque. Among the many pieces that he wrote was a *tafṣīr*, commentary, on the Qur'ān which remained incomplete.[12] As he carried out his duties, Abū ʿAbd Allāh, who was the great grandfather of our al-Mazdaghī appointed his son Abū 'l-Qāsim to the post of *khaṭīb*, and they worked together until their respective deaths.[13] In 694/1294 the Marīnids appointed his son, Abū 'l-Ḥasan al-Mazdaghī as *khaṭīb,* to succeed his father. Three years later, in 697/1297, when the *imām* of the al-Qarawīyīn died, he also became *imām,* uniting the two positions in his own hand. When it became too arduous for him to perform the *khitāba* because of his advanced age, the sultan Abū 'l-Ḥasan appointed his son, Abū 'l-Faḍl, *khaṭīb*.[14] From his father's death in 726/1325, until the event in question, Abū 'l-Faḍl was a central figure in the social life of Fez, frequently visiting the court and serving as an intermediary between the people and the authorities.[15] We do not know whether his huge fortune came from an inheritance, or was accumulated while in office, but contemporaries report that in addition to his income from the mosque, he also owned land which he cultivated, and that the fortune he amassed over the years permitted him to have his own little court where poets sang of his generosity in eloquent terms.[16] He could not endure the grief of his disgrace and died in 748/1347, two years after the event came to light.[17] Nonetheless, his name remained immortalized in Fez, chiseled in the foundation inscription on the wall of the *medresa* al-Misbaḥiya, following a list of properties which Abū 'l-Ḥasan endowed as *waqf* in 747/1346, for the maintenance of this *medresa*.[18] His is the only name associated with that of the sultan, and A. Bel, who deciphered and published this inscription, suggested that on this occasion he was also appointed the administrator of the properties, which might indicate his reintegration into the public administration.[19] This is the story of his fall from grace, as told by Ibn Marzūq:

> This is the affair of the respected *khaṭīb* Abū 'l-Faḍl Muḥammad, the son of the pious *khaṭīb* Abū 'l-Ḥasan al-Mazdaghī, a *khaṭīb* in the mosque of al-Qarawīyīn in Fez. According to everyone, they were the most admirable people. I am telling here a singular detail of the life of our master and his kindness, may God be his benefactor.
>
> This *khaṭīb*, may God have mercy on him, had the nobility of a strong horse, always looking to perform good deeds, a devoted friend, always offering hospitality, loving his children and protecting them. Thanks to his position and his enormous wealth he was chosen to administer the inheritance money of the orphans, which was deposited with him in his capacity as a legal guardian, and also the income from the endowments, *waqf*s. He faced enormous expenses because of the needs of his children and the buildings which they had started to build. He was obliged to use the money deposited with him and hope that he would be able to repay it from the revenue he anticipated deriving from his holdings and his lands. This is why he had borrowed money from the deposits at his disposal, and transferred both the deposits and the interest gained on them, to his own account. He did all this in secrecy and operating from his own account, until he eventually exceeded the limit; the sum of money owed became bigger and

bigger and went beyond his capacity to reimburse it. At this point he stopped because he was afraid that his fraud was going to be discovered, but he could not see any way out. According to what he said, he had debts of approximately thirty-thousand gold dinars.

And so, one night when I was with our master, may God accede on his behalf, he asked me to go to Oujda to bring the great chandelier that belonged to the big mosque of New Tlemcen [al-Mansūra] which his uncle, the sultan Abū Yaʿqūb, may God have mercy on him, had originally made to put in the mosque in that city's Casba.

I departed at dawn. En route to Oujda I met the *khaṭīb* al-Mazdaghī coming from Fez. He saluted me, and greeted me, but he was very, very sad. I asked him, "What is the problem?"

"I would prefer you to be there when I arrive at the court," he said.

"Oh," said I, "people like you and I don't need intermediaries at our master's court, he is on your side."

"Well, I came on very important business," he said.

"As far as his grace is concerned, every business is very important, and every big business is minimal," I said.

"Nonetheless, I hope that you won't stay too long," said he.

"I hope so too," I responded.

I stayed two days at Oujda and when I came back on the third day, I met one of our friends who told me: "Something very bad has happened here."

"What is it?" I asked him, and he answered,"Our master, God be his protector, is very, very sad and depressed. It is already two days since he last ate and we don't know the reason."

When I entered and saluted him, I noticed that the situation was indeed very, very bad, even worse than they had told me. I went home. When it was time for evening prayer, I entered and found him, may God protect him, in the big council hall, which he had inaugurated in old Tlemcen, and which was attached to his magnificent palace. Several of our colleagues were already seated. So he asked me, "Are you aware of it?"

I answered "I'm not aware of anything except for the fact that I see that you are in a very bad state of depression and sadness."

"Yes, this is true," he said, "this is the third day on which I have not touched food. I'm afflicted by what has happened to this person, the disappearance of the morality which all the world recognized in him, and by the decline of someone whom I have trusted, and placed in such a high position."

"Who is this person, may God protect you?" I asked, and he responded; "The *khaṭīb* al-Mazdaghī."

I went on to ask, "What is the matter?"

"He obliterated the Muslims' money."

"How did he do that? Did he steal it? Did he lose it?"

"If it was only that. By God, By God! If he could have let me know about it I would have reimbursed everything, but he disgraced himself and also greatly embarrassed me because a large number of people are aware of this business. If nobody had been informed about it, I would have paid in his place but I asked him where things are, and he told me that he told several people in the Casba."

Then all the people who were present, including myself, started to calm down our master and minimize the gravity of the affair until the time of the evening prayer.

When he left the prayer hall we asked him to enter, he entered the palace and then left after a while. We were told that he took a little soup. After he left, we discussed his intentions relating to this affair. In the morning he asked us to assemble at his place, and appointed the jurists ʿAbd al-Muhaymin and the *qāḍī* Abū Isaq Ibrāhīm b. Abū Yaḥyā, as well as Ibn Yarbūʿa, Ibn Tadarart, and his secretary, the author of this work, to deal with it.

ʿAbd al-Muhaymin and the *qāḍī* expressed very negative opinions about the *khaṭīb*, but when the jurist Ibn Tadarart addressed the assembly, he spoke kindly about him. Later on, the *khaṭīb* was interrogated about the use he had made of the money and he explained what had happened. He was told, in an accusing manner, that he was responsible for the money deposited with him. Trying to justify himself, he brought up an argument which was even worse, may God forgive him. He said,

"I had a lot of grain in store, waiting for the price to go up. When I went to inspect it, I discovered that my children had spent a great part of it and what was left no longer belonged to me. So I have come today to request that the sultan awards me three gold charges which I will take to the inn of the Shammāʿīn, in Fez and I will repay the money I owe to each and every one of my debtors. I'll pay everyone what I owe him."

There were some people among us who condemned him, and declared that we would not accept his request, but others excused him and supported him. Then we came to our master, may God protect him. He said,

"By God, by God! If I didn't know for a fact that his children have wasted a large part of that money on frivolities and luxuries, I would be one of those who accept his request. But he was so unethical, that it would be even more unethical to reimburse this money with money belonging to the Muslim community than it would be to do so with money from my own treasury. My decision is, therefore, that I will personally replace the money owed to the fund for my servants' orphans, but, so far as the money from the deposited *waqf* income from endowed properties is concerned, we shall calculate the value of the properties he bought, and sell them to pay his debts. As for the *khaṭīb*, we shall leave him enough money for living quarters and to provide for his children and for his servants. I will provide him with a pension in order to acquire land for his needs, which he will cultivate but, in the name of God, I don't want to see him. I'm too ashamed on his behalf."

Then the *khaṭīb* wrote and requested an audience but he, God may protect him, said, "By God, by God! I'm too ashamed to see him, I'm so ashamed for him."

Then he ordered the people to return to Fez, assemble the jurists and the pious people, and make them aware of this event, and to propose reimbursing whatever the *khaṭīb* had spent and keeping him in his post. He said, again, may God protect him,

"Our ancestor, ʿAbd al-Ḥaqq, may God protect him, has instructed us and we have followed his command that there are three positions of government you should not give to the people: *raʿiya*, commander of the Casba, chief of Police, and governor of the city, and there are three positions which will go to the people: *imām* and *khaṭīb*, *qāḍī* and the supervisor of public morals, *muḥtasib*."

Then the jurist, Abū ʿAlī b. Tadarart left to fulfill this mission, to which I was initially assigned. He arrived in Fez and gathered together those which were to be gathered in cases like this, but the people were divided. Finally they agreed on their decision and waited for the arrival of the *khaṭīb*. He was given what was his, and the share of the *waqf* which came to him from the income of the properties was calculated exactly, then the jurists returned to Tlemcen. During this time, the *khaṭīb* was in the palace of our master, may God defend him, in the small apartment called the "apartment of the secretaries." He was treated with all the honors due to people of his importance whether they are at home or traveling. The only honor never accorded him was that our master, may God guard him, never received him, because of the shame that he felt and had mentioned to me earlier.

When the jurist Abū ʿAlī returned to the court, the *khaṭīb* was authorized to leave, but he did not want to leave until he had been received by our master. So the sultan received him at night, keeping himself hidden from sight by the light of the candles. With his usual kindness, he said goodbye to him, crying all the time, then the *khaṭīb* left.

In spite of his sympathetic tone Ibn Marzūq was not an impartial observer. He was careful to leave us the details of the fraud, which came to light during the interrogation to which the *khaṭīb* was submitted, and the court's resolution of it, to show that he was critical of his colleague's financial dealings. He made clear that in his financial deals, al-Mazdaghī committed a double offence when he relied on benefiting from speculation in grain, and stole money for this purpose from deposits and from *waqf*'s endowment income. The offence was against the Islamic legal principle which forbids usury on moral grounds, since speculation was proscribed by Islamic jurists, who saw in it unjust enrichment, as well as against the principle which forbids making use of an item given for safekeeping, whether the item was liquidated by the use or not. In the *khaṭīb*'s case, such items were used to increase the capital with which he bought grain and properties. His deed is even more revealing about his privileged position. Storing a large amount of grain in order to sell it at a profit during years of drought, indicated that he could speculate with grain when the sale and export of grain to the Christian merchants was a government monopoly. Al-Mazdaghī must have used his favored position at the court to benefit from it.[20] The argument which he put forward in his defense, that his children wasted the majority of these resources, and that he was powerless against them, might have been made to reflect the tumultuous relationships Abū 'l-Ḥasan had with his own sons, but it did not find a sympathetic ear with the monarch, nor did it justify him in the eyes of his audience. Nonetheless, the affair took its toll on the sultan, who abstained from eating for three days, and was clearly distraught by it. Ibn Marzūq hints that he did not think Abū 'l-Faḍl was worthy of even the little kindness he received, but we should not ignore his motives in proclaiming Abū 'l-Ḥasan's devotion to his loyal servants and those of the dynasty. The *Musnad* was written and presented to Abū Fāris, Abū 'l-Ḥasan's younger son, in the hope of obtaining his favor and regaining his position in the Marīnid court.[21] If the Sultan demonstrated such loyalty and devotion to al-Mazdaghī, who, according to Ibn Marzūq, clearly did not deserve it, it would be hard to deny it to Ibn Marzūq, who never betrayed the royal trust.[22]

Beyond the frustrated personal ambitions, intrigues and accounts settled, which formed part of the lives of the elite at the Marīnid court, this story raises some important questions regarding the government structures of the

Marīnid state. First there was the legal aspect of the affair.[23] Was the *khaṭīb* accused of committing a crime? What about the procedure? Why was not he charged and brought before a court of justice, or can we read into this episode a description of the *maẓālim* court's session headed by the sultan? Legally speaking, delinquent administrators and petitions from the public against state officials were addressed only by this court and this should have been the institution before which Abū l-Faḍl would have been brought and tried, as this was the usual practice in the state. Ibn Baṭūṭa described how the *maẓālim* court functioned a few years later, under Abū ʿInān, Abū 'l-Ḥasan's son: "He used the early afternoon hours to listen to the women's complaints, and the hours after prayer for listening to the men's."[24] Yet, neither Ibn Marzūq nor al-Jaznā'ī mentioned the *maẓālim* court, nor was the expression 'court of law' ever used. Perhaps, a monarch of Abū 'l-Ḥasan's stature would not normally be expected to be distracted on his campaign with presiding over this court. Instead when having to deal personally with dishonest individuals implicated in fraudulent activities, Abū 'l-Ḥasan resorted to a special conflict resolution mechanism, incorporating both Islamic and Berber notions of justice, which was in tune with the public policies of the Marīnid state.

While he reserved the right to have the final say in the matter himself, Abū 'l-Ḥasan resorted to an institution, not even remotely resembling the Islamic court but reminiscent of the tribal assembly of peers and elders. He created an ad hoc committee to investigate and recommend action, made up of al-Mazdaghī's equals, members of families close to the Marīnids among them a *qāḍī*, a *faqīh* and a *khaṭīb*. Familiar with Berber notions of justice, they were resolved to handle the affair in accordance with a public policy which was now in place in the Marīnid state. Reimbursement of the stolen money would not come from the state's treasury, the *Bayt al-māl*, since the public should not suffer because of the impropriety of an individual who was the sultan's direct appointee. All the missing deposits, including those of the orphans and other private individuals, would be reimbursed from the sultan's treasury. The personal liability was retained, however, since the income from the endowments used by the *khaṭīb* to purchase grain would be reimbursed through the sale of properties which belonged to him. The *khaṭīb* himself would receive a pension as well as some land, and this would enable him to satisfy his personal needs.[25] After the decision was taken, Abū 'l-Ḥasan had the message passed on to the authorities in Fez and gave orders to reinvest al-Mazdaghī with his old functions.[26]

Ignoring the required legal procedure of an appearance before a *qāḍī* and a court, did not mean that Abū 'l-Ḥasan completely abandoned Islamic notions. On the contrary. The *Musnad* reads like an agenda for the behavior of a monarch intent on building a state shaped by Islamic principles, and to be sure, such behavior dominated this monarch's private life. Ibn Marzūq's memoir depicted Abū 'l-Ḥasan as being solely motivated by the desire to maintain the Islamic character of the Marīnid state. We are informed that on his access to power Abū 'l-Ḥasan abolished all non-Qur'ānic taxes, transcribed Qur'āns and sent them to Mecca, enabled his mother to travel on pilgrimage, and preferred to dispense with the medical advice from a Jewish physician who refused to convert to Islam.[27] But his devotion to seeing the ideal Islamic state he wanted to preside over, was mitigated by reality. The resolution of the affair shows that upholding Islamic conduct in the state's public life was a declared Marīnid policy, and that this policy was enacted with varying degrees of consistency at different times. As anywhere else, Islamic norms, whether legal or moral, were articulated and diffused from the mosques and expressed in public manifestations. The Islamic character of the Marīnid state was maintained thanks to the clergymen who pontificated in the mosques and the jurists who ruled in the courts. They populated the urban centers and applied Islamic principles to the lives of individuals and institutions, but they were also powerful and influential and had to be closely watched. What Ibn Marzūq depicted as friendship and loyalty to one's employees, was in fact three different policies which the Marīnids implemented side by side, appointment and patronage of selected families, institutional supervision and maintenance of Islamic norms. Policies were implemented with the intention of acquiring a pious image for the monarchy, bent on upholding the Islamic nature of the state via the increased role given to the clergymen in public life, while at the same time making sure that they did not become too independent, too influential and disobedient. By the time the first policy, a close supervision of appointments to public institutions, was implemented the struggle between the first Marīnids and the religious milieu of Fez, which raged during the second half of the 13th century, ended in the state's favor. By the time Abū 'l-Ḥasan came to power the right to make appointments to the religious institutions, in particular to the mosques, which had been disputed, had become the prerogative of the sultans.[28] The Marīnids developed a system of political patronage, through which key positions in the public domain, such as preacher, prayer leader, judge, market supervisor, were given to individuals who could be trusted. Ideally, the Marīnids sought individuals with similar backgrounds to the ruling family, such as those in military command, with Berber roots and tribal support. But the positions within the administration of justice and religion required education, knowledge of Islamic Law and training. The policy which was developed, separated two categories of administrative functions, the sword and the pen, or rather, religious and secular institutions, by creating a correlation between ethnic background, function and social organization. In order to legitimize and sanctify this policy it was quoted as a dictum from the mouth of ʿAbd al-Ḥaqq, the saintly founder of the Marīnid dynasty. This dictum, which put limitations on the clergy's power, sanctioned the military power given to the families related to the ruling house. Al-Mazdaghī was of Berber origin, albeit remote by now, a descendant of a family which had been associated with the regime and religious services for generations. His appointment was in recognition of a long standing service and loyalty to the state.

As the case of the al-Mazdaghīs shows, the implementation of this policy was facilitated by apprenticeship with one's father, and enhanced by the hereditary transmission of positions and functions, a pattern long established in other Islamic societies. Religious duties and appointments, like manual trades, tended to become hereditary in all Islamic cities, but under the Marīnids the transmission of a public administrative position from father to son, whether in the mosque or in the government, became institutionalized. This pattern was favored by the oral transmission of knowledge and practice, and through apprenticeship with a family member, which remained the most common channel for professional instruction despite mounting evidence of a large number of professional manuals, composed for trades such as secretarial, bindery, cooking, calligraphy etc. As everywhere else the policy had good and bad implications for the regime. While acting as a stabilizing factor in terms of providing administrative services to the public, this pattern contributed to the centralization of power into the hands of a limited number of individuals or families, led to the abuse of power and impeded free social mobility. This resulted in a system of close supervision of the families who monopolized the management of the religious life. As the case of the Azefīs of Ceuta has shown, the appointment of clergy had to be closely monitored, because these long established clergy families with a traditional hold on judicial power in cities, tended to take over the government when circumstances permitted.[29]

Another reason for the court's desire to control appointments to religious institutions, was the financial resources they controlled. The mosques in the Marīnid state, like other religious institutions, subsisted on financial contributions provided by income from endowments made by private individuals.[30] Allowing the clergy to control this income gave them the power which would usually be vested in the hands of administrative staff centered in the court. The enormous funds deposited with al-Mazdaghī, which he used for speculation, were both a reminder and a demonstration of why such a policy was needed. These resources were collected as income from properties endowed for the support of the Qarawīyīn mosque and other institutions attached to it. The rest of the lost wealth consisted of property, cash, jewelry or precious objects which had been inherited by orphans who were still minors and could not take possession of it. The fact that these assets were public property explains why they were deposited with the *khaṭīb*. In addition to being the guardian of these funds one of his official duties as administrator of the mosque, he was also trusted to be above suspicion because of his dignity, family standing and personal wealth.

Al-Mazdaghī's fall from grace and the way it was handled by the Marīnid state, can be read as the sad, private story that it was, according to Ibn Marzūq's account, but in many respects it was also the story of the Marīnid system of government itself. Marīnid policies were conceived under the constraints of a society undergoing acculturation to Islamic norms and institutions and had to counter the pressure which they put on them. In the third part we shall examine how the Marīnid state proceeded to implement Islamic institutions and manipulate them for its own survival.

IMPLEMENTING ISLAMIC INSTITUTIONS

CHAPTER 7

The Introduction of the *Medresas**

The *Medresa al-ʿAṭṭārīn* in Fez built by the Sultan Abū 'l-Ḥasan while still a Crown Prince, circa. 1321.

Islamic institutions, in particular the religious ones, conferred legitimacy on the Marīnid state. In that respect, the mosques, through the weekly address, the Friday *khuṭba* were the most important tool in diffusing legitimization and good will towards the regime. But institutions also confer legitimacy, and thus power, on the individuals associated with them, those who serve in them, and the institutionalized clergy were extremely powerful in Fez. The Marīnid rulers, some more than others, clearly cared about their image as being devoted to the Islamic cause and displayed it in a series of military campaigns in the Iberian Peninsula against the Christian armies,[1] and through the religious monuments they erected in Morocco and elsewhere, and the endowment of property for their upkeep. But assessments of the Marīnids' religious image fluctuate among historians. Some claimed they had only a general notion of the Islamic religion, while others claimed them as the "unconditional champions of the Mālikī restoration".[2] In fact the Marīnid state's policies sometimes reflected a religious policy determined not by principles, but in reaction to events and social conflicts, conceived not out of unconditional religious zeal but dictated through by interaction with the religious institutions and their milieu. Both the earlier and later chronicles provide plenty of evidence about the struggle between the regime and the religious milieu and clergymen over resources, control of public opinion and Islamic legitimization. This struggle highlights the role of the religious institutions in the Marīnid state and explains the desire to control them.

The first three rulers, Abū Yaḥyā, Abū Yūsuf, and Abū Yaʿqūb were alerted to the power of the clergy by a number of uprisings.[3] Following the revolt in 648/1250, the activities of the clergy were closely monitored by the court. The *imāms* had orders to inform the authorities about all assemblies which took place in the mosques, especially those which attracted numerous participants. Preachers and other clerics and religious personali-

**Studia Islamica*, XLIII(1976): 109-18.

ties whose sermons and teachings in the mosques drew large attendances, sometimes, thousands of people, were invited either to be paid by the State for their services or to cease their activities. In 651-52/1253-54, a lecturer in the Qarawīyīn mosque became very popular and the *imām* thought that he had better denounce him. The ruler ordered that this individual should be assigned wages, to ensure that he was identified as an employee of the administration and prevent him from engaging in adversarial activities.[4]

Not all clergy agreed to accept the state's wages and be silenced by the state's wishes. Even the al-Mazdaghīs were not always in good grace. The Andalusian al-Nubāḥī recalled that Abū Ja'far al-Mazdaghī had initially refused the judgeship in Fez when it was offered to him, and had been forced to accept it under pressure from an earlier Marīnid ruler, sometime before 669/1270.[5] The supervision of public lectures and mosques continued and became public policy. In 749/1348, a teacher of the Qur'ān, who was normally surrounded only by children, began to attract adult students as well, and "a great disorder ensued".[6] When the affair was reported to the *sheikh* he related it to the authorities, the sessions were interrupted, and later forbidden, and the crowd forced to disperse. However, the government chose to keep the lecturer on the payroll, and assigned him the wages and other benefits which were due to scholars of the rank to which he belonged.

The Marīnid government also challenged the appointment of clergy to positions in the religious institutions which were made by the notables without consulting the court. This was a pattern which had evolved earlier, under the previous dynasties. The Almohads had a policy whereby they championed Berber language and institutions, and the very moment they entered Fez, they replaced the existing preachers, local *khaṭīb*s who preached in Arabic, with ones who could preach in the Berber language, *al-lisān al-barbarī.*[7] The Almohads removed the *khaṭīb* Abū Muḥammad al-Mahdī, who spoke perfect Arabic, from his job after five months, and appointed Abū 'l-Ḥasan b. 'Aṭiya who spoke Berber: "In fact," said al-Jaznā'ī "the Almohads appointed to positions of *imām* and *khaṭīb* only individuals who could recite the *tawḥīd* in Berber."[8] However, since the Almohad court resided in Marrakech for most of the 12th and 13th centuries, the Fezī religious establishment was apparently free to make such appointments as *imām*s, prayer leaders, and *khaṭīb*s, preachers from among their own members. The list of employees in the Qarawīyīn mosque shows that a cluster of families, named by the author of the *Qirṭās* as *fuqahā* and *ashyākh*, monopolized the decision making process.[9] The author of the *Zahrah* referred to them as *qāḍī*s and *wujūh al-madīna*, the notables of the town, but did not dispute their power.[10]

Once the Marīnids arrived in Fez they reverted to the Almohad practice of making appointments to the religious institutions themselves. In 679/1280, the sultan Abū Yūsuf appointed the *faqīh* Abu ʿAbdallāh Muḥhammad b. Abī Zarʿ to the post of *khaṭīb* of the mosque of Fez Jdid, the new capital. Following a period when the positions of *imām* and *khaṭīb* remained vacant, the *fuqahā'* and *ashyākh* named Abū 'l-Qāsim b. Mashūna *khaṭīb*, and Abū 'l-ʿAbbās b. Abī Zarʿ, *imām*. These two had exercised their functions for about sixty six days when an order came, from the sultan Abū Yūsuf, according to the *Qirṭās*,[11] or Abū Yaʿqūb according to the *Zahra*,[12] that the two positions should be combined in the hand of Abū ʿAbdallāh b. Abī 'l-Ṣabr. The text of the order given in the *Zahra* indicates that this appointment took place in 689/1290, and that the man appointed by the Marīnids was a member of the Nafsaja Zanāta tribe.[13] The two individuals who were removed from their posts were members of families who had continuously provided candidates for posts in the mosques. In 695/1295-96, the same two positions were amalgamated in other mosques, and the author of the *Qirṭās* says that Abū ʿAbdallāh b. Mashūna was the *imām* and the *khaṭīb* of the al-Andalus mosque in Fez. The Marīnid rulers acted swiftly to eliminate individuals judged dangerous to the regime, and, according to the chroniclers, rewarded the officers who came under government control.[14] In 696/1296-1297, the *qāḍī* of Abū Yaʿqūb in the old city of Fez was Abū Ghālib, son of the *qāḍī* Abū ʿAbd al-Raḥman al-Maghīlī, who had been executed in 648/1250 by the amir Abū Yaḥyā[15] From then onwards the appointment of *imāms* and *khaṭībs* became the prerogative of the sultans.[16]

The next step taken to control the religious institutions and their personnel was to remove their freedom of action over expenses. During the Almohad period, government intervention in financial matters was minimal, but under the Marīnids, all decisions about renovations made to the mosques had to be referred to the *qāḍī* of the city. He in turn consulted the court, which frequently made changes, not only when there were insufficient funds for the project and a royal contribution was required, but also on other occasions, even though a project was being financed through public money. The clergy was forced to seek approval of expenditures before using revenue from the mosques. The authors of the *Zahra* and the *Qirṭās* describe incidents during the years 682-700/1283-1300, when the sultan Abū Yaʿqūb's approval for renovations in the Qarawīyīn mosque was sought on at least seven occasions.[17] This sultan refused to allow the use of a new door to the mosque, which had been built without consulting him.[18] The liberties taken by the religious dignitaries clearly displeased the authorities, who chose to intervene when it seemed necessary. Even the pious sultan Abū 'l-Ḥasan was not free of suspicion. He had a group of clergymen accompany him for the duration of his campaign in the Eastern Maghreb, no doubt because their presence legitimized his removal of neighboring Muslim rulers, but also wanted to control their activities during his absence from the capital. The traveling retinue included the judiciary, *mufti*s and *qāḍī*s, both of the capital and of the court, scholars, *fuqahā'* and *ulamā'*, as well as descendants of the many noble families of Fez. These people paid a heavy price for their adventures. They were displaced from their homes, taken away from their families, students, libraries, teaching and writing, and died prematurely, either in the Black Death in Tunis, or by drowning.[19] It was against this troubling and unstable background that the introduction of the first *medresa* to Morocco took place.[20]

The first *medresa* in North Africa, an institution of higher learning which prepared jurists for diverse careers, was established in Tunis under the Ḥafṣids in 647/1249.[21] The Marīnids followed suit, even though the sources disagree about when the first *medresa*, the *al-Yaʿqūbiyya*, was introduced. According to the *Zahra* it was in 670/1271-72, but according to the *Dhakhīra* in 680-81/1280-81.[22] In later years the Marīnid *medresas* became a symbol of Marīnid art and architecture,[23] the most beautiful specimen by Abū 'l-Ḥasan and Abū ʿInān,[24] dated from the 14th century, which led Ibn Marzūq to say that building *medresas* was an unknown activity in the Maghreb before the time of Abū 'l-Ḥasan.[25] As we can now see from the stormy atmosphere surrounding its foundation, there is no reason to doubt that the incentive to establish a *medresa* in the latter part of the 13th century came from Abū Yūsuf Yaʿqūb himself:

> When the amīr al-Muslimīn Abū Yūsuf ordered the building of the *medresa* al-Yaʿqūbiyya which is situated south of the al-Qarawīyīn mosque, 670/1271-72, this is what had happened. The person charged

> with fixing or deciding on the *qibla* was the *muʿaddil*, astronomer, Abū ʿAbdallāh Muḥammad ben al-Ḥabbāq, and nobody else among those people knowledgeable in the astronomical sciences was associated with him; it appeared that the orientation of the *qibla* in this *medresa* was not like the one of the al-Qarawīyīn mosque. The affair was brought to the attention of our master, the amīr al-Muslimīn, Abū Yūsuf. On the other hand, an ordinary person, whose opinion would not be taken into consideration in such matters, declared that in certain mosques in Fez, the orientation of the *qibla* was not the same as in this mosque either. The sultan had the idea of uniting all the reputed legal scholars amongst the Zanāta people to examine the question. The legal scholars from the Zanāta, together with the ruler, reacted firmly; the *qibla* of the *medresa* was fixed according to that of the al-Qarawīyīn, which was determined by Idris. Condemning it as incorrect implies stigmatization of the holy *qibla*. By this judgement, the legal scholars of the Zanāta nation wanted to convey the message that the sultan had decided to establish the medresa as he wanted it, and would not back down.[26]

There was always a basic antagonism between religious persons, who claimed high standards of uprightness, and their rulers whom they considered corrupt and offensive, ignoring the word of God. The clashes with Muslim rulers were common, not only in the West but throughout the Islamic societies everywhere.[27] In the case of the Fezī clergy and the Marīnids, the religious establishment felt, correctly, that the new institution would challenge their authority. They retaliated with an attempt to discredit the new institution's ability to provide training by charging that the *medresa* had a wrongly oriented and therefore unorthodox, prayer angle to which the ruler retorted by bringing together the religious scholars of the Zanāta nation.[28] Tempers cooled after the initial showdown, and the *medresa* was officially inaugurated, but the Fezī religious milieu's alienation remained unabated, and was even heightened by the incident. As a result, the director of the new *medresa*, the *qāḍī* al-Dila'i, was a foreigner, originally from Almeria in Spain, rather than a local jurist.[29] The dispute surrounding the direction of the *qibla* reflected the opposition of the religious milieu of the city, who did not participate in the foundation of the *medresa*. Whether motivated by the hostility of the clergy towards them, or for the sake of obtaining unconditional support by having new clergy, the Marīnid regime embarked upon the formation of Berber clergy through the new religious institution, the *medresa*. The Marīnid rulers continued to speak mostly Berber and not Arabic at the court, as did most of their tribesmen. This was evident in the 13th century: Al-Malzūzī, "the poet of the sultan Abū Yūsuf", mixed Arabic with the Zanāta language, *al-lisān al-zanātī,* when he addressed the sultan.[30] Significantly enough, Ibn al-Khatīb, who spoke Arabic at the court in Granada, was sensitive to the difference when he came to Fez and commented that the rulers were still addressed in both languages well into the 14th century.[31] The issues of Berber origin and the Berber language were central to the regime. The person who replaced Ibn Abī Zarʿ and Ibn Abī Mashūna was a 'Zanāta Berber'.[32] As noted earlier, the poet al-Mazūzī, also a Zanāta man, was another person closely associated with the Marīnids and officially appointed to the court. He had the right to pronounce *fatwā*s, although we are unsure about his qualifications as a jurist.[33] The early and vacillating appearance of the first Islamic jurists described as being of Zanāta origin, as well as those who were brought over during the crisis over the *qibla*, show that it was imperative for the regime to produce new clergy possessing the right qualifications who could legitimize their rule by appropriate Islamic legal and religious training. The policy underlying the establishment of the first *medresa* is clear enough. The state needed to produce jurists who would be able to challenge the privileged position of the established religious milieu of Fez as the only people who could apply Islamic norms and by association, the only ones who could provide legitimacy. For Abū Yūsuf the founding of a *medresa* was a means of generating a new group of Berber speaking Islamic clergy, who would be devoted to him and at the same time, educated and qualified enough to stand up and even replace the prevailing religious milieu of the city, but especially to fill up the normative Islamic institution with loyal elements. Some decades later, the unwillingness of al-Abīlī, Ibn Khaldūn's admired professor, to assume a teaching position in the Marīnid institution, and his criticism of the political authorities' strict supervision over its activities, bears witness to the fact that the Marīnid *medresa* was a state institution.[34]

The events involving the religious milieu of Fez and the Marīnids in the historical introduction of the *medresa* to Morocco, shows the power generated by institutions in the Islamic state. In the case of the *medresa* the struggle with the religious milieu was over power, over control of the normative authority, setting, upholding and sanctioning Islamic norms. In the next chapter we will examine another institution, the royal *waqf*, endowment for the public good, which was of a longer date and more widely used than the *medresa*, but where the struggle between them revolved around control over the resources generated under Islamic norms.

CHAPTER 8

Royal *Waqf* in 14th-century Fez*

A Berber rug from the High Atlas mountains.

The examination of Marīnids' acculturation to Islamic institutions, which began in the previous chapter with the study of the Marīnid *medresa*, will proceed here with the study of the *waqf* institution. No other institution better portrays the way in which the Berber-Islamic state, and for that matter any Islamic state, struggled with acculturation to Islamic norms, than the *waqf*, endowment for the public good.[1] In the pre-modern state, where support of municipal life, health, religious services and education was not built into the system, the *waqf* institution supplemented this task in a less than satisfactory manner. It became a private act on the part of individual monarchs and not a matter of dynastic policy. It thus involved many personal decisions on a multitude of levels, which were all inspired by Islamic norms but carried out in a variety of patterns and under different circumstances and conditions. Acculturation to this institution meant making normative decisions every step of the way, ranging from what constitutes a public good cause to the choice of objects for endowment, from deciding what and how much to endow, to keeping control over the revenue from endowments. But following the letter of the law in daily practice, especially when the state used it as a framework for interaction with its subjects, was not easy, and the legal inquiries show that all concerned had difficulties adjusting to its legal norms.[2] By the time the Marīnids came to power, the practice of endowing property by the state to support public institutions was well entrenched in Morocco and widely practiced everywhere. The state and individuals adopted the institution enthusiastically, adapting it to their particular needs. Whether providing maintenance for public, religious and municipal institutions, or as an arrangement for intergenerational property transfer, this unique Islamic institution gained considerable economic dimensions, and became a major, integral part of the Muslim propertied existence. Here, the acculturation process is examined by studying the Marīnid endowments' patterns, size, identity of donors, objectives, the legal

**Anaquel de Estudios Arabes* 2(1991): 193-217.

problems surrounding them and the administrative organization which handled them.

The documentation available is literary and empiric, drawn from chronicles, inscriptions, books, and legal documents.[3] In spite of the large assets endowed, which required registration, no registers have yet been found, or published, even though A. Bel indicated that *ḥawāla*, or *habous* documents from the Marīnid period had survived, and were being transferred to Rabat at the time when he was writing his classic "Inscriptions arabes de Fès".[4] R. Brunschvig also noted that fragments of *waqf* registers of the Ḥafṣids in Tunisia may have survived if they were kept in the central mosque of Qayrawān.[5] In general, few archival *waqf* records for this period from other regions of the Islamic West have survived, and Naṣrid Granada's *waqf* holdings, which were registered by the ecclesiastical authorities after the liquidation of Islamic rule in the city, were the exception which proved the rule.[6] No registers which would compare to those of Egypt were ever found.[7]

Two special undertakings stand out in the Marīnid *waqf*, *medresas* and books, but the perception of individual or dynastic commitment to endowment took sometime to develop.[8] The chronicles, which provide precious, yet fragmentary and sporadic information, speak only about the humble beginnings of endowments made by the Marīnid rulers. The first Marīnid known to have built several unnamed monuments in Fez, was Abū Yūsuf Yaʿqūb, 651-685/1253-1286. Among those was the first mental asylum and hospital in the city, financed by the head tax levied on the Jews, *jizyat al-yahūd*. He made property endowments, not for Fez, but for *zāwiya*s, hospices for religious orders, which he built in the desert for use by passing travelers.[9] Although, as discussed in the previous chapter, Abū Yūsuf Yaʿqūb built the first *medresa* in Fez, we do not know whether any endowments were made on this occasion.[10] However, following its introduction, the *medresa*, became a special cause with the Marīnids and from the first quarter of the 14th century onwards, a number of *medresas* were built, with a massive stream of endowments for them. A cluster of Marīnid rulers favored the *medresa*s more than any other institution in the city. Five of them were built in Fez over the 35 year period, between 721/1321 and 756/1356, following the institution's introduction to the city. They were: the Dār al-Makhzen *medresa*, 726/1325, and the al-Ṣihrīj *medresa*, 721-23/1321-23, both erected by Abū 'l-Ḥasan while still a crown prince; the al-

ʿAṭṭārīn *medresa*, 726/1325, built by his father, Abū Saʿīd; the al-Misbaḥiyya *medresa*, 747/1346, built by Abū 'l-Ḥasan; and the Bū ʿInāniyya *medresa*, 751-56/1350-55, built by his son, Abū ʿInān. These five, plus others in different cities in Morocco and the central Maghreb, are well documented because of the inscriptions which the Marīnids regularly affixed to the entrance door. The inscriptions reproduced a segment of the *waqfiyya*, the notarized act of endowment, registered with the bureau of properties which included not only the donor's name and the date of the building, but also a precise description of the properties endowed for the maintenance of each of the five, their exact location, and the share—if not wholly donated. The following is a list of assets endowed by the Marīnid Abū 'l-Ḥasan, for maintenance of the *medresa* of the Dār al-Makhzen in Fez Jdid. It is reproduced here as a sample of the size of the properties endowed for *medresa*s by the rulers mentioned earlier, and is part of the comprehensive list of all endowments given in Appendix B.[11]

1. The *madshar*, village, of Abū Zayd, in the territory of Fez, bordering Rās al-mā', which includes 35 *athra*. Two parts of this village which belonged to Abū 'l-Ḥasan's late mother, are now equally endowed by him.

2. In the old city of Fez, the *ḥamām al-sultan* situated in the quarter of the kharrāṭīn, near the mosque of the Shurafā'.

3. The *ḥamām* of the Darb al-ṭawīl situated at the end of the trail of the same name.

4. The constructions built above these two *ḥamāms*.

5. The yearly rent of three large houses, two of which were built on the top of the *ḥamām* al-sultan and the other on the *ḥamām* of the Darb al-ṭawīl.

6. Sixteen boutiques built on the spring of al-Jūṭiyya, located to the left on entering the square, on the second street going toward al-Jūṭiyya, from the beginning of ʿAin ʿAllūn.

7. 7/8 of the Darb al-Ghorba' inn, located in the slaughtering place.

8. Mill located on the spring of Qamīma, which includes two stones.

9. A large oven in Fez Jdid and the two boutiques which are connected to it to the south, as well as the constructions built above them.

10. A boutique situated on the right side when leaving the *medresa* through the door on the *qibla* side.

The other four *medresas* in Fez, and the *medresa* built by Abū 'l-Ḥasan in al-ʿUbbād, today's Algeria, were endowed in a similar manner.[12] There are also directions for the exact allocation of wages and maintenance, as well as the endowment of housing units to be rented out to the personnel attached to the service of the *medresa*. As we have seen, the Marīnids had valid political reasons for introducing the *medresa*, and by combining it with the benefits of *waqf* revenue they gave the institution some economic muscle. But in the 14th century the motivation behind the building of *medresas* changed. The three Marīnid rulers who built them, clearly thought that *medresa* building was a tribute to Islamic religious life, a meritorious act which reflected the eminence and glamour of their own reign.[13]

The second area which stands out in the Marīnid endowment's patterns were the books which carry their signature. Inscriptions commemorating the acts of endowment, *waqfiyyas*, which appear on books dating from the Marīnid period and have recently been discovered in different libraries and mosques in Morocco, reveal that the Marīnids endowed books not only as an appendage to the foundation of the *medresas*, but also for support and development of libraries, and for encouraging book production and intellectual life. This *waqf* pattern was inaugurated in the East in the fourth *hijrī* century, and the first library to be constituted entirely as *waqf* was the one built by Ibn Siwār in Basra sometime before 372/982. Public libraries in mosques or *medresas* appear as public institutions, dependent to a large degree on the ruler procuring premises, acquiring books, and maintaining staff. This pattern reached Morocco around the 10th century, and is illustrated by copies of books executed for the Almoravids, who also built libraries to house them; their example was followed later by rulers from other dynasties.[14] The Marīnid endowment of books was inaugurated by Abū Yūsuf, who deposited the books seized during his conquests in Spain in the *medresa* al-Ṣaffārīn, built in 684/1285, about which we know so little. In 728/1327 Abū 'l-Ḥasan endowed, no doubt among many others, two books which have survived.[15] The first was a copy of *Kitāb al-tamhīd li-mā fī 'l-Mutwaṭṭā' min 'l-maʿānī wa 'l-asānīd* by Ibn ʿAbd al-Barr, and the second, a copy of the *al-Bayān wa 'l-tahḥṣīl* by Ibn Rushd, for use by the *medresa* students attached to the al-Andalus mosque.[16] In 745/1344 Abū 'l-Ḥasan endowed another college with a copy of al-Qurṭūbī's *Tafṣīr*.[17] His son, Abū ʿInān endowed the *medresa* of the al-Manṣūr's mosque in

Marrakech with a copy of *Mashāriq al-anwār* by Qāḍī ʿIyāḍ, al-Ṭabarī's *Tafṣīr* and the *Kitāb al-taʿrīf* by Ibn al-Ghallāb.[18] For the Qarawīyīn he endowed a copy of the *Muwaṭṭā'* in 750/1350.[19] A later Marīnid ruler, Abū ʿAbd al-Muntaṣir billāh, son of Abū Sālim, endowed a copy of the *Jāmiʿ al-bayān ʿan ta'wīl āyyāt al-furqān* by al-Ṭabarī for the Qarawīyīn mosque.[20] In 816/1415, the Marīnid ruler, Abū Saʿīd ʿUthmān, built a library in the Taza mosque, commemorated by an inscription.[21] The Marīnid governor, Abū Muḥammad al-Ṭarīfī, endowed many books for the mosque he built, which explains the salary of 12 dinars which he ordered for the librarian.[22] Al-Ṭarīfī also endowed the Qarawīyīn mosque with a copy of the *Mahādī al-Muwaṭṭā'*,[23] and allocated a sum of 6 dinars a month to the reader who would read from the *Kitāb al-Shifā'* in his mosque.[24] In a similar act, Mankulī-Bughā, the Mamlūk governor of Aleppo, built a mosque in Aleppo in 767/1365 and endowed its library with books.[25] Other contemporary endowments of books were found in the central and Eastern Maghreb. A Zayyānid ruler built a library in the great mosque of Tlemcen,[26] while another, Abū Zayyān Muḥammad, endowed the central mosque in Tlemcen in 801-802/1389-99 with copies of the *Saḥīh* by al-Bukhārī and the *Kitāb al-Shifā'* and also with a copy of the Qur'ān.[27]

The power of acculturation is visible in the kind of books endowed. They were either *tafṣīr* or *fiqh*, which suggests a link with the doctrinal movement to the use of *furūʿ* in teaching Mālikī law.[28] The process began under the Almohads, with a copy of the *Mudawwana* written in 517/1123, which carries the name of the teacher for whom it was copied, and was maintained up to the end of their rule, when the last Almohad caliph, ʿUmar al-Murtaḍā, 640-65/1242-66, endowed a copy of the *Muwaṭṭā'* for the al-Siqāya mosque in Marrakech.[29] Rulers in the Maghreb had a pattern of involvement in doctrinal matters and Al-ʿUmarī reported that the Ḥafṣid ruler was regularly informed about the needs of the library,[30] and it would seem that the need for a particular book in the institution for which it was endowed would be brought to the attention of the rulers. The Marīnid rulers also consulted the scholars teaching in the *medresa* before ordering a book to be copied when they were approached to do so. That arrangement corresponded to the *curriculum* and the method of the *medresa*, which consisted of teaching one single text at a time.[31] The endowment of books as *waqf* was also practiced by authors who endowed their own works. The most famous act of endowment of this kind in 14th-century Fez was Ibn Khaldūn's *Kitāb al-ʿibar*, which he sent from Egypt in 799/1396 as *waqf* to be deposited in the Qarawīyīn mosque's library.[32]

Was the contribution of the book itself as a source of revenue completed when it was deposited in the library?

The development of the public library through its own resources was never anticipated, and rulers were expected to continue to provide financial support, hence the continuous endowment of books.[33] But books themselves could be used as a source of income if fees were charged for copying them. A *fatwā*, recorded by al-Wansharīsī in his *Miʿyār*, suggests that books in Marīnid Morocco were sometimes endowed in order to become a revenue source for the library. This can be deduced from the following case submitted to al-Qabbāb, a 14th-century jurist in Fez, who was requested to decide the fate of a book endowed by a person who did not specify what use was to be made of it. "If the donor has indicated certain ways of using the books as though he would have said, 'to read and consult them', it is forbidden to make copies of it. This would be allowed only if the donor said: "..and other ways of making profit from it."[34] It would seem however, that making copies for further use did not constitute a source of income for the library or owner, as it did for private owners in medieval Europe, because books on religion and religious subjects should not be used as a source of revenue. Yet, we should distinguish between copying books for profit and deriving revenue from lending them for a fee, and book endowment in general, particularly that of the *maṣāḥif,* Qur'ān volumes, which were clearly not intended to produce income.

An expression of acculturation to Islamic norms is reflected in the endowment of Qur'āns, and Qur'ān copying. This type of endowment should be viewed as a special category within the Marīnid book endowment, especially in view of the dimensions it assumed. The practice began as early as the 8th century but did not become a common feature of libraries before the 4th/10th century.[35] Endowments of Qur'āns in the Maghreb began as early as the 11th century in Ifrīqiya.[36] Pre-Marīnid rulers in Morocco used to create a separate section in the libraries solely for endowed Qur'ān copies. The last Almohad caliph, ʿUmar al-Murtaḍā, 640-65/1242-66, endowed a 10-volume set of the Qur'ān in Marrakech in 656/1258.[37] In 709-10/1309-10 Abū Yaʿqūb sent copies of the Qur'ān to

Mecca, but we do not know what endowments were made for their upkeep.[38] In the middle of the 14th century, the Marīnid Abū ʿInān built a library attached to the Qarawīyīn mosque where he dedicated a room solely for copies of the Qur'ān. The chronicler al-Jaznā'ī, who reported this, tells us that Abū ʿInān himself designed the special, richly decorated section, which he filled with sumptuously made copies, and on which he traced the *waqfiyya* with his own hand. He also nominated a clerk whose duty it was to register the books when they were in use, and endowed the library with assets to pay for its maintenance.[39]

The act of copying a Qur'ān in one's own hand, endowing it, and providing for readers to read from it was an even a stronger personal acculturation pattern on the part of the monarchs. Inaugurated, or made famous by Nūr al-Dīn, d.567/1171, it was elevated to a highly pious act. Under Abū 'l-Ḥasan, such Qur'āns became the subject of close correspondence between Marīnid and Mamlūk authorities. Abū 'l-Ḥasan sent Qur'āns several times, and both Ibn Khaldūn and Ibn Marzūq, in their respective chronicles, give long, elaborate descriptions of the enterprise.[40] According to Ibn Marzūq, the first copy made by Abū 'l-Ḥasan was deposited as *waqf* in Chella, today, Salé. However, from 740/1339 onwards, he produced more copies, each time calling on professional copyists to verify his work. He sent two of these copies to Mecca and Medina as *waqf* and bought land in Egypt and Fez in order to pay for the professional readers who would recite from his copies. Correspondence kept by the Egyptian chancellery testifies that the Mamlūk administration authorized the establishment of the Marīnid *waqf* in Egypt for the purpose of providing funds for the upkeep of this copy and for readers to read from it.[41] Ibn Marzūq mentioned that Abū 'l-Ḥasan finished another copy in 745/1344, and this was deposited in the al-Aqṣā mosque in Jerusalem.[42] 25 volumes of this 30-volume set, protected and preserved in their original leather binding, are still housed today in the Ḥaram al-sharīf in Jerusalem.[43] This act, too, was accompanied by the endowment of properties in the East to pay for the special readers. The Mamlūk sultan, in a document dating from the same year, gave the Marīnid ambassadors permission to buy property and endow it in order to provide readers for this copy.[44] The revenue from this *waqf* was in addition to that derived from *waqf* endowed in Morocco for the same purpose. In Egypt, a secretary was appointed to supervise the use of the properties and to choose a proper manager for them.[45] The governors of the provinces where the properties in question were located were informed about them, and the official writing the letter confirms their prosperity and guarantees their protection.[46] An unfinished copy of the Qur'ān was destined for Hebron. Abū 'l-Ḥasan began it while staying in the vanquished city of Tunis. His defeat by the Bedouins immediately afterwards explains why this copy was never finished. The sultan wanted to buy lands in Syria and around Cairo and make endowments in order to pay for the readers. Ibn Marzūq concluded: "we heard that the copy in question was at last finished by his son, the sultan Abū Fāris, 768-44/1366-72, and was about to be sent to its original destination".[47]

In great contrast to their devotion to *medresas* and books the Marīnids did not endow very much for the mosques, the long established institutions, and particularly for the two main mosques of the capital, the Qarawīyīn and al-Andalus.[48] It could be that they judged that the mosques had sufficient income and no more revenue was needed for their maintenance, but, on the other hand it also could be that they detected opposition to their rule there, and curtailed further support.[49] Using the numbers provided by the chroniclers, we shall examine both reasons. In 529/1134-35 an assessment of the *waqf* property of the Qarawīyīn mosque was carried out by order of the Almoravid *amīr*. The accounting produced an estimate of 24,000 silver dinars, *dinar fiḍḍī,* according to al-Jaznā'ī,[50] and 80,000 drawn from urban and rural sources, according to Ibn Abī Zarʿ.[51] Funds from the *waqf*'s revenue were continuously used for construction. In 505/1111-12,[52] *waqf* revenue was used to rebuild the western door of the mosque and in 518/1124, to rebuild the big gate of the Shammāʿīn inn. The *amīr* ʿAlī b. Yūsuf also made endowments for the mosque, during the years 528-37/1134-43.[53] This money was administered by the *qāḍī,* who actually controlled the *waqf*'s funds.[54] Under the Almohads, however, the Qarawīyīn *waqf* revenue diminished and did not reach even 10,000 dinars, either because of the alienation of the endowed properties referred to above, or because of corruption and misuse by the personnel responsible; as Ibn Abī Zarʿ said: "The supervisors ate it all." In 538/1144, after the Almohad occupation, a new minbar was erected for a cost of 3.800 and 7/8 dinars.[55] The lack of sufficient income from the *waqf*'s properties brought an appeal for state involvement in the financing of the mosques and thus, by the back door, state intervention and control of the *waqf*'s revenue. In 600/1203-1204, the state had to provide for the construction of a door.[56] The building of the second large mosque in Fez, the al-Andalus mosque, between 600-604/1203-1207 was undertaken by the Almohad al-Nāṣīr, although it is not clear if he endowed his own resources for this purpose, or used funds of the *bayt al-māl*, or *waqf*'s revenue from other institutions.[57] The property endowed included flats for living quarters for the *imāms* and other personnel of the mosques. A *khaṭīb* died in one of those in 615/1219 and in 563/1255 another refused to live in the official residence but was persuaded to do so, in order not to cause the cancellation of the endowment.[58] This pattern of building accommodation for the *imāms* and *khaṭībs* in the mosque, financed by *waqf* revenue,[59] was followed by Abū 'l-Ḥasan in the *medresa* al-Sīhrīj and by al-Ṭarīfī in the mosque he built in Fez Jdid, mentioned in the inscription.[60] In spite of the initial generous property endowment for the mosques, the revenue was not sufficient by the time the Marīnids came to power and Abū Yūsuf Ya'qūb had to provide for its maintenance in 688/1289.[61] The amount of revenue must have increased considerably in the following years, since that source provided, among other things, the oil used for lighting the mosque during *Ramaḍān*, as well as funds for transforming the large church bell from Gibraltar, which had been transported to Morocco following the Marīnid conquest in 737/1337, into a huge candelabra for the mosque.[62] Marīnid endowment continued but not for the mosques: After the wave of *medresa* foundations in 1352/3, endowments were made for a *zāwiya* and a hospital near Taza, in northern Morocco.[63] Abū 'Inān endowed a *ḥamām* in Salé in 755/1354-55, to pay for the maintenance of his father's tomb, after he chased him to his death in the mountains.[64]

If the capital amassed through the endowments' revenue was not sufficient and the Marīnids were asked to contribute, their hesitation and reluctance to do so had us believe that the revenue of the Qarawīyīn mosque's *waqf*, gave the clergymen influence, independence and power and that the Marīnids resented it. The quarrels between the Marīnid rulers and the religious milieu over decisions concerning the mosques, discussed in earlier chapters, reveal a struggle between the two over the income from the *waqf*, betraying the dynasty's apprehension over the power accumulated at the hands of the clergy and their desire to curtail it. They refused to allow the clergy to use the revenue from *waqf* to pay for alterations and repairs, and the Marīnid Abū Yaʿqūb, 685-706/1286-1307, even ordered that a new door built in the al-Qarawīyīn mosque, be closed because he had not been previously consulted about it.[65] The Marīnid rulers' move to control the *waqf* income of the mosques spilled into other areas, as some members of the dynasty withdrew money from the public treasury, the *bayt al-māl*, in order to make *waqf* endowments.[66] Al-ʿAbdūsī issued a *fatwā* on this matter denying the rulers' claims, even theoretical ones, over the public treasury revenue for the purpose of *waqf* endowments, saying that: "If the sultan in question makes endowments for the public utility from funds of the public treasury, claiming that those funds belong to him, the endowment becomes null."[67] The fact that money could legally be taken from the public treasury for other reasons, for example, for the Holy War against the infidels, made it hard for the jurists to maintain a unanimous front against the rulers use of funds from the public treasury for other purposes.[68] Thus the same al-ʿAbdūsī admitted that, if the practice of a ruler borrowing money from this fund was a long established tradition, it could be permitted. Another jurist was less categorical. When consulted about a governor who borrowed money from the public treasury in order to build benches around the mosque, he declared the act legal, since it was for the benefit of the community. Yet another jurist decreed that the same applied to a sultan who used the public treasury funds for *medresa*, *ribāṭ*, hostelry, hospital, and *zāwiya*. The Marīnid sultan Abū 'l-ʿAbbās Aḥmad, 775-87/1373-84, 789-96/1387-93, is reported to have endowed a garden whose revenue belonged to the public treasury, as *waqf* for the maintenance of his father's tomb. His son, however, probably as the result of pressure from the public and jurists cancelled the endowment and returned the asset to the public treasury.[69] Not all Marīnid rulers considered the public treasury, *bayt al-māl*, as their private bank. As we have seen in the story of al-Mazdaghī, Abū 'l-Ḥasan certainly did not, but others felt they could use it as a source for future endowments.

The issue of management and control of the *waqf's* revenue were directly related to the particular Mālikī legal norm which prevented the endower or his family from managing the revenue and supervising the assets he endowed, something which the Ḥanafī school permitted. As a result the administration, management, registration and accounting of revenue was independent of the state's domain. The Marīnids' attempts to control the public treasury went against the established norms regulating the activities of the institution. Construction and renovation of the mosques were to be financed by *waqf* revenue, regardless of whether the endowments were made by the rulers or by others. The revenue from the endowed properties which was earmarked for individual religious institutions and specific projects, could not be used for other purposes. For the sake of efficiency and to maximize benefit of the *waqf*'s revenue, the jurists entertained a proposal to unite the revenue from all the mosques into one single treasury and administration during the Marīnid period. The legality of such an act, which altered the expressed will of the endower was questioned, and the jurists disapproved of the practice of spending revenue from one mosque in favor of another.[70] Since not all revenues in the *bayt al-māl* came from *waqf* endowments, this might have resulted in a state attempt to control it.

Marīnid endowment had other problems with the legal norms. The lack of any indication of the act of buying, or ownership in the Fezī *medresas* inscriptions raises the question of whether or not the Marīnid rulers actually owned, or bought, the urban properties which they endowed. This was an important issue because chroniclers often stated that the rulers bought properties in order to make endowments, and while some inscriptions proclaim this fact explicitly, other do not. The founding inscription of the al-ʿUbbād *medresa*, near Tlemcen, endowed by Abū 'l-Ḥasan in 747/1347, indicated the name of the previous owner of the property endowed, and specifically mentioned that each asset was *bought*.[71] This was also the case in the Mustaghanim inscription from 741/1340, which recorded that Abū 'l-Ḥasan endowed the mosque of Mustaghanim with two stores in the central market, two bread ovens and three oil containers.[72] The insistence in these cases is understandable since Tlemcen was conquered by the Marīnids following a long siege, and the property might well have fallen to the sultan by right of conquest, which is contradictory in normative Islamic terms to what Abū 'l-Ḥasan was doing in the Maghreb. But Abū 'l-Ḥasan was particularly concerned to abide by Islamic norms as much as he could, given his conquests in the central Maghreb. Jurists did consider some of the royal endowments illegal because they were made with property acquired through confiscation or containment, something which was condemned when it was done for the public benefit. The practice occurred in other regions. In al-Andalus the Naṣrids' private treasury, from which they made endowments, was largely fed from the confiscation of subjects' properties, and there is no reason why this would not have happened in Morocco as well.[73] But did the Marīnids in Fez use their privilege as rulers in Morocco, and as conquerors in the central Maghreb, to endow properties which they had snatched from the public treasury, in the first case and confiscated from the locals, in the second? An investigation of the status of real estate in Fez and the jurists opinions will help answer this question.

In two instances, endowments made by Marīnid governors from properties acquired while in office were declared null by the *muftī,* because they were made from properties illegally acquired. One of the jurists consulted insisted that all endowments made by governors, tax collectors, or Makhzen administrators, from properties which they acquired while in office, were illegal. The notion that officials acquired property in an unjust manner was prevalent among the jurists. Ibn Marzūq, himself a jurist, who served as grand vizir in Fez under Abū Sālim, 761-63/1359-61, referred to the problem when, in exile in Tunis, he requested that the revenue from properties which he had acquired in Fez during his time in office be sent to him: "these are all properties which I acquired with my own money, there is nothing illegal about them."[74] The Zayyānid Abū Ḥammū also made endowments for a *zāwiya* attached to his father's tomb, and made it clear in the foundation inscription that all properties endowed were legally his own, and did not belong to the public treasury.

The legal status of the urban assets endowed by the Marīnids in Fez was indeed a complicated issue, which could not be easily resolved. The royal *waqfiyya*s in Fez contain no information about buying property, and the inscriptions did not state the legal status of the assets they endowed. As in most Islamic cities, stores and workshops, as well as other commercial units, such as inns, belonged in principle to the state, which built them in order to derive income from the rents. In his *Zahra,* Al-Jaznā'ī speaks about the confusion regarding urban property in Fez, which, he explained, following some unnamed sources, resulted from a promise made by Idrīs, founder of Fez in the 3rd/9th century, that all buildings inhabited and gardens cultivated before the walls were erected could become private property. Subsequently, all other properties, whether land or buildings, were the state's property and could be leased from it. This was a long standing urban practice in the Maghreb and according to al-Jaznā'ī stores built in Fez by

Idrīs or Dūnās b. Ḥamāma, and other Zanāta rulers during the 9th-10th centuries, bear witness to it.[75] Only when the owner died without leaving an heir could the State take possession of it and rent it out.[76] This was the explanation given to a Marīnid governor who inquired why certain houses were *jazā'*, state's domain, rented out on a long term lease, while others were private property and the state could not rent them out. However, al-Jaznā'ī's account of the circumstances surrounding the rulers' endowments leads us to believe that private ownership in the city of Fez during the 14th century went beyond common practice. This situation evolved over a period of time, because as the capital had moved to the south and the center of government had been at distance for over 200 years, there was enough time for these establishments in Fez, initially state owned, to become privately owned. The Almoravids and Almohads, who ruled the city from their capital Marrakech in the south, probably did not exercise sufficient force to prevent transfer of property from the state's domain to private hands, and stores, houses and workshops, within the city of Fez, formerly state owned, were taken over by individuals. Al-Jaznā'ī, speaking about the Almoravid period, 5th-6th/11th-12th centuries, said that: "They, (the *qāḍī*s), informed him (the Almoravid ʿAlī b. Yūsuf) that many of the habous properties were illegally in the hands of inhabitants of Fez, who derived profits from them as though those were their private property."[77] As a result, properties such as stores, bakeries, mills and houses, were privately owned, and the Marīnids, on their arrival in Fez, found out that they could not endow them but were faced with either having to build or buy rentable properties for this purpose. Al-Jaznā'ī recounted that Abū Yaʿqūb was forced to repair and renovate the large al-Shammāʿīn inn, the inn of the wax-makers, for the benefit of the Qarawīyīn mosque nearby, by the *qāḍī*, who ordered the renovations and by doing so, aroused the ruler's ire. The *qāḍī* insisted that this inn was a property which had originally belonged to the ruling dynasty, but was not endowed, and its revenue belonged to the Qarawīyīn mosque. He expressed the hope that the sultan would honor the tradition and confirm the endowment.[78] The physical location of the *waqf*'s revenues was in itself a symbol of its independent status. In Umayyad Spain the *bayt al-māl*'s *waqf* funds were kept separately, in the grand mosque, independently from the *khizānat al-māl*, and were controlled and operated by the *qāḍī* assisted by a supervisor, a *nāẓir al-awqāf*.[79] In Ifrīqiya the *bayt al-māl* was simply the treasury fed by the revenue from the *waqf* and from inheritances derived from individuals who died without a will.[80] The Ḥafṣid public treasury was not separate from the ruler's private treasury, nor from funds coming from other public sources. In Almohad times, a safe was built under the floor of the Qarawīyīn mosque to guard the money and other deposits and valuables belonging to the mosque, including the orphans' inheritance money: "Five windows all protected by cast iron and three iron doors protected the entrance to the room. Three keys, held by three different men were made for each door. A big iron safe, *ṣundūq,* with ropes all around it, protected the deposited money both of the endowments and of individuals. Needless to say, the room was broken into", continues al-Jaznā'ī "and all its contents stolen."[81] That event took place sometime before 599/1202.[82] The choice of a preacher, not a *qāḍī*, to take charge of the *waqf*'s revenue deposited in the grand mosque of the Qarawīyīn, was also an Almohad practice. In Marrakech, a *khaṭīb* was entrusted with the supervision of such funds at that time.[83] Similarly, in the middle of the 14th century the *imām* of the al-Andalus mosque in Fez was entrusted with the handling of revenue from 2 stores endowed by Ibn ʿImrān for the purpose of educating children of poor families.[84] In the Marīnid case, the revenue collected was kept in a depository in the central mosque of the city and managed by the *qāḍī*, as was the custom in Spain. The debacle of the Qarawīyīn's *khaṭīb*, al-Mazdaghī, discussed in Chapter 6, who was entrusted with the supervision of these funds, and speculated with them, ultimately losing 30,000 gold dinar, shows the vulnerable side of public institutions, not just under the Marīnids. It was also not unlike the situation in medieval Egypt, recorded in the Geniza documents.[85]

A manager, *nāẓir,* specifically appointed for the task of administering the endowments, was usually entrusted with carrying out the directives and disbursements of the funds, under the supervision of the *qāḍī*, or preacher, of the mosque.[86] The author of the *Zahra* also confirmed that a *nāẓir* had been in position in earlier centuries.[87] As early as 688/1289, and again in 712/1312, a Marīnid *nāẓir* was appointed for general *waqf* administration, and another *nāẓir* for the mosques.[88] The official title, as it appears in the inscription of Bū ʿInāniya *medresa* was the *nāẓir fī 'l-ḥubūs bi-ḥaḍrat Fās,* and the occupational pattern of other offices repeated itself here, under the Marīnids, since the office of the *nāẓir* became an inherited one.[89] The existence of a supervisor, *nāẓir fī 'l-āḥbās,* to handle the properties of *waqf khayrī,* confirmed the wide use of the institution, mostly by individuals.[90] A number of *fatwā*s noted that the manager's duty was to make regular rounds of the properties and to produce a detailed statement of accounts for public inspection.[91] A later Marīnid chronicler has left a detailed description of the *nāẓir*'s duties in Fez at the end of the 15th century. He described the Qarawīyīn mosque's revenue and enumerated the staff assisting the manager of the endowments. Management was an elaborate task which required a large personnel: eight witnesses, six rent collectors, who were entitled to keep 5% of the money collected, as well as twenty workers who regularly tended to the gardens, stables and other enterprises.[92]

The acculturation process to Islamic norms as portrayed through their *waqf* policy was inspired both by political calculations and cultural mission, commitment to the public good, and personal motivations of all sorts. An echo of this policy is found in the description by Egyptian historian, Shihāb al-Dīn Aḥmad Ibn Faḍl Allāh al-ʿUmarī, 701-49/1301-49, of the Maghreb, where he said that the lack of *waqf* endowments under the Marīnids was related to doctrinal differences.[93] Ibn al-Khaṭīb, writing some twenty years later, when he was living in Fez as an exile from his native Granada, said, *awqāfuhā āriyyatan,* her endowments are numerous.[94] There is no discrepancy between the statements of two usually reliable observers, which both confirm what we have seen. In the early 14th century Al-ʿUmarī's informers reported few new endowments, but when those of previous dynasties were taken into account, the total number of endowments in Fez was great. Even a small new mosque was endowed with revenue from a new oven, a *dār*, a dwelling house, *maṣriya*, a flat, a stable, and a stable with another *maṣriya.*[95] This income was sufficient to provide wages for an *imām*, a reader, a *muadhdhin*, a janitor, and a supervisor, and to purchase oil for the lamps and other needs. In addition, housing for the *muadhdhin* and the *imām,* and a room in which to hold classes were provided. Two inscriptions from Tlemcen for endowments made by the Zayyānids, the ʿAbd al-Wādid dynasty of the central Maghrib, which was contemporary with the Marīnids, also provide a sample of generous endowments from the royal families in the neighboring region.[96]

Another problem related to acculturation was that there was no consensus in the Maghreb about what items were considered "public good", and what public institutions deserved support from the rulers. In the time of the Almoravid ʿAlī b. Yūsuf there was a levy, *waẓf*, on the people of Fez to pay for the building of the city's walls, and no *bayt al-māl* funds were used.[97] The practice continued when the Marīnids came to power and decisions about what the community considered the public good were subject to negotiations with the dynasty. For instance, since no *waqf* money was available the people of Fez agreed to pay voluntarily for the maintenance of the clock, *majāna*, but Abū ʿInān agreed to pay the supervisor's wages.[98] The abstract notion of a public good was not a norm which would produce an explicit policy of endowments on the part of the dynasty, as part of its Islamic identity, but the *waqf* was more of an individual gesture. The Marīnid rulers' policy of endowing a public institution was selective, sporadic, practiced by individual monarchs only and restricted to a small number of institutions. Concern for the public good could be acquired through the acculturation to Islamic norms, but could not help being influenced by personal goals and specific conditions.

The historical pattern of Marīnid endowments, was one which took place within a limited period time, and was restricted to a small number of rulers, was also visible during the Almohad period. All Almohad monumental structures, mosques, palaces, walls, date from a 50-year period which corresponded to the prosperous and stable rule of the first Almohad caliphs, 552-604/1157-1207. Clearly certain material conditions, political ambition, and personal vanity were the driving force behind royal *waqf*. The rulers also needed to posses certain cultural attributes in order to make endowments for the public good. Prosperity was a fundamental factor. Economic and political gains also influenced these decisions and during the period in question, Marīnid military and economic power was at its peak. From the politically stable and expansionist base, the Marīnid state went on to occupy the central Maghreb, reconquer the "gold road" from the Sudan to the Mediterranean, and establish commercial relations with European countries across the Mediterranean.[99] Marīnid endowments made an important contribution to the economic life in Fez. The economic incentives provided by the establishment of new institutions and the endowment of property for their upkeep contributed to the economy of Fez in two ways. Firstly, the creation of the *medresa* brought additional consumer groups—students, teachers and staff—into the city, either from the countryside, or from other cities or lands. These individuals had certain material needs which had to be met by the city's manufacturers: Food, and shelter had to be provided, books had to be copied for them, and additional buildings were erected in order to house them. The endowments contributed to the city's development into a major commercial, administrative and cultural center by the 14th century, and Fezian medieval urbanism became a model to be emulated in other Moroccan cities.[100] Urban life in Fez under the Marīnids has gained a reputation of unprecedented glamour, to which the Marīnid historiography, with its collection of the city's chronicles, is a standing testimony.[101]

Among the Islamic public institutions, the *waqf* was more powerful as an acculturation tool than the *medresa*, which helped reinforce cultural norms alone, because the *waqf* brought the strong muscle of economic rewards to bear upon acculturation to these norms. In the development of the last institution, the state's domain, we shall see the state's acculturation to Islamic norms solely on the economic level, with legal and administrative patterns which will enable us to put the entire acculturation process into perspective.

CHAPTER 9

The State's Domain: Land and Taxation*

The *Medresa Bū 'Ināniyya* in Fez built by the Marīnid Sultan Abū 'Inān in 1350-1355.

The state's domain was the vast area of economic resources and revenues, which the state controlled, including sectors such as land, both agrarian and pastoral, ores and metals, monopolies on selling and buying, taxation over rural and urban production, rent from commercial units and taxes on the person.[1] The Marīnid state, like other Islamic states and non-Islamic pre-industrialized large centralized societies, aspired to organize and control these resources which formed the core of the state's treasury, to the best of its ability, in order to maximize revenue. What made the situation of the Islamic State unique here, in comparison to other pre-modern societies, was precisely its acculturation to the Islamic norms, which produced a common and unified legal and normative framework, which other medieval states lacked.[2] As happened with the *waqf* institution, the domain also had to adjust to legal norms, but these norms were practiced by administrations across the Islamic world, and were based on similar legal assumptions. It did not matter that the laws governing economic activities were formulated by jurists who were not initially attached to the state's administration, because they were shaped and regulated by universal Islamic legal code. This legal framework, while inhibiting somewhat the freedom of the state's actions, also provided a unifying and stabilizing factor in its social and economic life. Even though, with the exception of Egypt, no other Islamic state was ever able to effectively control the entire domain system,[3] legal sources, and in particular a collection of legal opinions, *fatwās*, will provide the general context, and as in the case of the *waqf,* substantiate statements and suggest missing links. The best treatment so far given to these questions as they affect the Maghreb, can be found in the monographs devoted to the dynasties of Ifrīqiya,[4] which individually and collectively depict an evolutionary process in the Eastern Maghreb which can also be observed in the

*This is an unpublished study incorporating material from "Unity and Variety of Land Tenure and Cultivation patterns in the Medieval Maghreb," *The Maghreb Review*, Special Issue, 8(1983): 24-28, and from "Land tenure in Muslim Spain and North Africa: The Legal Evidence," Paper presented at the ICANAS meeting in Hong-Kong, 1993.

Western Maghreb. Since many questions are not sufficiently documented, nor fully understood in the Marīnid case, the discussion will benefit from comparison with other regions, especially Egypt and North Africa.[5]

The first question concerns the right to the land, who owned it and how these rights were acquired.

The development of the concept of land ownership among early Muslims resulted from the convergence of two different approaches, the nomad and the peasant. Private land ownership was unknown among the Bedouins, as the nomad society only recognized a certain kind of ownership: the collective ownership over the land which the tribe regularly camped on, or cultivated, known as the *ḥimā'*; activities such as measuring land or determining borders were unknown.[6] Among the settled populations land ownership was known and all its related activities practiced. Before the Arab conquest much of the land in Iraq belonged to the Sasanid state, and private land ownership was a common concept. Those who practiced cultivation on the state's domain contributed one third of their produce as rent and taxes, and these norms persisted after the conquest of Iraq, serving as background to the Islamic legal norms of landholding.[7] Strong central state before the Arab conquest existed also in the Maghreb, so patterns of land ownership must have been entrenched there as well. Equally, following the Eastern pattern, the rights to the land were renegotiated in the aftermath of the act of the conquest itself. Theoretically speaking, the right to the land was invested in the state by God, since the Islamic State was the embodiment of the religion, the monarch was the head of State and religion and there was no antagonism between the two. In that respect, Islamic states differed from the other medieval state which was formed through conquest in the area, where there was a struggle to prevent the church from possessing the land, the Crusader states in 12th-century Syria.[8] Islamic jurists, who by the 9th century, were writing from within a centralized State, concluded that it was the Arab conquest of North Africa in the 7th-8th centuries, which entitled the Berber-Islamic state to own, give away, cultivate and excavate ores from the land. Because the Islamic principle was directly derived from the acts of war and conquest, there was, however, a need for a definition to establish land ownership in cases where the Islamic State, which was the legal heir to all the rights invested in the state by conquest, conflicted with the rights of individual previous owners whichever were maintained in their former status as owners through their conversion to the new religion. As a result the actual problem became to determine whether North Africa was conquered and settled by peaceful negotiations, *ṣulḥan*, which would enable new converts to retain private ownership, since conversion to Islam entitled its subjects to retain private ownership, or by force, *ʿanwatan*, which would establish the right of land ownership entirely with the state. In that respect the traditions about the Berbers' conversion before the Arab conquest, could be used to claim previous rights to the land. In the East rulers struggled with those problems at an early date: Caliph ʿUmar II (99-101/717-20), was opposed to the distribution of the state's land to individuals, as private property, but was helpless to recover lands which had already been given away.[9] He sent a letter to the provinces' governors saying that local inhabitants who had accepted Islam before the conquest could keep their property, but those who converted after the conquest forfeited their right to their land and property, and those who submitted to the Arabs, but did not convert, had to pay the *jizya*.[10] How much change in landholding patterns did the Islamic conquest really cause?

Hardly anything is known about the land holding patterns in Morocco immediately after the Islamic conquest. The actual land distribution differed from that in the East, because conquest, pacification and finality of land distribution, occurred in different sequence. According to the description of the process in the *Kitāb al-amwāl*, the Western equivalent of the *Kitāb al-kharāj* in the East, the Arab conquest in the Western Maghreb initially produced chaos, which was aggravated by the conquest's erratic nature.[11] Al-Dāwudī, writing at the beginning of the 11th century had this to say: "Concerning Ifrīqiya and al-Andalus and Ṣiqliya, Sicily. The accounts of the land tenure in Ifrīqiya are contradictory, some say it was conquered *ṣulḥan* other say *ʿanwatan*...regarding al-Andalus some claim it was wholly conquered *ʿanwatan*, or mostly".[12] ʿAbd al-Ḥalīm defined the status of the land of the Maṣmūḍa and Marrakech as "neither conquered by force nor by peaceful means, namely that the inhabitants simply converted to Islam and thus gained rights over the land."[13] Several military campaigns were required and there is no evidence that a definitive allocation of lands took place early in the conquest.[14] Had there been one, the lands would have had to be re-allocated after each new campaign, given the state of chaos which ensued. So far as we know, it appears that the land was distributed rather arbitrarily. Some was given to Arab soldiers and settlers, while some remained in the hands of individual owners who converted to Islam at an undisclosed date. The Marīnid chroniclers of the 13th and 14th centuries repeated the essentials of this debate in an attempt to sort out past events and legalities, but without providing any new insight.[15] Al-Jaznā'ī, quoting Abū 'l-Ḥasan ʿAlī al-Qābisī, a Mālikī jurist from Qayrawān, 324-403/935-1012, who, himself, projected historical circumstances from the current land situation in the Maghreb into the past, said that since the right to derive revenue from mined ores was exercised by the ruler, it followed that the area had been conquered by force.[16] A *fatwā* by Ibn Abī Zayd, d. 386/996, reveals that in the region of Gafṣa in the 10th century, the state did not own a single piece of land which it could rent out. This fact, which seems unusual for the time, was explained by the jurist who said that the inhabitants of the area must have submitted peacefully to the Muslims, and therefore could retain their property.[17]

Even if the Islamic conquest in the Maghreb was indeed the disruptive force that the jurists would like us to believe it was, the Islamic legal system, this egalitarian unifying front to which we referred earlier, effaced it. Many of the genuine details of the conquest were also obliterated by attaching to it terms borrowed from the conquest and settlement of the Eastern regions.[18] In the case of Ifrīqiya, where the Roman patterns were more deeply entrenched, they have persisted. The dominant land holding patterns of late antiquity consisted of vast domains, primarily owned by the emperor, but also by wealthy individuals, some living in Africa, others living in Rome or Constantinople, who left the administration to contractors, or communal bodies such as cities and churches.[19] Land was cultivated by free peasants who were either native or immigrant ex-soldiers and who lived on the land as tenant-farmers, paying rent in proportion to the harvest. Small holdings were in the minority to begin with, and the free peasants' independent status slowly deteriorated, hastening the incorporation of these small private lands into the larger estates. By the 4th century, the division was, rather, between large and small size estates, both private and state owned.[20] Immediately after the conquest, in the 8th and 9th centuries, the patterns of the Roman system remained in force in Ifrīqiya, consisting of large estates cultivated by an agricultural slave labor force, together with medium and small lots cultivated by tenants who paid rent.[21]

The significance of the legal debate about the conquest should not be seen merely as a fiction, not only because, in the eyes of the jurists, it was the event that *de facto* entitled the state to the divine right over the land, but especially because later events in the Maghreb prove that landholding reforms could be anticipated only in the aftermath of a conquest, even if that conquest was by fellow Muslim rulers. In fact, both attempts at landholding reforms in the Maghreb occurred following a conquest. The first occurred in 554/1159, in the aftermath of the conquest of the Maghreb by the Almohad ruler ʿAbd al-Mu'min.[22] The second reform came some 200 years later, in 748/1347 after the Marīnid ruler Abū 'l-Ḥasan, conquered Ifrīqiya, and was an attempt to retrieve *the iqṭāʿ* land that had been ceded to the Arab nomad tribes.[23] Like all changes in land tenure patterns, Abū 'l-Ḥasan 's attempts to take over the prerogatives of the reigning dynasty were meant to redistribute wealth and benefits to newcomers, rather than to unify landholding patterns across the Maghreb.

In fact, the evolution of landholding patterns in the Maghreb had little to do with the conquest, and everything to do with the new legal system and the nature of the state's power. Following the transition period, a slow, but unmistakable shift, towards unique Islamic patterns, emerged. This included the first two categories inherited from the Roman and Byzantine State: private land, *mulk*, and the public domain, sometimes referred to as *jazā'*, and in Marīnid Morocco, the State's land and the domain, the *makhzen*. A third category of land, *ḥabous* or *waqf*, endowed land, whose legal status as a species of private property frozen in time, lay between the other two, had existed in principle from the beginning, but increased considerably in later centuries,[24] as the result of the Islamic inheritance law.[25] A fourth category, land held in common, or tribal land, term *mubāḥa*, non-propertied, was not mentioned by the Marīnid sources or the Marīnid *fatwā*s. On the other hand, a description of "revived" land, found at the limit of settled areas, *aḥyā' f īmā qarb min al-ʿumrān*, appeared in a *fatwā* from Tlemcen.[26] In addition to the state's lands which were dead land, *mawāt*, the domain also included another category of land, less fertile than the *jazā'*, which paid *ḥukr* tax. The cultivator of *ḥukr* land was not allowed to built on it or to plant it, but could raise it to the level of cultivated land by paying a *jazā'* tax on it. This was the case in Ifrīqiya, at least.[27] Landholding patterns continued to evolve in a different manner, and subsequently acquired a separate history and terminology. The existing structures had to be justified each time a struggle over property rights with the state occurred, and were justified by calling upon Islamic norms. In the Marīnid West, a *fatwā* described a tax imposed on *jazā'* land in Fez, an orchard whose owner had to pay a *jazā'* of 1/2 dinar a year in the 15th century. This could have been tax, rent, or crop-sharing with the state.[28] Both in Ḥafṣid Ifrīqiya and in Morocco under the Marīnids, the term *jazā'* land was used to denote not only State land but also the rent paid on it and the tax paid on land in general, both of which were to go to the public treasury, the *bayt al-māl.* As a result, the use of this term is always accompanied by uncertainty about precisely what the sources meant. The confusion is aggravated by the unclear use of the term *kharaj,* and whether or not it was used in the same manner as in the East, or whether the term *jazā'* was the only one used to refer to land tax.[29]

The conquest was not an apocalyptic event which introduced deep changes in landholding, but, by imposing the new Islamic norms, existing patterns slowly, although not immediately, changed course. The basic division of land lingered on, retaining the State's domain on one hand and private domain on the other, but the theoretical discussion of rights over land had given way to an actual evolution in landholding patterns. By the time the acculturation to Islamic norms was completed, and reflected in the legal sources of the 14th century, the change was evident and affected the relative size of the private domain as it grew in relation to the state's domain. Even if a definitive answer to this question could be provided, it would sit well with the protagonists of *longue durée* theory, who object to the idea of a split between the classical period and the medieval one. The effect of the conquest is a question of form, not of substance, because we cannot invest the conquest with such a disruptive force.

As the evolution in the legal status of the lands in the state's domain continued, the land which was rented out to cultivators began to disappear into the private sector, as renters began to sell the land they cultivated under the assumption that they owned it. The battle over the right to the land was fierce. In a series of *fatwās* from Granada, Fez, Tlemcen, and Tunis, all relating to this problem, we see a battle raging between the state's domain and private citizens over land, with the jurists taking the side of the state, and defending its right to retain the *jazā'* land and to benefit from the rent collected on it.[30] The jurists' defense did not result necessarily from approval of the state, but because land was the eternal resource of the community, represented by the *bayt al-māl,* the public treasury.[31] The Marīnid *makhzen* was not the only administration which had to fight the alienation of State lands. A *fatwā* written by Ibn Lubb in 14th century Granada, defined the rights of the person who rented *jazā'* land, or land of the sultan, as it is referred to in Spain, from the state.[32] In Tlemcen, Ibn Marzūq even gave a court decision, *ḥukm*, on the subject.[33] In another *fatwā* in Tlemcen, written by al-ʿUqbānī, there was again a question about land rented out and cultivated by an order of the sultan, *amr sultani*.[34] A family member planted it with different kinds of trees, then his heirs sold it to others, who continued to derive profit from it for a long time, until the land was claimed. Yet the ruling was unequivocally in favor of the state; the land belonged to the authorities, *a'ima*, and had been given only for cultivation, not ownership. It belonged to the Muslim community, *jamāʿat al-muslimīn,* and the right in it was not specified, or, if it was, then the imam was "to derive usufruct" while the land belonged to the *bayt al-māl*. Under Mālikī law, the person who rented the land could build, plant an orchard and pay rent on the produce to the state; he had the right to sell the harvest or to uproot the trees, as he saw fit. According to other opinions, the cultivator of the domain land had the right to purchase the buildings and the plantation at a lower price, when they were offered for sale.[35] The state treasury also considered itself a partner in all crops or revenue recovered from the gardens, houses, orchards, vineyards, or any other constructions or other enterprises undertaken on the domain's land, no matter how long ago the land had been rented out or how sharing the revenue would affect the cultivators. The sale of such land, even when carried out with the knowledge of those who had given it, was still a legal offence.

The continuous use of the state's land by individuals over a prolonged period of time represented a real danger for the state. Unless there was an organized system of administration and land registration in place to enforce the norms, the state would not be successful in claiming its share or ownership, and the expansion of the private domain at the expense of the public one would continue.

Opinions vary among modern historians about whether there was regular land registration in North Africa. Hopkins suggested that "The turbulent history of the country gave no opportunity for the establishment of a lasting fiscal tradition. Tax collection, like the other functions of government, was generally organized ad hoc".[36] Claude Cahen was of the opinion that "The source of land ownership, the cadastral survey, namely the assessment of land tax, which became a fiscal cadaster known as *qānūn*, seemed to develop slowly and to have been less precise. It is possible that it was not introduced to Morocco before the Almohad period, being brought back by Ibn Tūmart from his journey to the East, and not all estates were covered."[37] Talbi spoke about a land register of Ifrīqiya without providing any details,[38] and Brunschvig thought that the land, at least that which belonged to the *jazā'* category, was never registered as such but was always "considered" as such.[39] However, we know that in the later Middle Ages, Ifrīqiya had a land registry, which the great grandfather of the historian Ibn Khaldūn described in a manual for scribes he has written.[40] This man served as a supervisor under the Ḥafṣids, and described the existence of three revenue registers, which included estimates on crops.[41] Whether or not there was a cadaster, a land register, in Marīnid Morocco is not clear, but we can conclude from the evidence provided in the *fatwā*s that some registration of the domain land did exist, since the state could make ownership claims based on some legal documentation, even though no direct reference to a cadaster, whether termed *dīwān* or *qānūn,* occurred. Despite the passing of several generations, during which the land was bought, sold and cultivated as if in private ownership, the state's administration did not lose track of it, retaining the legal documents relating to the transaction and claiming a share of the revenue derived from investment made in it.

As observed in the *fatwā*s, the cultivation of land on the state's domain was organized either through renting the entire plot, or by crop-sharing with the state. In Marīnid Morocco, the state became a legal partner with individuals when state land was rented to share croppers. Legal arrangements in this case were the same as for privately owned land and hired labor. The major crop-sharing contracts were *muzara'a*, pertaining to cereals and the *musāqa* and the *mughārasa,* pertaining mainly to vegetables and orchards, although some irrigated crops, grown together with the trees, were sometimes allowed. All contracts were conceived as a partnership between the owner of the land and the laborers. The latter brought not only his labor but sometimes, the animals and the seeds also. Each of these contracts had numerous variations in the share given to the parties. In private land, it was obvious that the owner was working side by side with his hired journeyman. Another popular system, which fell between crop-sharing and hiring, was the *khimāsa*, concluded by an oral agreement, according to which the *khamās* often received more than the one-fifth implied in the contract's name, sometimes as much as a quarter, although the jurists particularly objected to this form of business because of its ambiguous nature. Simple agricultural wage labor was also recorded in the *fatwā*s. If the crop-sharing partnership contracts failed, a move could be made into wage labor. Night and day watchers always received wages and were usually paid in kind. Wages could be calculated either for a certain amount of labor or for a determined period of time. The law also provided instructions for the division of crops between partners. Although it usually forbade the approximate measure of crops, the *fatwā*s detailed conditions for such divisions when they were necessary. In many cases, the allocations made to share croppers differed according to the nature of irrigation available to the land, its quality, and the kind of crop grown. In general, the jurists looked askance at agricultural contracts, because they shunned any contract which included unclear clauses and therefore implied one side taking advantage of the other. Projection of the crops could not be made as precisely as it was in Egypt. However, such contracts were common, and so, too was the state's partnership in cultivation, and even in the 50/50 contract of cultivation, whether for grains or fruits.[42] Partnership with the state did not absolve renters from paying the land tax, the *zakāt* and the *ʿushr*.[43] The 50/50 arrangement described in the *fatwā*s was unique and was not included in the Andalusian notarial formularies. Certainly, nothing remotely resembling Egypt's land registry system ever existed in Morocco.[44] The anticipated revenue of the crops could be calculated in Egypt, the norm requiring complete knowledge of the details of the contract, because of the stable condition of the agriculture there. The *qānūn* registered lands had their taxes assessed based on the agricultural production according to the quality of the land, availability of irrigation and the crop cultivated, with the state's agent registering all parcels' size, fertility, allocation and designated crop.

The lack of social unrest in the rural areas seems unique. Rural unrest was common in the East under the ʿAbbāsids during the 8th and 9th centuries, and in Egypt during the Ayyūbid and the Mamlūk periods, but was absent from the Maghreb. In contrast to the frequent urban agitation, there were no peasant uprising under the Marīnids. Does this indicate that the rural sector in the medieval Maghreb was not subject to the extreme exploitation, which occurred in the Muslim East? Could the land holding patterns under the Marīnids, a majority of small private land plots and the elimination of the large estates be credited with making this possible? This was a reversal of the process which occurred in the Islamic East, where small landowners preferred to become share croppers and give their land to the large landowners, in order to receive protection.[45]

From the domain holdings, the Marīnid state made land and tax grants as concessions to individuals or tribes. The beneficiaries were politicians, exiled dignitaries and Arab and Berber chiefs, but not soldiers. When Ibn al Khatīb, the exiled vizier from Granada, came to Morocco, he received the taxes from the city of Salé as *iqṭāʿ*.[46] When land was given, the size of *iqṭāʿ* land appears to have varied considerably.[47] The Almohad *sheikh*s in Ifrīqiya received between 60 and 120 hectares each, not necessarily in a single lot, and the kind of land was unspecified.[48] Unlike the private, family, *waqf*, which always included agricultural plots, the royal *waqf* rarely included agricultural land. In fact, the only occasion when endowment of land was mentioned as part of a Marīnid royal *waqf* was when Abū 'l-Ḥasan was reported to have bought lands around Marrakech, in the East, and also near Tlemcen, to create a revenue source for a *waqf ḥaramayn*. In Marīnid Morocco, the mercenary cavalry received wages, *rātib*,[49] while the local chieftains received landed *iqṭāʿ* worth 20.000 gold *mithqāl* in taxes and kind, which they had to collect from the tribes. According to al-ʿUmarī, soldiers only rarely received *iqṭāʿ* land. Others, such as the chief *qāḍī* and the head of the chancellery, received wages and a small amount of *iqṭāʿ* land. The first received 1 *mithqāl* a day, and the second, 2 *mithqāl* a day, but he also received 2 villages from the domain as a concession. The availability of cash strengthened the Marīnid state because it prevented the creation of the strong military absentee landlords who proved ruinous to the peasants in other areas, and particularly in Iraq and Mamlūk Egypt.

The modest land concessions made by the Marīnids to soldiers and commanders stands in great contrast to the practice in the East, and leads us to look at the relationship between the state and its army in a new light. By the time the Marīnids came to power the use of the state domain lands to maintain a standing army had become a long standing Muslim practice. In the East, *iqṭāʿ* land was initially given as temporary payment for certain *ad hoc* services, in many cases, but not exclusively, military service, and was supposed to revert to the state's domain either later or on the death of the ruler who had awarded it.[50] In cases of weak central government or during a political crisis, *iqṭāʿ* lands tended to remain in the hands of their holders and to become *mulk*, private property. The Marīnids had a standing army composed of Christian and Muslim mercenaries but paid them in cash.[51] The Christian militia was not a Marīnid innovation. It was a Maghrebi tradition, which began under the Almoravids.[52] The Marīnid recruitment of Aragonese cavalry began in 1274 with a treaty between Abū Yūsuf and Jacques the Conqueror. Five hundred Christian soldiers and 10 war vessels and 50 other boats would cross the strait to Morocco. Each soldier was to be paid the amount of 2 besants a day in the form of gold dinars. Their commander was to be paid 100 besants, and if the war continued for more than a year, an additional 200,000 besants would be paid to the Aragonese king.[53] Abū Yaʿqūb Yūsuf also paid Jacques II, 10,000 gold dinars for a detachment of Christian troops. From 1306 the Marīnid army included regular Castilian and Portuguese soldiers, whom we know were paid wages. Some of its members gained influence in the court and were conspicuous by their presence at some key events.[54] In the first half of the 14th century, al-ʿUmarī, gave the numbers in the standing Marīnid Marīnid army: "Many Arab tribes, 1500 *Ghuz* arrow-shooting cavalry of Turkish origin, 4000 Frankish cavalry, 500 *ʿulūj* Muslim cavalry, more than 1000 Andalūsī arabaletiers shooting arrows from a footbow, and a large group of Berber tent dwellers."[55] The Christian mercenaries, whether French or Spaniards, who numbered around 5,000 under the Marīnids, together with the Muslim units, received payment in cash every few months. Other soldiers, presumably locals and natives, received 60 gold *mithqāl* a month, others received 30 *mithqāl* a month, and the lowest rank received 6 *mithqāl*,... "and no land was given to them".[56] It seems that the Marīnid state's treasury never lacked precious metals with which to pay for its troops and the recruitment of mercenaries. At the same time the Marīnids did not lack manpower to enlist in their army. They constantly sent their own soldiers as mercenaries across the strait to be employed by their Christian and Muslim neighbor states and sometime enemies. In 1285, for instance, Marīnid Zanāta cavalry participated in the Aragonese war against France, and in 1303, 7000 Marīnid soldiers served in Naṣrid Granada, however, this policy could be explained by a desire to keep turbulent elements out of the army.

The sultan's ability to pay wages in money or gold distinguished the Marīnid from other states, and gave it a unique status among its medieval contemporaries. The abundance of gold in its treasury remained a constant and beneficial factor to the Marīnid state. It lasted for at least a full hundred years, from the 1270's onwards, from the time of Abū Yūsuf to Abū ʿInān, who bought the city of Tripoli for the Muslims for 50,000 dinar of pure gold.[57] The price of gold, highly valued in the Mediterranean trade, with its new international monetary system, was constantly increasing during the 13th and 14th centuries, and dictated Marīnid policies.[58] The Islamic norms gave the state the revenue from gold, since extracted ores belonged to it, but the Marīnids also needed to acquire control over the gold routes and outlets to the Mediterranean ports. The conquest of the triangle Sijilmāsa, Ceuta, al-Manṣūra, which later extended to Tunisia, shows the importance of the gold factor in Marīnid policy.[59] Thanks to its control over Sijilmāsa, the Marīnid state could keep a regular supply of gold from across the Sahara, and prevent any other state from exporting gold from the Maghreb to Europe. The abundance of gold documented in the Arabic sources and Aragonese archives supports R. S. Lopez's hypothesis that the frequency by which Genoese traders focused on Ceuta in the 13th century was related to this city's situation as a Mediterranean outlet for the Saharan gold.[60] The principle which established the state's right to the land also permitted it to share in the exploitation of its riches, whether extracted from the land or from the seas. The Marīnid state considered the natural resources such as ores, petrol, amber, fish etc. as a state's domain and received one third of the proceeds from all mining operations and silver, as well as iron and other ores, were mined in the Moroccan mountains.

The area of tax collection was the one where the Marīnid state transgressed Islamic legal directives heavily, and extended the reach of the state domain into areas where it was not anticipated. The tax portion of the domain can be conveniently split into rural and urban taxes, or taxes imposed on cultivation and those imposed on manufacturing. The collection of taxes in the rural areas was less structured and less effective than in the cities. A precious text by Ibn Marzūq, which actually described the taxes abolished, gives what seems to be only a partial view of the array of illegal taxes in the mid-14th century.[61] When recounting Abū 'l-Ḥasan's tax reform, Ibn Marzūq spoke about different taxes which were imposed in addition to, or replacing, the basic canonical taxes of *kharāj* and *ʿushr*, both in the city of Fez and in the countryside.[62] In the case of the first, this referred to the *khirās* tax on fruit trees, which was "like the *jazā'* in Ifrīqiya", mentioned earlier.[63] According to Ibn Marzūq, this tax, was so heavy that many people in Fez sold their fruit trees. In Sijilmāsa, the tax imposed on agricultural products was termed *jamūn*, collected from the sale of dates and cereals. Ibn Marzūq remarked that as appropriately for a town on the trans-Saharan gold route, this tax was paid to the central treasury in several loads of gold each year. Abū 'l-Ḥasan abolished this tax and returned it to the canonic *kharāj*. The rural areas paid several other levies called respectively *khirās, burnūs, ḍiyāfa, inzāl, qaʿa, khatīʿa*, whose meaning is open to interpretation. As Ibn Marzūq explained, both rural and urban residents in Morocco had to pay the *qānūn*, similar to the *jizya*, the long established poll-tax which states imposed on the *dhimmis*, and was levied from all kind of property.[64] Abū 'l-Ḥasan abolished this tax as non-canonical, but it must have been in use earlier, since it was mentioned by several other historians before Ibn Marzūq explained it.[65] A supplementary tax was imposed on irrigation, whereby water users needed a license, *barāʿa*, to prove that they had paid their dues for water in order to have access to irrigation. Another rural tax was called *al-ḥibl* or *al-matāwī*. This also appears to have been a sort of poll-tax, since peasants who left their villages, either for lack of livelihood or any other reason, found that their families had to pay the tax on their behalf, while they were also taxed in their new location. Either Abū 'l-Ḥasan's abolition of these taxes was temporary or Ibn Marzūq was badly informed, since only a few years later, Ibn Baṭūta reported that Abū ʿInān had removed several onerous taxes, *maẓālim*, from the people, even though these taxes, among them the dues collected along the roads, brought in a huge amount of money, *majba ʿaẓīm*.[66]

Collection of taxes on urban production was easier to organize and supervise, even though such taxes were even less grounded in Islamic legal norms than the taxation on the land. It is hard to establish how well organized the tax collection was before the Marīnids, but the Marīnid state inherited an orderly register of urban establishments, workshops and public commercial buildings on state land, or on public land in the cities from which rent was collected.[67] These properties were registered in a ledger kept by the central administration of the domain and were supposed to pay rent, and tax on any transactions concerning them. A list drawn up by the Almohad administration, enumerating the rent and tax paying establishments in 13th-century Fez, shows the exceptional urban development of the city.[68] The list included 785 mosques, 93 public bathing houses, 80 fountains, 17,040 large dwelling units, 472 mills, 89,236 houses, 467 inns, 9,082 shops, 2 *qaysariyas*, 2 minting houses, 1,170 ovens, 3,490 looms, 47 soap making shops, 86 tanneries, 116 dye houses, 12 copper foundries, 11 crystal manufacturing stores, and 188 potteries. The Marīnid administration inherited both the properties and the register from the Almohad administration, and was able to increase both the number of establishments and the revenue collected. As elsewhere, the taxes on financial transactions in Marīnid Morocco were collected in cash, whereas taxes on agricultural produce were collected in kind, except in the case of 14th-century Sijilmāsa, mentioned earlier.[69]

The Marīnid state was not unique in its orderly management of urban property. The Egyptian administration kept details of the stores, inns and workshops and of food production establishments, from which it regularly collected rent.[70] In Ifrīqiya the Ḥafṣid state collected thousands of gold dinars in revenue from transactions concerning sheep, food, oil, salt and vegetables, which took place in the market place,[71] even though the jurists criticized this practice on legal grounds.[72] Yet, as we have seen in the discussion of the Marīnid endowments in Fez, the same process of alienation of the domain property into private hands persisted there as well.[73] Thus, while Mālikī law effectively regulated the land ownership and other related aspects of land and cultivation transactions, including inheritance, sale, endowment, etc., as well as crop sharing and hired labor, and stood by the state in its struggle to regain control over alienated properties, it could not interfere with non-Qur'ānic taxes imposed by the state.

The attempts of the state to organize the domain and maximize revenue reached into two additional areas. Both monopolies and tax farming were irregular as far as Islamic legal norms are concerned, but both were widely practiced. In addition control over the resources given to the Islamic state, also did not enable the Marīnids to effectively impose monopolies over the buying and selling of certain items as part of its drive to maximize revenue from the domain. In Ifrīqiya,[74] and Egypt,[75] state monopolies were feasible because geographical and demographic conditions favored state control and centralization of revenue collection. This policy reached its pinnacle in the Mamlūk state's attempt to monopolize the revenue from the huge sugar industry, and to force the buying of meat and grain at fixed prices from the state's agents.[76] The Ḥafṣid state monopolized soap production, and fishing became a state monopoly by the 14th century. In 686/1287, the sale of wine imported and sold as a monopoly by the *qabāla* office, brought 120 gold dinar to the state treasury of Tunis in clear violation of the norm forbidding wine drinking among Muslims.[77] In the case of Morocco, it is not clear whether there was a strong tradition of state monopolies among the dynasties preceding the Marīnids,[78] but there were certainly attempts to establish such monopolies. One such area where the state managed to impose a monopoly was over the sale of its grain for export, but it probably did not do so for trading in local markets. As demonstrated in the case of al-Mazdaghī, the European grain trade in the western Mediterranean was active and lucrative, and Marīnid subjects participated in it.[79] Documents issued by and for Christian merchants, who carried most of the Marīnid grain in Catalan and Majorcan ships, imply that grain was cheaper in Morocco than in Ifrīqiya, and in general cheaper in the Maghreb than in Catalan and Aragonese lands.[80] Speculation in this commodity was shared by Moroccans as well as by traders from Barcelona, who would sometimes buy in Morocco in order to sell it back there.[81] Whether or not taxes were farmed out, *ḍamān,* to agents, *wulāt*, or directly collected by the administration is an important issue because it reflects the state's capacity to organize an effective tax collection system based in the court and maximize the usefulness of these taxes. Unlike the practice in the East, there are indications that there had been attempts to abolish tax farming in the Maghreb and replace it with direct collection by the state. In Ifrīqiya, Ibn Ḥawqal, writing about the 10th century, said, "under the Fāṭimids tax collection was direct, *bi 'l-amāna*, but later, the taxes of the city of Barqa were farmed out," constituting a unique case in the history of the Maghreb.[82] Later, speaking about the year 336/947 and enumerating a long list of taxes, he provided a minute description of how the taxes were paid in advance by the incoming officials. No direct evidence is available about the Marīnid practice, and we can assume that like everywhere else in the Islamic world, tax farming was the rule.

Unlike the intellectual malaise which acculturation to the Arabic language and Islamic history provoked among the Berbers, the acculturation of the Marīnid state to public institutions and especially the domain, appears to have taken place without agony and compared to the debacle around the *medresa* and the *waqf*, without a struggle with the subjects. It was less antagonistic, less intrusive and less disruptive. What was also unique to the Marīnid situation was its situation vis-à-vis the state's domain in the East. There bigger and bigger estates were created, while in the Maghreb, smaller private lots became common. In fact, the state had to fight hard to regain control over lands which had been originally part of its domain and were lost.[83] This was not necessarily a bad omen; the placidity of the agrarian system contributed to the security of the political regime in Morocco, while the urban unrest destabilized it.

TRADE AND THE MEDITERRANEAN WORLD

CHAPTER 10

Marīnid Fez and the Quest for Global Order

A Long-Term Quest

On April 25 1348 the mighty Marīnid army, led by the sultan Abū ʻl-Hasan and stranded far away from home in Tunisia, suffered a momentous defeat at the hands of a coalition of nomadic tribes in the battle of Qayarawān.[1] The tribes were Arabic speaking, which distinguished them from the Berber speaking tribes of Morocco, and they rebelled against the Marīnid plans for fiscal reorganization in their newly created empire, repossessing *iqtāʼ*, grants of land and the right to collect taxes from their tenants, which the tribes had secured under a weaker Hafsid central government. Put in place after the conquest of Tlemcen,[2] the Marīnids tried to implement a policy of administrative re-organization, with strong financial institutions in the conquered territories.[3] The adversarial relationship between central governments and the nomadic tribes in North Africa was nothing new to its rulers, and for later observers was described and commented on by Ibn Khaldūn in his *Kitāb al-Ibar*. This time, however, it was happening on a much grander scale, as befitted an empire. Empires seek to control resources, and the Marīnids were set to do just that on the final stage of realizing their long-term dream of building an empire. The nomads might well have never won the battle of Qayrawān if the Marīnid army had not succumbed to the Black Death, which arrived in the port of Tunis a year before it reached Fez.[4] Spread by a rodent, the black rat, found in all types of grain storage, the disease quickly affected urban and rural areas, while sparing the nomadic population.[5] The fate of the Marīnid army only serves to illustrate the degree to which it was integrated into the global order. It should not obscure the significance of its existence as a forerunner, a harbinger of the Portuguese, Spanish and Dutch Atlantic Ocean empires in the following centuries.[6] The hasty, disorganized retreat of the ailing troops back to Morocco, triggered the rejection of Marīnid sovereignty in the newly conquered towns along the Mediterranean coast. In a quick reversal of fortune, the great Abū ʻl-Hasan went from a conqueror to a fugitive. Indeed, not only his life but even his defeat after his army's demise, evokes 'Napoleonic' proportions: alone, abandoned by his soldiers, chased by his son across the Maghrib, he died hiding in the mountain of the Hintata in Morocco. What he may not have fully realized at the time, was that the Black Death which caused the collapse of his army and his dream of an empire, was a personal tragedy shared by many others.

Abū 'l-Hasan may have been the most successful of the 'quest for empire' drive but the rise of 14th century Marīnid Moroccan empire had significant predecessors with various degrees of duration and continuity. Through political and military campaigns the Almoravids, 1061-1146,[7] and the Almohads, 1147-1269,[8] achieved limited success in their drive for empire, repeatedly attempting to expand southward to Africa, northward to Spain and eastward to Tunisia. Yet, in the 14th century, local and global conditions made the empire dream more plausible. From the instant he came to power, Abū 'l-Hasan saw himself and his country holding a global vocation and systematically acted to achieve it. At no point in time, was Western North Africa, the Maghrib with its capital Fez, closer to accomplishing its quest for empire. It was at this mid-fourteenth century point that the region's long standing economic, demographic and political advantages, culminated in forging a new regional and international power. Led by three ambitious and visionary long- reigning monarchs, Abū Said, his son Abu l'Hasan and grandson, Abū Inān, 1325-1361, used their country's strategic advantages to realize the empire dream with military might, and as empires do, pay for the monumental buildings erected in their capital, Fez. During this period, Fez also became a center of intellectual creativity, attracting many of the great minds of medieval Islam, including Ibn Khaldūn. Ibn Khaldūn was an observer of current affairs. Born in 1332 in Tunis, he spent several years in the Marīnid court in Fez, and thus witnessed it first-hand. "With the conquest of Tlemcen, Abū 'l-Hasan greatly enlarged his empire; from being the king of the Banū Marīn he became the king of all the Zanatas and after he became ruler of the Maghrib he found himself in control of both sides of the strait", he wrote in the *Kitāb al-'ibar.*[9] "Driven by ambition and pride, Abū 'l-Hasan sent ambassadors carrying sumptuous gifts to rulers in Africa, (the famous Mansa Musa,) and to the Mamlūks in Cairo, and received the Castilian ambassadors in 1347, after the capture of Oran and on his way to conquer Tunis." Across the strait, the Granadan Nasrids were intimidated by the economic and military power of the

Marīnids. Beforehand, Abū 'l-Hasan consolidated his position in the Western Mediterranean with an extraordinary victory at sea in April 1340, over combined Christian armada from Castile, Portugal and Aragon, all maritime powerhouses in full expansion. To ensure Marīnid victory, Abū'l-Hasan crossed the straits escorted by 60 galleys, which he leased from Genoa. The visit of the Castilian ambassadors to the Marīnid court confirmed that the victory made him a figure of global stature and the subject of talk among kings and Popes alike.[10] The ongoing hostilities between the Iberian powers ceased in 1337 in anticipation of an attack by the Marīnid troops crossing the straits. In April 1339, the Aragonese king Peter wrote to Pope Benedict XII to say that the king of Morocco, having captured Tlemcen, has turned his eyes to Spain. He feared that a North African invasion would stir up the Muslims of Valencia, who at that point in time constituted one third of the population, some 170,000 souls.

Abū 'l-Hasan's imperial aspirations to integrate the conquered Atlantic African shore and to colonize the Maghrib did not expire with his death. His son and heir, Abū ᶜInān. d. 1358, regained control of the central and eastern Maghrib, fighting both Muslim and Christian armies in the process. In the South, Moroccan expeditions continued into the 16th century.[11] In what follows I describe and analyze a set of economic factors that enabled the Marīnids to achieve their goal of building an empire. These were in order of discussion, their demographic strength, their control over the West African gold, their participation in the Mediterranean grain trade, and their institutional reforms.

The Demographics of the 'Quest for Empire'

The Marīnid defeat in Qayrawān gives us a convenient departure point for the discussion, illustrating how closely linked was the Islamic Mediterranean to the new economic order emerging in Europe. Tunis was a major grain shipment center, importing and exporting grain to Mediterranean destinations, which made it a natural host to a Sicilian ship carrying grain, or an Italian cargo ship from Alexandria with sick rats and their fleas on board.[12] Alexandria was infected earlier by an Italian ship bringing Circassians and Turkish slaves, new army recruits from the Black Sea sold to the Mamlūk rulers of Egypt. The rapidity and ferocity through which the Marīnid army was decimated by the Black Death in 1348, illustrates the mortality rate for Europe: between 60% and 65% for the years 1346-1353, or 50 million out of a general population estimated at 80 million, were killed by the plague.[13] As no records exist for the mortality rate in the Middle East and North Africa regions, the same study suggests a mortality rate similar to that of Europe. In our case it would have meant that Marīnid Morocco would have suffered a loss of about two thirds of its population.[14] However, the long term vicissitudes of the Maghrib's demographics and the demographic history of Morocco in particular, and that of its various regions in general, remain somewhat confused. North Africa's population declined with the rest of the Mediterranean lands well before the Arab conquest of the 7th century due to a previous plague, the Justinian plague, 6th-8th century. Estimates for the year 1000 suggest a total of between 2 and 5 million for North Africa, distributed at a rate of 2:1:1, meaning that historical Morocco always had double the population of the other two regions, central and eastern North Africa.[15] Population estimates for Muslim Spain suggest about 8.3 million in the 11th century, then decline to 7 million by the 12th century, probably because of internal wars, but otherwise inexplicable. However, North Africa is believed to have followed the pattern of Arab Middle East, where the population declined even before the arrival of the Black Death and remained low. According to Muhammad Talbi, the population of Tunisia, for instance, declined considerably because of the nomadic invasions in the 11th century.[16]

Human ecology in Morocco suggests otherwise, however. Areas of the mountains where tribal population was concentrated followed a trajectory of slow population recovery beginning with the eleventh century. Three centuries of uninterrupted military exploits that followed one after the other throughout the Almoravid, Almohad and Marīnid rules, demonstrate its strength. Abū l'Hasan, like the Marīnid sultans who preceded him, had enough combatants to send some to Muslim Spain, where they remained permanently. He may have had additional reasons for sending them overseas - these were turbulent tribal elements - nonetheless, the fact that he could dispense with soldiers is sufficient proof that he had plenty under his command. In 1339 Catalan merchants reported that Abū 'l-Hasan crossed the strait with an army of 8,000-10,000 men, to join another contingent of 4,000 men already stationed in Ronda. Abū 'l-Hasan was also able to staff his galleys with new recruits from Tunis and Bougie, the newly conquered territories. Each of the 44 galleys and 35 other boats he used for the crossing, carried between 300 and 400 men including some 200 archers and cross-bowmen stationed in three castles in every ship. With the final addition of troops from Granada it could be estimated that he had mustered an army of between 18,000 and 20,000 men. The ethnic composition of the Marīnid army is also of interest as it shows that recruits came from everywhere. According to al-Umari, an historian contemporary of the events, "there were many Arab tribes, 1500 *ghuzz* arrow-shooting cavalry of Turkish origin, 4000 Frankish cavalry, 500 *uluj* Muslim cavalry, more than 1000 Andalusi shooting arrows from a foot bow and a large group of Berber tent dwellers."[17] Abū 'l-Hasan's Marīnid army was a reflection of armies made up of natives and mercenaries, where Arab, Turks, Berbers and Europeans, all speaking different languages and trained in different warfare techniques, drawn and kept together for several years, fight together and achieve victory. Some of the Spanish mercenaries even remained in the country and played a role in successive palace politics. Notwithstanding, population growth continued. In 1342, despite of years of ongoing warfare, government agents fanned out across the country, mostly in the tribal areas of the Rif and Atlas mountains, to raise more troops; clearly the State administration believed that manpower was still available there.[18] This suggests that the demographic trends of 14th century Morocco were probably closer to those of Europe, which enjoyed a century of rapid demographic growth up until the Black Death, rather than that of the Arab or Middle Eastern Islamic regions, to which it is normally compared. [19] It may also be true that because of limited maritime trade, rates of infection were lower in Morocco.

There were additional factors in the demographic picture. Black Africa became a major supplier of manpower and the Atlantic coast was destined to play a decisive role in the slave trade in the years to come.[20] Morocco's strategic location on the Atlantic Ocean raises the question of whether black slaves played a role in the Marīnid army. Indeed, one of the ways in which the Islamic state in general handled a chronic manpower shortages, was through a sustained purchase of slaves, white from Russia, Central Asia and the Caucasus, and black from sub-Saharan Africa, areas not affected by the early plague. [21] The dependency of the Mamlūk regime in Egypt, a contemporary of the Marīnids, on the supply of slaves highlights the degree to which Genoa, by ensuring the military slave supply, enabled the survival of the Mamlūk regime.[22] Austen demonstrated that a regular yearly supply of slaves from sub-Saharan Africa was in place in earlier years. Some slaves arrived in the Mediterranean ports, while others were sold in East African ports. Since European demand for slaves vanished in the early Middle Ages, demand must have come from the Islamic Middle East.[23] Austen estimated that the entire slave trade between the years 650 and 1500 AD, provided 5 million slaves, of which at least 2 to 2,5 million were taken captives directly from the regions bordering the Red Sea, thus avoiding the "Western" road, via Sijilmasa and Fez, the gold export route.[24] According to E. Savage, this import, was managed single handedly by the Ibadi slave traders of Ifriqiya in the early 8th-10th century.[25] Black soldiers were a common phenomenon in the Islamic armies of North Africa, particularly in Ifriqiya where the dynasties more commonly employed black soldiers. While Austen estimated that the Almoravids employed some 2000-4000 slaves, he could not find indication that either the Almohads, or the Marīnids used black army slaves.[26] He therefore concluded, that "the Moroccan military need for slaves would not seem to have induced as massive slave trade as was the case in Egypt,".[27] With the demographic conditions prevailing under the Marīnid, there was no need for black slaves, who nonetheless, were bought for domestic use. No Atlantic slave trade before the arrival of the Portuguese in the 16th century.[28] In conclusion, despite an historical association between Western Africa, the Atlantic shore and slavery, it was never a factor in the Marīnid 'quest for empire'.

African Gold and the Return to Gold Minting in Europe

African gold was another matter, and under the Marīnids it facilitated and was instrumental in Europe's return to gold coinage. The supply of gold and silver, precious metals supply needed for coinage, was determined by trade interaction between the Islamic and European economies.[29] Thus, silver, which was scarce in Europe between the 8th and 10th century, while plentiful in Islamic lands became plentiful in Europe in the thirteenth century, but scarce in the Islamic lands. The Islamic silver financed the early economic growth of the Islamic lands, while some claim that it also affected the European economy when it passed through the northeastern routes.[30] Gold on the other hand, was always available in the Islamic lands.[31] It came from the Arabian Peninsula and the Red Sea region, as well as from West Africa. The routes supplying the African gold shifted to Qayrawān during the 10th century and no longer ended in Fez for reasons of security but shifted back again in the 11th century after the Hilalian invasion of 1050.[32] By the end of the eleventh century, Nul, Aghmat, Sijilmasa, Fez and Marrakesh, all Moroccan cities clustered along the gold route, became involved in the gold supply to Europe. European gold coinage decreased early in the medieval period to an end in 7th century in England and France, and 8th in Italy and Spain. [33] From then until the beginning of the 13th century, a period of about 500 years, Europe had no gold coinage. New gold minting in Europe began in the regions close to North Africa, modeled on the Islamic dinars, even inscribed in Arabic. The earliest gold minting took place in Southern Italy in the 11th century. First the dukes of Apulia and later Robert Guiscard in Sicily, began minting *rubais* and *taris*, small gold coins, using African gold. Al-Andalus played its usual 'bridge' role as the supplier of gold to Europe, even though very little gold minting took place in al-Andalus itself before the 10th century. Later, and with a large amount of West African gold flowing, the Cordovan armies could afford to hire Catalan mercenaries. By late 1030 Barcelona's mints were supplied with ingots coming from Ceuta and gold dust which came through Sijilmasa, the Moroccan desert trade outpost. The gold metal arriving at Barcelona, contributed to the revival of the monetary economy there in the mid-11th century.[34] Barcelona itself may have not adopted gold coinage until the 14th century,[35] but in 1052 count Ramon Berenguer established money fiefs based on an annual payment of 10 ounces of gold to his vassals, a rent which could reach up to 100 gold ounces.[36] Between1062 and 1071 he invested 10,000 ounces of gold in purchasing castles and acquired the counties of Carcasonne and Razes. By the second half of the 11th century more than 87% of the land transactions in Barcelona were recorded in *mancusos*, imitations of Islamic gold coins. By the 12th century increased amounts of African gold appeared in Europe. In November 1190, Richard I of England received 40,000 ounces of gold from King Tancred of Sicily in the form of 1,200,000 *tarie,* which he carried to Acre and divided equally with King Philip of France. With the *tarries* standard, if not the *tari* coin, being used from Palermo to Acre, eventually the Latin empire in Constantinople switched to using African gold, rather than the Byzantine gold, which all but disappeared with the last emperor.[37] Between 1235-1250 the crusaders states in the Holy land, which used gold before the rest of Europe did, participating in gold coins transactions with their neighbors, finally switched from the *hyperperion,* the Byzantine gold coin or the Crusaders Bezant, to the *tari* standard. In Spain, with the Reconquista in progress, the Islamic cities of al-Andalus, now under Christian rule and where gold was always used in commercial transactions, contributed to gold provisioning of Christian Spain. West African gold continued to flow into the Iberian Peninsula, allowing Castile and Portugal to begin minting gold in the 12th century, while keeping the Arabic script on their respective coins. By the 13th century the *doblas,* imitating the Almohad double dinar, replaced the Morbetinos in Castile, where they were described as the 'standard' gold coin of Castile from the 13th century onwards.[38] The Italian cities led the Christian Mediterranean adoption of commercial practices based on an internally accepted gold coin.[39] Since1180 onwards, the Genoese, who were trading between Tunis and Sicily were bringing Tunisian gold to Sicily while exporting Sicilian goods to Genoa. By 1220, when Tunis replaced Ceuta as the major trading post with the Genoese, grains and gold dust, *paiola*, as well as minted gold, were exported. By the mid-13th century, there was enough African gold accumulated in Genoa and Florence to allow these cities to begin minting their own gold coins, the *Florin* and the *Genovino*. The newly minted coins were related to the existing currency system of Genoa and Tuscany,[40] and were no longer imitations of the Islamic dinar. By the 14th century gold coinage was common in the Mediterranean economy. In Northern European countries such as France and England even though regular minting of gold coins did not take root, [41] gold bullion availability in the economy, increased.

The Venetian ducat replaced the Islamic dinar in the 14th and the 15th century in trade transactions with the Egyptians. The Islamic world learned to accept the new Venetian ducat as pay for the purchases of Oriental goods in Syria and Egypt, though they preferred payment in silver, of which there was a shortage in the Islamic East. The payments in silver enabled North African dynasties dealing with the Europeans to resume silver minting at an accelerated scale and once again changed the balance of payments. From the mid-13th century onwards, North African states began minting their own silver dirhams, *millares,* using European silver. In the meantime, the Europeans continued their time- honored practice of minting Islamic coin imitations and voluntarily engaged in shipping their own imitations instead of the Islamic original coins.[42] Again Tunis played a central role. The availability of African gold changed the ratio of gold to silver in the Middle East and North Africa, where part of the exported gold ended. By the end of the 13th century North African ports were flooded with silver paid for by gold and other raw materials as well as manufactured goods. By the beginning of the 14th century gold was cheaper in Bougie because it lay close to Sijilmasa, while silver was cheaper in Tunis, where European silver was most easily found. The amount of silver paid for gold in Tunis "was so high, at least temporarily, that Tunis was drawing in not only fresh West African gold, but also gold that had been to Europe before coming back to North Africa," [43]

At the Marīnid court in Fez there was an awareness of the changes in global economic realities. Gold, very much in demand in both Europe and in Egypt and further east, in India, was the obvious commodity available to them, which they were quick to exploit. According to Ibn Khaldūn there were two routes, one leading directly to Egypt, through which 12,000 camel caravans passed annually, the other through Timbuktu to Fez. As the Marīnids established control over the sub-Saharan gold outlets, Fez eventually became responsible for the long-term stability of gold prices in European specie-markets during the mid-fourteenth century (1325-1375). The stability of a delicately balanced bi-metallic flow within and between a series of autonomous specie markets was possible thanks to the Marīnid policy of providing security and efficiency to the Saharan gold trade. They also maneuvered to control the ports, where the benefits of the international trade, including their gold, were accumulating. The gold trade made them rich. They had plenty of gold for minting the beautiful Marīnid gold dinars, some of which have survived in mint condition, a demonstration of their superior quality compared to those of their contemporaries in the rest of the Islamic world.[44] For instance, the treasury had sufficient reserves to pay cash wages to the army, instead of giving them land resources as *iqtā'* as the Mamlūks have done. Lacking an appropriate naval fleet of their own, the Marīnids could afford to rent one as mentioned earlier. There are no numbers for how much Abū 'l-Hasan paid in March 1339 for the rent of 40 Genoese galleys, or the fleet of 48 galleys which he had been preparing elsewhere, but a combined force of 80 galleys assured him domination of the waters of the Western Mediterranean. As mentioned earlier, the gold also enabled Abū 'l-Hasan to hire and maintain a large mercenary army for the long-term. The chroniclers tell us that the Christian militia in Fez numbered around 5000, including mercenaries from Aragon, Castile and

France, and that for their services the Marīnid sultans before and after Abū 'l-Hasan, paid wages in gold every few months, in addition to a fee paid to their Christian lords. The price of 50,000 gold dinars paid by the sultan Abū Inān for ransoming the city of Tripoli in modern-day Libya, was deemed by him 'a trifle" , as indeed it was when compared to Ibn Hawqal's report that in the 10th century the city of Sijilmasa drew 400.000 gold dinars each year from the trade. There is no surprise that a detailed manual on minting techniques was written by the royal mint director in 14th century Fez.[45]

The role of the Marīnids in maintaining the stability of gold supply to Europe has not been properly recognized. The account of Europe's return to gold has focused on the Almoravids and the Almohads and their relations with the Italian republics, even though, as Walker admits, "the disintegrating Almohad state may have helped to cause a temporary break-down of the long-distance gold trade."[46] When the Marīnids came to power in the 1250, a date corresponding to the so called 'revolution' of 1252 that resulted in gold minting in Europe, they took over the 'disintegrating structures' of the Almohads, ensuring stability of the gold trade. [47]There can be no doubt that the uninterrupted provision of gold across the Sahara for the next 200 years, from second half of 13th to the 14th century, had more effect on the sustainability of the 'revolution' and its overall sway and that had to do with Marīnid rule rather than anything else. The long-term impact of a centralized and well-integrated Marīnid state, and with functioning state and institutions, guaranteed the safety of the gold trade over hazardous and difficult terrain inhabited by hostile nomadic tribes. By controlling the regular shipment of gold bullion and gold dust from West Africa, Marīnid Morocco played an unrecognized role in the global economic order. [48] The supply of gold continued unabated: "As late as 1343 the problem in Venice was still how to help the mint to cope with the enormous quantities of gold being imported into the city from overseas."[49] Until 1252 the Islamic gold currency with its various regional coins provided the models for European coins but West African gold provided sufficiently sustained level of precious metal stock to permit European return to gold. Walker's theory, namely that a growing, sustainable amount of gold answered the growing demand for a recognizable, reliable and international coin to facilitate exchange, was a trigger of the revolution, is correct but not without Marīnid support. [50]

Ian Blanchard suggested that the trans-Saharan gold route changed after 1375. [51] Modification in weather conditions led to further desiccation of the environment increased the difficulties in securing adequate water supplies for the caravans. With nomads attacking the Caravans, gold shipments increasingly avoided the direct routes across the arid zones, altering the basic structures of the trans-Saharan trade. The deterioration in security along the routes was not the only cause – a succession crisis within the Marīnid dynasty beginning after 1361, with palace revolts and insurrections limiting the state's power to protect the gold carrying caravans. Yet, it would be inaccurate to end it with the Almohads, since the entire supply of gold that fed it and allowed it to prosper, originated in Marīnid North Africa.

Grains and Merino Wool

Recent explorations of the archives of Barcelona, Genoa, Venice, Florence and Pisa, show that international traders favoured the Eastern Maghribi Mediterranean ports, rather than the ports of Morocco on the Atlantic shores, Anfa, Arzila and Salé.[52] Among the different products exported across the Mediterranean through the ports of Tunis and Bougie, two items in particular, grain and wool, played a major role. North African grain trade was the most lucrative and at its highest point between the 13th and 15th century.[53] North Africa provisioned Europe's Mediterranean countries during years when their own crops failed and imported grains from them when the reverse situation occurred. Thus, the Maghrib, which was an importer in the 13th, century, became an exporter of grain to the cities of Genoa and Florence in the 14th century, while in the 15th century, thousands of tons of grain arrived in Genoa from Tunis, Bone, Stora, Bougie, Alger, Oran, Tenes. Marīnid Fez shows limited participation but not unawareness. The lucrative grain export did not escape the attention of individual Moroccan entrepreneurs with easy access to capital. The case of al-Mazdaghī a *khatib*, preacher, one of wealthiest men in the city, described by Ibn Marzūq, chronicler of Abū 'l-Hasan exploits across the Maghrib. As discussed earlier, because of his wealth he was entrusted with guarding the inheritance money of orphans in the city and with the mosques' *waqf* revenue funds, which were deposited in his hands in the mosque, the famous al-Qarawiyyin. However, as he later admitted when the fraud was discovered, he used the money to purchase grain for speculation, "He had a lot of grain in store, waiting for the price to go up.", wrote Ibn Marzūq. For some reason the grain he stored disappeared and was no longer available when he wanted to sell it. It had most probably been sold by his sons without his knowledge, he explained. Abū'l-Hasan, who then resided in al-Mansūra, decided to replace the missing funds, "so that the people will not suffer from the greed of individuals", but refused to grant him an audition.

Maritime trade in Ceuta was frequent enough to accommodate Marīnid Morocco's export of some raw materials and manufactured goods, most notably sugar.[54] Still, Mediterranean and Atlantic shipping was fragmentary for Morocco. Overland trade, was more prominent with regional framework. The Sus region enjoyed commercial relations with the big cities of the Sahara and sugar and salt were exchanged for precious metals and slaves. From their perch in inland Fez the Marīnids witnessed the largest trade expansion in North African history and were fully aware that they were left behind; the Marīnid port of Ceuta no longer captured enough of the returns of expanding Mediterranean trade. They were strategically disadvantaged as a large portion of the Mediterranean trade eluded them, but determined to change it. Given this background, the attraction of capturing Bougie and Tunis becomes clear and the integration of the eastern port cities into the Marīnid economy, obvious. The empires that emerged later on the Northern shores of the Atlantic ocean demonstrate how access to maritime trade may be a requirement for expanding economies.[55] Though landlocked empires appear in world history, for example, the Mongol Empire in the 13th-14th century,[56] the Marīnids were aware of their disadvantage and tried to fix it by conquering the coastal cities in the central and eastern Maghrib.

A sense of lost opportunity also accompanies the story of Merino wool, which as the name suggests, was a product associated with Marīnid Morocco. Christian Spain was always a thinly populated country with a particular human ecology, which made the co-existence of nomadic and settled habitation possible. The general expansion of herding, especially accommodated by this ecology, began in the 11th-12th centuries and followed the military frontier as it shifted southward with the Reconquista. By the late 12th century, a time of population surge and economic growth in many areas of Europe including Spain, pressure on the resources increased, as did the flocks' size.[57] By the 13th century the patterns of the long-distance movement between seasonal pastures along habitual routes, which made the Spanish wool industry so profitable, were in place. The post plague depression of the mid-14th century reduced the pressure on farmland and thus allowed sheep farming to increase even further. But it was the introduction of the merino breed of sheep from North Africa which made the entire wool industry in Spain a success story and changed its fortunes. By the end of the 14th century Spanish wools were still the cheapest and less coveted kind in the wool markets of Italy, England and Belgium but in the 15th century, after the cross breeding occurred, it began to capture an increasing share of the market for fine wool. By the beginning of the 16th century, Merino wool was known all over Spain and the number of sheep is estimated at 3 million. Years of experimentation by the Castilian sheep breeders went into developing the initially extremely fine wool into a short, less than 5cm, strand of very fine wool. The production of fine merino wool was so successful, to the point that "from the mid-fifteenth to the mid-eighteenth century Spain, thanks to her virtual monopoly of the breed, dominated the world market of wool,"[58]. Soon, in Spain "The entire economic and social structure of the country both its assets and liabilities was etched by merino sheep grazing," [59] Producing merino wool was transformed into the largest and most profitable manufacturing enterprise.

The circumstances which made merino wool into the most expensive and sought after wool in the world were linked to the Marīnids and their historical role in Spain, but the circumstances of its introduction into Spain remained a mystery until quite recently. In a 1953 article, the Italian-American economic historian Robert Lopez, suggested that the name Merino sheep was derived from the Moroccan rulers' tribal name, the Banū Marīn, and that the sheep itself was a 14th century crossbreeding of the North African Barbary ram with the indigenous Spanish sheep. Lopez could establish a link between the name and the wool using a document dated 1307 in the Genoese archives that for the first time mentions of the import of merino wool from Tunis. The fact that the wool was exported from Tunis, not from Western North Africa, where Marīnid Zanāta herds would be normally grazed in the Northern Rif mountains, should not cast doubt on the attribution. Tunis was the major export port of North African products. After that early mention, merino wool disappeared from the Genoese records until the fifteenth century, when it surfaced in Spain. This time with the Marīnid troops who initially crossed the straits in the late 13th century but later reported to have warfare booty including captured Marīnid flocks. Another incident established yet another link, this time through the record of Marīnid rams being imported by the Castilian monarch Pedro IV around 1336-87. [60] The debate over who was responsible for the introduction of the Merino sheep also saw the role of Genoese merchants, who brought an existing Merino breed to Southern Spain and persuaded Castilian rulers and administrators to develop it.

The new global economic order reserved a place of honor for wool production and export, but again the Maghribi wool, whether shipped from Ceuta or from Bougie, was not of high quality.[61] The history of the humble Marīnid ram, which roamed the mountainous homeland of the Marīnid tribes unnoticed for hundreds of years until it gained a place of honor in the annals of Spanish history, illustrates the point that economic growth requires a combination of technical knowledge, availability of transportation and markets, economic links which Marīnid Morocco did not have. Another global situation in which the Marīnids played an important part, albeit, unknowingly.

Institutions and Empires

The rise of empires, the factors driving it, and the institutions that account for their economic growth, are subject of interest in recent years, in particular their role in the rise of empires bordering on the shores of the Atlantic Ocean.[62] Among all factors mentioned, institutions, economic or legal, state or private, are at the center of attention.[63] In the case of the Atlantic empires, change in political institutions allowing economic actors the freedom to interact with state powers, thus optimizing the conditions for success in trade, is highlighted.[64] Institutions undergo change through a 'self-reinforcement' process, beginning with negative feedback to the point of self-destruction, leading to the development of new institutions, better suitable to accommodate the needs of the economy. However, as European institutions became "self-destroying" and on the path towards regeneration, Islamic institutions were described as stagnating with no sign of modified institutional behavior and no sign of negative feedback, which prevented them from performing at their optimal capacity. The most obvious example, Islamic law.[65] While it adapted well in its formative period to the needs of the economy in the Middle East, Islamic law failed Muslims later. Timur Kuran argued that partnership arrangements in Islamic law are a good instance of stagnation. In light of this paradigm the question needs to be asked: what about Marīnid institution and the Marīnid 'quest for empire'?[66] Did Marīnid institutions contribute to the achievement of an empire, or did they hamper it? Were they stable, efficient, well-functioning, or help in the empire's disintegration?

Morocco was an institutional rarity. Since its conquest to Islam, Maghribi institutions develop and mature through a process of adjustments and adaptation to Berber norms, but as the eastern parts Islamized and Arabized to a greater degree, the conflict subsided. Berber institutions acculturated to the legal, religious, cultural, political and intellectual norms that came with Islam and its language, Arabic. In Morocco it was an evolutionary trajectory, with institutions borrowed from al-Andalus and the Middle East trying to mitigate the power of a more numerous Berber population. The institutional history of the Marīnid state began through rule of individual dynasties, but became exceedingly accommodating under the last three dynasties with Berber affiliations. By the mid-fourteenth century the Berber/Islamic state in Morocco had its unique cultural and institutional shape, with an array of Berber-inspired institutions and Islamic structures that could flourish under the rule of the Almoravids and the Almohads. Despite this unique institutional mix the Moroccan state was sufficiently centralized to exercise control over its resources. A reorganization of the tax system carried by the previous administration, that of the Almohads, provided the urban fiscal and taxation patterns, that through written records, a list of tax paying establishments, was used by the Marīnid administration in Fez. The public good *waqf,* which controlled a large amount of property and revenue, applied the rules of the Maliki law, so it was supervised by the mosque's personnel, and opened it to various degrees of abuse. The religious institutions, like the mosques and *medresas,* were closely watched by the court, and their personnel, who were rebellious and bellicose under the Almohads and early Marīnids, eventually submitted to the state who took over the payment of their salaries. The introduction of the institution of the *medresa* in Marīnid Morocco by the state, maintained this institution under state supervision that guaranteed that religious personnel remain obedient.

As seen earlier, the intellectual malaise among the Berbers, aroused by the need for acculturation to Islamic and Arabic norms, lingered in the Berber/Islamic state and remains so today. Through a myth of Arab origin, re-writing the history of the Berbers, and the recognition of the Berber language by the administration, though still needs to be written in the Arabic script but being spoken at the court, and under the Almohads in mosque services, the Marīnids achieved a national coherence. The tension further subsided when the new *medresas* began accepting Berber students, who later took their place among the judges and muftis. The support offered to the religious monuments, mosques and *medresas* by the Marīnids, also ensured that the State would exercise control over religious leaders. Securing the support of the Zanāta Berber tribes, ensured that a succession of long reigning monarchs, ambitious and visionary like Abū Said, his son Abū l'Hasan and his grandson, Abū Inān, would secure strong state, lengthy reign, leading to the realization of the 'quest for empire'. On the contrary, Isamic/ Berber institutions, played a constructive role in the process. The reconciliation that occurred between Berber and Islamic identities under the Marīnids in 14th century Morocco, may have begun among the elites, religious and political, but it triggered downward and spread geographicly, so that it was effective in offering stability. The intellectuals exiled from al-Andalus who found refuge at the Almoravid and Almohad courts kept coming under the Marīnids. Ibn al-Khatīb came from Granada, Marzūq from Tlemcen and Ibn Khaldūn from Tunis, but all spent time in Fez provoking and cultivating a new intellectual climate. And then there were the monuments – cultivating a sense of pride and loyalty among the masses – a common feature to all empires. The Marīnids had their own monumental architecture of *medresas*, mosques, walls and gates, markets and mausoleums. Entire cities throughout the entire Maghrib bear the testimony to the Marīnid 'quest for empire'.

In conclusion, the Marīnid quest for empire had a great deal in common with the great Atlantic Ocean empires but unlike Spain, Portugal, France, Holland and England, it was not meant to be. The Marīnid dream was brought down by rats and fleas, and probably by the climate change, lack of the resources, technological innovations, institutional change and a new economic order that permitted the others to succeed. A quest for empire needs all of that before it runs out of steam.

Conclusion

The objective of this book has been to reconstruct several aspects of the Marīnid period's contribution to the history of the Berber-Islamic state of Morocco. It has highlighted the transformation by focusing on some of the principal paradigms through which the Marīnid state navigated the difficult water of governing. This was not a peaceful process, since such paradigms as the strength of the state institutions were confronted by individualism and heightened self-awareness. The book has also described how the Marīnids themselves, both the ruling family and the Berber tribes who supported it, reacted, interacted and were transformed by the process. The former became sophisticated Islamic monarchs, the latter, military and political pillars of the state. In addition, the book has explored the dimensions of the cultural and normative world of the Berbers themselves, and the resistance offered, especially by those who were more acculturated to the Islamic norms. This resistance shows that the 'African particularism', namely the resistance to acculturation, observed during earlier and later historical periods, remained a constant component of Berber history during the Islamic period.

Within the Berber-Islamic state, however, this resistance was subtle and was much less fierce and militant than under Roman rule. This might have been because the rulers went through the same process of acculturation as their subjects, and individually experienced the same intellectual onslaught of the Islamic and Arabic norms. They shared with their people the same characteristics which were perceived as handicaps for the image they wanted to adopt as good Muslims: little or no Arabic, little or no knowledge of Islamic principles, literature and culture, and a historical image of renegades.

Beyond its immediate medieval context, the legacy of the Berber "unofficial" history has a message for modern Maghrebi historians. Manifestations of medieval Berberhood and its anguished relationship with the Islamic state and Arabism have not always been recognized for what they were, even though they did not pass unnoticed in the literature and historiography of the pre- and post-independent Maghreb, and contemporary Maghrebi writers. The nationalist discourse interpreted the story of the *Kahina*, the 8th century Berber woman leader and the Berber struggle against Islam and the Arabs, as a struggle for independence, and used it as a symbol in their resistance to French domination.[1] The Berbers were depicted as having been liberated by the Arabs, who brought Islam and therefore equality.[2] Today, native historians of the Maghreb feel that the true nature of their history has been falsified and misinterpreted by colonial European historians in order to spread disunity, helplessness, a sense of futility, and most of all, dependence and self effacement before French culture and political dominance. While perfectly valid, this complaint and the demand to "decolonize" Maghrebi history were the same as those formulated by the Berbers, who also tried to "decolonize" their history from what they considered to be "Arab falsification". Both examples demonstrate the importance of history in the creation of national identity, but also demonstrate how difficult, if not impossible, is the task of evaluating its true impact.

Appendix A

Historians of the Berbers in the *Kitāb al-Ansāb*

ORIGINS AND DATES

AUTHORS	***PLACE OF ORIGIN***	***DATES***	***SOURCE OF IDENTIFI-CATION***	***KITĀB AL-ANSĀB***
AL-BALĀDHURĪ AHMAD B. YAHYĀ B. JĀBIR B. DĀWŪD	**EAST**	**3rd/9th**	**EI²**	**FOLS. 19, 109,** ***44****, ***252*** * ITALICIZED PAGE NUMBERS REFER TO THE PRINTED EDITION.
AL-BAKRĪ, ABŪ UBAYD B. 'ABD AL-'AZĪZ B. MUHAMMAD B. AYYŪB	**MUSLIM SPAIN**	**D. 487/1097**	**EI²**	**FOLS. 5, 8, 16, 17-20, 22, 23,** *22, 37, 39, 45, 51-53, 55, 88.*
IBN HAZM, ABŪ MUHAMMAD 'ALĪ AHMAD B. SA'ĪD	**MUSLIM SPAIN**	**384/994-456/1064**	**EI²**	**FOLS. 20,23,** *46, 53, 245, 248, 368.*
IBN RUSHD, ABU 'L-WALĪD MUHAMMAD B. AHMAD B. SA'ĪD	**MUSLIM SPAIN**	**520/1126-595/1198**	**EI²**	**FOL. 33,** *70.*
AL-TĀDILĪ, YŪSUF B. YAHYĀ B. 'ĪSĀ B. 'ABD AL-RAHMĀN	**MAGHREB**	**D. 627/1230**	**AL-ZIRIKLI II, 258**	**FOL. 34,** *72, 214, 219.*
AL-MUSABBIHĪ, MUHAMMAD B. 'UBAYD ALLĀH B. AHMAD	**EAST**	**366/977 420/1029**	**AL-ZIRIKLI I, 259**	**FOL. 85,** *189, 190.*
MUSLIM B. AL-HAJJĀJ B. MUSLIM AL-KUSHAYRĪ	**EAST**	**204/820 261/875**	**AL-ZIRIKLI II, 221**	**FOL. 32, 35,** *69, 73, 330.*
SA'ĪD B. AL-MUSIB (MUSIYYIBB) B. HAZN B. WAHB AL-MAKHZŪMĪ	**EAST**	**13/634-94/713**	**AL-ZIRIKLI III, 102**	**FOL. 8,** *25.*
IBN AL-JAWZĪ 'ABD AL-RAHMĀN B. 'ALĪ	**EAST**	**508/1114 597/42-1**	**EI²**	**FOL. 33, 46,** *70, 98.*

AUTHORS	***PLACE OF ORIGIN***	***DATES***	***SOURCE OF IDENTIFI-CATION***	***KITĀB AL-ANSĀB***
IBN HAMMĀD, MUHAMMAD B. 'ALI	**MAGHREB**	**617/1120**	**GAL SUPP. I, 555**	**FOL. 44,** *93.*
AL-MAWĀ'I, OR AL-MAWA'INĪ, ABŪ 'L-QĀSIM MUHAMMAD B. IBRĀHĪM	**MUSLIM SPAIN**	**D. 564/1168**	**PONS BOIGUES, 227**	**FOL. 112,** *257.*
AL-WARRĀQ, MUHAMMAD B. YŪSUF	**MUSLIM SPAIN**	**292/904-363/973**	**PONS BOIGUES, 80**	**FOL.79,** *174, 182, 193.*
AL-FURGHĀNĪ, AHMAD B. 'ABD ALLAH	**EAST**	**327/398-939/973**	**AL-ZIKRKLI I, 156**	**FOL. 85,** *189, 224.*
AL-GHAZĀLI, ABŪ HĀMID B. MUHAMMAD	**EAST**	**450/1058**	**EI²**	**FOL. 128,** *333.*
AL-WĀQIDĪ, ABŪ 'ABD ALLĀH, MUHAMMAD B. 'UMAR	**EAST**	**130/747 207/822**	**EI²**	**FOL. 37,** *77.*
AL-IDRĪSĪ, ABŪ 'ABD ALLĀH MUHAMMAD B. MUHAMMAD, AL-SHARĪF	**MAGHREB**	**493/1100 560/1165**	**EI²**	**FOL. 22,** *50, 51.*
AL-KALBĪ, HISHĀM B. MUHAMMAD B. AL-SA'ID	**EAST**	**120/737-204/819 OR 206/821**	**EI²**	**FOL. 38,** *79.*
IBN 'ABD AL-BARR AL-NAMARĪ, ABŪ 'UMAR YŪSUF B. 'ABD ALLĀH	**MUSLIM SPAIN**	**368/978 463/1071**	**EI²**	**FOLS. 33, 41,** *69, 85.*
ABŪ 'L-SALT, UMAYYA B. 'ABD AL-AZĪZ B. ABĪ L-SALT	**MUSLIM SPAIN**	**460/1067 529/1134**	**EI²**	**FOL. 86,** *191.*
AL-THA 'ĀLIBĪ, ABŪ MANSŪR, 'ABD AL-RAQĪQ B. MUHAMMAD	**EAST**	**350/961 429/1038**	**EI¹**	**FOLS. 6, 15,** *22,* **30,** *38, 61.*

AUTHORS	PLACE OF ORIGIN	DATES	SOURCE OF IDENTIFI-CATION	KITĀB AL-ANSĀB
IBN 'ATTIYA AL-MUHĀRIBĪ, B. GHĀLIB B. 'ABD AL-RAHMĀN ABŪ MUHAMMAD	MUSLIM SPAIN	481/1088 541/1145	PONS BOIGUES, 207-208	FOL. 6, *22.*
AL-JAYHĀNĪ, ABŪ 'ABD ALLĀH	EAST	9TH CENT	EI² SUPP.	FOLS. 48, 49, *103, 106.*
IBN SAHNŪN, MUHAMMAD	MAGHREB	D. 256/870	TALBI, L' EMIRAT, 9	FOL. 53, *112.*
'UMĀRA B. WATHĪMA ABŪ RIFĀ'A B. MŪSA B. AL-FURĀT	EAST	D. 289/902	GAL, SI,217	FOL. 29, *63.*
AL-TABARĪ, ABŪ JA'FAR MUHAMMAD B. JARĪR	EAST	D. 310/923	GAL, I, 148-9	FOLS. 14, 19, *44, 49.*
'ABD AL-MĀLIK B. HABĪB, AL-SULAMĪ AL-MIDRĀSĪ AL-ILBĪRĪ	MUSLIM SPAIN	D. 180/796	GAL I, 156	FOL. 53, *114.*
AL-RĀZĪ, ABŪ BAKR AHMAD B. MUHAMMAD B. MŪSĀ	MUSLIM SPAIN	D. 325/937	GAL, I, 156	FOL. 45, *97, 205, 206.*
AL- MAS 'ŪDI, ABŪ L-HASAN 'ALĪ B. AL-HUSAYN	EAST	D. 345/956	GAL, I, 150 , 151	FOL. 9, *28.*
AL-SUHAYLĪ, 'ABD AL-RAHMĀN B. 'ABD ALLĀH B. AHMAD	MUSLIM SPAIN	508/114- 581/1185	PONS BOIGUES, 249	FOLS. 14, *16*, 17, 18, 19, *41, 44, 64, 66.*
AL-TURTŪSHĪ, MUHAMMAD B. AL-WALĪD	MUSLIM SPAIN	451/1059 520/1126	PONS BOIGUES, 181-4	FOL. 34, *115, 261.*
IBN YŪNUS 'ABD AL-RAHMĀN B. AHMAD, ABŪ SA'ĪD	EAST	281/894- 347/958	PONS BOIGUES, 413	FOL. 33, *70.*
IBN AL-WAKĪL	MUSLIM SPAIN	7/13TH CENT.	TALBI, L'EMIRAT, 12	FOL. 111, *112, 256.*
ABŪ L-TAQĀ ' TĀHIR B. 'ABD AL-RAHMĀN	MUSLIM SPAIN	7/13TH CENT.		FOLS. 111, *112*, 148, 149, *287, 352, 356.*

AUTHORS	***PLACE OF ORIGIN***	***DATES***	***SOURCE OF IDENTIFI-CATION***	***KITĀB AL-ANSĀB***
Ibn Hamādū, Abū 'Abd Allāh, Muhammad b. 'Alī b. Hammād b. 'Īsā b. Abī Bakr al-Burnūsī	**Maghreb**	d. 628/1231	EI²	fols. 29, 44, 113, 90, 93, *180, 185, 199, 207.*
Ibn Bashkūwal Abū l-Qāsim Khalaf b. 'Abd al-Mālik b. Mas'ūd b. Mūsā	**Muslim Spain**	494/1101 578/1183	EI²	fol. 45, *96.*
Ibn Abī Zayd al-Qayrawānī Abū Muhammad 'Abd Allāh b. Abī Zayd, 'Abd al-Rahmān	**Maghreb**	310/977-386/996	EI²	fol. 51, *92, 204.*
Ibn Qutayba, Abū Muhammad 'Abd Allāh b. Muslim al-Dīnawārī	**East**	214/828 276-889	EI²	Fol. 4, 5, 13, 69.
Ibn Bassām, Abū l-Hasan 'Alī b.Bassām, al-Shantarīnī	**Muslim Spain**	D. 543/1147	EI²	fol. 87, *194.*
Ibn Hayyān, Abū Marwān Khalaf b. Muayn B. Hayyan	**Muslim Spain**	377/987	EI²	fols. 58,153, 150, *206, 271, 383.*
Ibn Hamādūh, Abū l-Hasan al-Sanhājī	**Maghreb**	13th cent. 616/1219	EI²	fols. 94, 100, *191, 208, 222.*
Ibn al-Sayrafī, Abū Bakr Yahyā b. Muhammad b. Yūsuf al-Ansarī	**Muslim Spain**	467/1076	EI²	fol. 91, *201.*
Al- 'Udhrī, Imrān b. al-Hasan	**Muslim Spain**	610/1213	Gal. SI,555	fol. 113, *253.*
Ibn Sāhib al-Salāt, 'Abd al-Malik Abū Marwān	**Muslim Spain**	d. 578/1182	Pons Boigues, 245-6	fol. 117, *269.*
Yūsuf b. 'Umar Abū l-Hajjāj	**Muslim Spain**	7/13th cent.	Pons Boigues, 514	fol. 117, *269.*
Ibn al-qattān Hasan Abū 'Alī	**Maghreb**	7/13th cent.	Makki *Nazm*	fol. 25, *55.*

AUTHORS	PLACE OF ORIGIN	DATES	SOURCE OF IDENTIFI-CATION	KITĀB AL-ANSĀB
IBN AL-RAQĪQ ABŪ ISHĀK IBRĀHIM, OR ISHĀK	MAGRHEB	D. 418/1027-28	EI[2]	FOL. 112, *257*.
IBN 'ALQAMA TAMMĀM, ABŪ GHĀLIB	MUSLIM SPAIN	187/803 283/896	EI[2]	FOL. 111, *257*.
IBN AL-'ARABĪ, ABŪ BAKR MUHAMMED B. 'ABD ALLĀH AL-MA'ĀFIRĪ	MUSLIM SPAIN	468/1076 543/1198	EI[2]	FOL. 119, *278*
IBN RASHĪK, ABŪ 'ALI HASAN, B. RASHĪQ AL-QAYRAWĀNĪ	MAGHREB? MUSLIM SPAIN?	390/1000 -456/1063-64	PONS BOIGUES, 303	FOL. 91, 201, 372
AL- TURTŪSHĪ, MUHAMMED B. AL-WALĪD	MUSLIM SPAIN	451/1059 520/1126	PONS BOIGUES 303	FOL. 34, 115, 261

Appendix B

Units and Properties endowed as *Waqf*

Establishment Town, Year Dynasty, Source	House (masr-iya)*	Square (tarbi'a)	Apartment (dar)	Store (hanut)	Stable (ruwa)	Bath (hammam)	Upper-flat (a'la)	Village (mad-shar)	Mill (raha) (hadjar) (tahun)	Garden (djan-nan)	Oven (kusha) (furn)	Inn (fundaq)	Hall (qa'a)	Varia
*Abu 'l-Hasan Mosque*** Tlemcen, 699/1296 Zayyanid (Brosselard)	1		2 (muadhdhin Imam)	20										
Dar al-Makzen Madrasa Fez, 720/1320 Marinid (Bel)	3			16,2,1		1,1	2,1	1	2	1		7/8		
Sahridj Madrasa Fez, 723/1323 Marinid (Bel)	1,1,1		1,1/2,2 Part, 1 duwayra	7,4,1 Part, 44 3		1			1/2,6	10		1	1/3,53	44 weaving stores (atriza)
'Attarin Madrasa Fez, 725/1325 Marinid (Bel)	1,1,1	1	1,1,1	13,3,4 4,4,4, 1,1,1,1,1			1		1,1		1	7/8,1/2	1,1/2	4 weaving stores (atriza) 1 soap factory
MOSQUE Mustaghanim, 742/1340 Marinid (Bel)				2							2			3 measures oil
*Abu 'l-Hasan Mosque*** Fez, 742/1341 (Maslow)				7		1	2(Imam, muadh dhin)							
Bu Madyan Madrasa 'Ubbad, 747/1346 Marinid (Brosselard)	1		1,2 1 duwayra			1,1/2			2,2	1,1,1,1 1,1,1,1/2 1,1,1,1,1				2 plots of land, 4 irrigated fields, 1,1, plot
Mesbahiya Madrasa Fez, 747/1346 Marinid (Bel)			1,3,3/4 1,3,3/4 2duwayra	1,13				1/2,1		4/7,1		6/8		plots of land
Zawiya Taza, 754/1353 (Maslow)								1		2				orchard

Establishment Town, Year Dynasty, Source	House (masr-iya)*	Square (tarbi'a)	Apartment (dar)	Store (hanut)	Stable (ruwa)	Bath (hammam)	Upper-flat (a'la)	Village (mad-shar)	Mill (raha) (hadjar) (tahun)	Garden (djan-nan)	Oven (kusha) (furn)	Inn (fundaq)	Hall (qa'a)	Varia
Hospital, Taza, 754/1353 (Maslow)									mills					enclosure
Bu 'Inaniya Madrasa Fez, 756/1355 Marinid (Bel)			1 durayra	74	2	1			1,1		1			
Zawiya Tlemcen, 765/1363 Zayyanid (Brosselard)				30			1		1,1,1 1 ma'sira	1/2,1 olive orchard	1,1			1 plot of land
Grand Mosque Fez Jdod 798/1395 (Maslow)				3,4,4,1							1			12 Qor'an readers paid 60 dirhams monthly
Lalla Ghariba MOSQUE Fez, 810/1408 Marinid (Bel)			1,1		1,1					1,1				monthly salaries 12,6,10,2,2 1/2 4 dinar 'ashri
Units endowed in Fez	9	1	22	222	4	5	6	2 1/3	12 1/2	16 4/7	5	1,7/8, 7/8,1/2, 6/8	54,1/3, 1/2	
Numbers of units in *** 7th/13th century Fez apud. *Qirtas*, 25-6, *Zahra*, 33	17,041		89,036 (89,236)	9082		93 93			400 472		135 kusha 1170 furn	467		3064 weaving 3490 47 soap factory

* The terms used to design the properties are identical to the Granadan endowments, as required in <u>Habices</u>.

** In order to demonstrate the importance of Marīnid property endowments in Fez, it was thought useful to compare them to those of comtemporary Zayyanid rulers, and to Marinid endowments outside Fez.

*** It is also useful to point out the numbers of units given in the *Qirtas* and *Zahra*, derived from the accounts kept by the 7th/13th century, which demonstrate that in comparison units endowed by the Marīnids were rather minute.

Notes

Introduction

1. *TLS*, October 18, 1996.
2. Foreword to Amar Ouerdane, *La Question Berbère dans le mouvement national algérien 1926-1980* (Quebec, 1990), 13.
3 Ibid., 14.
4. In his book Amar Ouerdane takes us step by step through the Berber representatives' negotiations with leaders of the Algerian National Liberation Front during the 50's and 60's, the years of the struggle for independence. See the analysis given to this aspect by William B. Quandt, "The Berbers in the Algerian Political Elite," in *Arabs and Berbers*, ed. Ernest Gellner (London, 1972): 285-303. Also Michael Brett and Elizabeth Fentress, *The Berbers* (Oxford, 1996), 193-199.
5. A vivid depiction of the lives lived by his and earlier generations of Kabylia Berbers, some of whom converted to Christianity under French influence, can be found in Fadhma A. M. Amrouche, *My Life Story*: *The autobiography of a Berber woman*, trans. with introduction by Dorothy S. Blair (London, 1988).
6. Not all four Maghrebi States experience today the same strife over the Berbers' identity question as Algeria does. Tunisia is hardly touched by it because the Berber element is demographically insignificant there. Morocco never experienced the fierce antagonism created by Arabization as Algeria did and Moroccan Berbers were granted greater accommodation on the part of the monarchy. See Brett and Fentress, *The Berbers*, 276.
7. In the introduction to his book, *African Resistance to Romanisation*, Marcel Bénabou explained why the term 'resistance' was an appropriate characterization of the Roman period in North African history. For him, "the term resistance can apply to three different forms of reaction to foreign rule; military, political and psychological, and the last means to protect one's personality against the influence of others". Marcel Bénabou, *La résistance africaine à la romanisation* (Paris, 1976), 17. On the Romans in North Africa see also Marguerite Rachet, *Rome et les Berbères*: *Un problème militaire d'Auguste à Dioclétien*, Collection Latomus 110 (Bruxelles, 1970). For North Africa in the classical period see Brett and Fentress, *The Berbers*, 10-79.
8. "Seen in such a light, those features of Donatism which so shocked Augustine ...showed that 'North Africa' could become 'Berbery'". Peter Brown, "Religious Dissent in the Later Roman Empire: The Case of North Africa,"

Religion and Society in the Age of Saint Augustine (London, 1972): 247. Originally published in *History*, 46(1961): 83-101. Heresies such as Donatism in North Africa and Monophysitism in Egypt, were rooted in 'secular grievances' and made the Copts in Egypt welcome the arrival of the Arabs in the 7th century. This interpretation also links the success of Christianity to the tensions between the Roman State in the centre and the provinces, to the loss of hinterland Africa to Roman civilization, and to the crisis in the pagan towns.

9. See W. H. C. Frend, "The Revival of Berber Art," *Antiquity* (1942): 342-52. Not all agree to see Donatism as an expression of deep anti-Roman feelings among the native population. See B. H. Warmington, *The North African Provinces From Diocletian to the Vandal Conquest*, (Connecticut, 1971), 99. Yet, Warmington fails to see that Donatism, as the natives' reaction to acculturation to Islamization and Arabization in the medieval period, are particular expressions of opposition, because they use the very terms and tools of the colonizing culture.
10. The weight and strength of the Berber input was equally felt in Spain, where historians designated the Islamic civilization which became familiar in Europe as Berbero-Andalusian rather than Hispano-Moorish. See "*Almohades*" (J.-Cl. Garcin) *Encyclopédie Berbère* (Aix-en-Provence, 1987), IV:534.
11. On related themes see *Individualism and Conformity in Islam: V Levi dela Vida Biennial Conference*, eds. Amin Banani and Speros Vryonis (Wiesbaden, 1977). On literary genres as expressions of individual and personal nature, see Jan Just Witkam, "The Human Element between Text and Reader: The *ijāza* in Arabic Manuscripts," in *The Codicology of Islamic Manuscripts*, ed. Yasin Dutton (London, 1995): 123-136.
12. For samples of Marīnid autobiographies by authors such as al-Ruʿaynī, al-Jadīrī, al-Ḥaḍramī, al-Tujībī, see Mohamed Benchekroune, *La vie intellectuelle marocaine sous les Mérinides et les Waṭṭāsides* (XIIIe, XIVe, XVe, XVIe siècles), (Rabat, 1974), 278, 249, 241, 225, respectively. Well known is Ibn Khaldūn's autobiography written in the same period, *al-Taʿrīf bi-Ibn Khaldūn wa-riḥlatuhu gharban wa-sharqan*, ed. Muḥammad b. Tāwīt al-Ṭanjī (Cairo, 1951).
13. On similar attempts under the Almohads see Dominique Urvoy, "La pensée d'Ibn Tūmart," *Bulletin d'Etudes Orientales* 28(1974): 29.
14. A detailed discussion of the Berber question in 10th-11th centuries al-Andalus in Peter C. Scales, *The Fall of the Caliphate of Córdoba: Berbers and Andalusis in Conflict* (Leiden, 1994), 142-181. The role of this legacy is discussed in chapter 3. Dr. Scales is also in agreement that "Berber hatred" for both "new" and "old" Berbers was evident and prevalent, see p. 67 note 107. Both the essay he refers to, as well as his comments reveal unawareness, or failure to take into consideration the evidence I have put forward in my historiographical study which traces the 14th century material to sources of the

10th-11th and 12th-13th Andalusian authors.

15. The French school claimed that the fractured political unity, the rise and fall of dynasties, and the rapid collapse of central authority in a repetitive manner, were indications of the inherent weakness of the North African State. See John Wansbrough, "The Decolonization of North African History," *Journal of African History* 9(1968): 643-650. Michael Brett, "Problems in the Interpretation of the History of the Maghreb in the Light of Some Recent Publications," *Journal of African History* 13/3(1972): 489-506. On the colonialist historiography of the Maghreb, and French colonial policies and statements see the relevant chapters in Laroui, *The History of the Maghrib*, 327 et sq., as well as in Brett and Fentress, *The Berbers*.
16. On the nomadic State building process in the Maghreb see Kathleen O'Mara, "The Kel Ahir Tuareg and the Problematic of Theories of the State," *The Maghreb Review* 19/1-2(1994): 173-189. Yves Lacoste, *Ibn Khaldun, naissance de l'histoire du tiers-monde* (Paris, 1966).
17. The centrality of Ibn Khaldūn's work to the formulation of this and other theories, was, in Michael Brett's words, 'A measure of his greatness, as well as of his ambiguity', but Brett suggested another interpretation for this account of the power of Islam in the fractured nature of authority of the Maghrebi State, attributing the division of power to the struggle between the secular and the religious authorities within the State. See Brett, "Problems," 490 and 505.
18. Yvon Thébert and Jean Louis Biget, "L'Afrique après la disparition de la cité classique: Cohérence et ruptures dans l'histoire maghrébine," *L'Afrique dans L'Occident romain*, Collection de l'école française de Rome, 134 (Rome, 1990): 576. I thank Professor Peter Brown for drawing my attention to this article.
19. For two instances reflecting the endurance of Islamic institutions past Christian conquest and colonization see Jonathan Riley-Smith, "The Survival in Latin Palestine of Muslim Administration," in *The Eastern Mediterranean Lands in the Period of the Crusades*, ed. P. M. Holt (Warminster, 1977): 9-22. Pierre Guichard and Denis Menjot, "Les emprunts aux vaincus: Les conséquences de la "reconquête" sur l'organisation institutionelle des Etats castillan et aragonais au Moyen Age," in *Etat et colonisation au Moyen Age*, ed. Michel Ballard (Lyon, 1989): 379-396.
20. Cemal Kafadar, *Between Two Worlds: The Construction of the Ottoman State* (Berkely and Los Angeles, 1995).
21. Henry Munson, Jr., *Religion and Power in Morocco* (New Haven, 1993).
22. "*al-Muwḥḥidūn*" *EI*[2] (Maya Shatzmiller).
23. Michael Brett, "Ibn Khaldūn and the Dynastic Approach to Local History: The Case of Biskra," *Al-Qantara* 12(1991): 157-180. The case chosen by Brett is not that of a Berber centred history, but focuses on State's structures in regard to taxation and land holding.

24. Jacinto Bosch Vilá, "Pour une étude historico-sociologique sur les Berbères d'"Al-Andalus", *Mélanges d'Islamologie dédiée à la mémoire de A. Abel,* (Bruxelles, 1976), 2: 58. Like most of the historians who saw the need to study the various aspects of the Berber existence in al-Andalus, Bosch Vilá wanted to address it by studying geographical, anthropological and linguistic aspects. On his concept of the history of the Berbers in al-Andalus see also, "A propos-ito de la berberización de al-Andalus," *Cahiers de Tunisie*, 26(1978): 129-131.

Chapter 1

Author's note: Manuscript Rabat K1275, which I first examined in 1983, is the primary source used throughout the next three chapters. M. A. Makki announced his intention to edit the work in the introduction to his edition of Ibn al-Qaṭṭān's *Naẓm al-Jumān*, (Rabat, 1968), 3, n. 1, but has not done so. The ms. was later the subject of a Ph.D. dissertation by Dr. Muḥammad Yaʿla at the Complutense University of Madrid, who edited and published it with a study in 1996 under the title *Tres textos Árabes sobre Beréberes en el Occidente Islámico*. References in this book are to the manuscript, as well as to the printed edition.

1. Évariste Lévi-Provençal, *Fragments historiques sur les Berbères au Moyen-Age: Extraits inédits d'un receuil anonyme compilé en 712/1312 et intitulé Mafākhir al-Barbar* (Rabat, 1934).
2. Évariste Lévi-Provençal, "Un nouveau récit de la conquête de l'Afrique du Nord par les Arabes," *Arabica* 1(1954): 17-43, especially, 23.
3. Évariste Lévi-Provençal, "Le titre souverain des Almoravides et sa légitimation par le califat ʿabbāside," *Arabica* 2(1955): 271. The text in question received much attention over the following years and was the subject of reprints and studies. See A. M. al-Abbadī, *Dirāsāt fī tā'rīkh al-Maghrib wa'l-Andalus* (Alexandria, 1967): 471-77. *Al-Wathā'iq*, majmūʿāt dawriya tuṣdiruhā mudīriyat al-wathā'iq al-malikiya (Rabat, 1976), 1: 204-219. María J. Viguera, "Las cartas de al-Gazālī y al-Ṭurṭūshī al soberano almorávid Yūsuf B. Tashufīn," *Al-Andalus* 42(1977): 341-74.
4. I have incorporated these assumptions in my analysis of 14th-century Marīnid historiography. See *L'historiographie mérinide*, 122-23, 129-30.
5. A second manuscript, D1020, seemingly a bad copy of K1275, is also located in the General Library in Rabat, Yaʿla, *Tres textos*, 28-30.
6. Fol. 3, and 18-19 of the Arabic text in the printed edition.
7. ʿAbd al-Ḥalīm was the author of a work dealing with the direction of *qibla*s which has further strengthened the claim for his connection to the present work. See infra note 13, Bencherifa, "Problems," 110.
8. Fols. 44-119, 125-272 of the printed edition.

9. Fols. 119-59, 275-383 of the printed edition.
10. For example we find references in the first part to the epistle of al-Ṭurṭūshī, which appears in full in the third part. There are also references in the introduction of the second part, the *Mafākhir al-Barbar*, to the epistle of al-Ghazālī, which is replicated in the third part, and references in the third to the geographical conditions in the Maghreb, which are treated in the first.
11. Quoted usually as ʿUbayd Allāh, but mentioned several times in full.
12. See his study of the manuscripts in the Spanish language section of *Tres textos*, 23-107.
13. Mohamed Bencherifa, "Problems of Attribution in Historical and Geographical Works," in *The Codicology of Islamic Manuscripts*, Proceedings of the Second Conference of al-Furqān Islamic Heritage Foundation, 1993, ed. Yasin Dutton (London, 1995): 109-12.
14. Lévi-Provençal, "Un nouveau récit," 23.
15. Francisco Pons Boigues, *Los historiadores y géografos arábigo-españoles* (Madrid, 1898), 323-26. Lucien Buvat, "Notice bio-bibliographique sur Athīr ad-Dīn Moḥammad ibn Yousouf Aboû Ḥayyān al-Gharnati," *Revue Hispanique* 10(1903): 5-18.
16. See references in Aḥmad b. Muḥammad al-Makkarī, *Analectes sur l'histoire et la littérature des Arabes d'Espagne*, eds. R. Dozy, G. Dugat, L. Krehl and W. Wright (Leiden, 1855-61), Rep. (Amsterdam, 1967), 2 vols.
17. Fol. 22, 51 of the printed edition.
18. *L'historiographie mérinide*, 124 et sq.
19. Fol. 94, 208 of the printed edition.
20. The list of the historians quoted in the *majmūʿa* is provided in Appendix "A" to Chapter 3.
21. On the anonymous author of this work see Bencherifa, "Problems," 112-15.
22. The anonymity of the *Dhakhīra*'s author is the exception that proves the rule. On this chronicle, see *L'historiographie mérinide*, 9-17. Mohamed Bencherifa illustrated the vast dimensions of this phenomenon in Andalusian and Maghrebi historiography by many examples. See Bencherifa, "Problems".
23. *Miʿyār*, 1: 186.
24. Robert Brunschvig, *La Berbérie Orientale sous les Ḥafṣides*, (Paris, 1940), 1: 1-40.
25. *Dhakhīra*, 101.
26. On these aspects see *L'historiographie mérinide*, 115 et sq.
27. Fol. 29, 62 of the printed edition. The passage is paraphrased, not translated word by word.
28. Fols. 32-33, 104-105, 67-71, 236-38 of the printed edition.
29. Fol. 23, 52-53 of the printed edition.
30. Fols. 104-105, 236-38 of the printed edition.
31. Fol. 26, 56-57 of the printed edition.

32. For instance fol. 37, 76-78 of the printed edition.
33. Lévi-Provençal, "Un nouveau récit de la conquête de l'Afrique du Nord," and Chapter 1. See also T. Lewicki, "Les origines de l'Islam dans les tribus Berbères du Sahara occidental: Musa Ibn Nusayr et ʿUbayd Allāh Ibn Habhab," *Studia Islamica*, 33(1970): 203-14.
34. They were reminiscent of the Almohads' proclamation of Berber institutions modeled and named after the Prophet's councils. The Almohad movement which legitimized the Berber language as the other official language, beside Arabic, had also conferred legitimacy on Berber institutions by assimilating them to the councils established by the Prophet. See "*al-Muwaḥḥidūn*," *EI*[2] (M. Shatzmiller).

Chapter 2

1. L. Genicot, *Les généalogies*, série typologie des sources du Moyen-Age occidental, 15 (Louvain, 1975). Ben Zion Dinur, *Dorot u-reshumot* (Jerusalem, 1978).
2. *L'historiographie mérinide*, 115-23. Modern authors who took interest in the Berbers' myth of origin have chosen not to look for its historical significance. H. T. Norris, *The Berbers in Arabic Literature* (London, 1982), 32-43. Also, Brett and Fentress, *The Berbers*, 131-35.
3. *Histoire des Berbères*, 1: 153-67, 3: 180-88.
4. For the anthropological examination of Arab genealogies and their usage, see *Al-Ansāb: La quête des origines. Anthropologie historique de la société tribale arabe*, eds. Pierre Bonte et al., (Paris, 1991).
5. On the relationship to biblical persons see M. A. Johnson, *The Purpose of the Biblical Genealogies* (Cambridge, 1969).
6. An Arabic genealogical work entitled *Tārīkh al-kanʿāniyyin wa 'l-ʿamāliq* was written by Abī Majd al-Maghīlī and is lost today. See fol. 23 of K1275 and 53 of the printed edition.
7. Hans Yohanan Levy, "Meriva al Karka'a shel eretz-Yisrael baet ha'atika," *Studies in Jewish Hellenism* (Jerusalem, 1960): 60-78.
8. Louis Gernet, "De l'origine des Maures selon Procope," *Mélanges de Géographie et d'Orientalisme offerts à E.-F. Gautier* (Tours, 1937): 234-44. H. Y. Levy, *Meriva*, 63-66.
9. Ibid., 62.
10. Ibid., 70.
11. Ibid., 60-62. Gernet, "De l'origine," 234-45.
12. "The homeland of the Berbers was Palestine, where their king was Jālūt (Goliath). When he was killed by David-may Allāh benefit him-the Berbers immigrated to the Maghreb." Ibn Khurradādhbih, Ibn al-Faqīh al-Ḥamadhānī

et Ibn Rustih, *Description du Maghreb et de l'Europe au IIIe-IXe siècle*, (Extraits), texte et tr. Mahammed Hadj-Sadok (Alger, 1949), 12-13.

13. "...The Berbers were in Palestine, their king Jālūt was killed by David, may God save him; they immigrated to the Maghreb...". Ibn ʿAbd al-Ḥakam, *Conquête de l'Afrique du Nord et de l'Espagne*, texte arabe et trans. Albert Gateau (Paris, 1948), 35.
14. "...The Jālūt in question was called Ouennour, son of Hermel, son of...son of Madghis al-Abter." *Histoire des Berbères*, 1: 175.
15. Thus al-Sūlī (d. 335/947): "He, Jālūt, descended from the Berbers, son of Kaslujim, son of Mesraim, son of Ḥam." *Histoire des Berbères*, 1: 176. The historical significance of the curse of Ḥam's biblical story was the topic of a panel in the 31st Annual Meeting of the Middle East Studies Association, entitled The Sons of Noah in Jewish, Christian, and Muslim Traditions. From among the papers read only one was available to readers, Sidney H. Griffith, "The Sons of Noah in Eastern Christian Tradition." For its relevance to contemporary Black-Jewish relations see David M. Goldenberg, "The Curse of Ḥam, a Case of Rabbinic Racism?," *Struggles in the Promised Land, eds.* J. Salzman and C. West (Oxford, 1997): 21-51.
16. "The tribes of the Kutāma and the Ṣanhāja do not belong to the Berber race. These were branches of the Yemeni tribes which Ifricos b. Sayf ī brought over to Africa with the soldiers that he left there in order to guard the country." *Histoire des Berbères*, 1: 170.
17. "The Berbers are a mix of Canaanites and Amalekites who were living in different countries after Goliath was killed. Ifricos, who invaded the Maghreb transported them from Syria and brought them over to Ifrīqiya, called them Berbers." *Histoire des Berbères,* 1: 175.
18. *Histoire des Berbères*, 1:176.
19. Fols. 6-11, 22-30 of the printed edition.
20. Fols. 14-16, 35-39 of the printed edition.
21. Fol. 19, 44 of the printed edition.
22. *Histoire des Berbères*, 1: 176-77.
23. *Kitāb al-Ansāb*, Manuscript K1275, fols, 48-49, 102-105 of the printed edition.
24. Jacinto Bosch Vilá, "La ciencia de los linajes y los genealogistas en la Espana musulmana," *Miscelanea de Estudios dedicados al Profesor Antonio Marin Ocete* (Granada, 1974): 69.
25. *Histoire des Berbères*, 3: 187, 1: 171."...Ibn Sabic and the genealogists of his school.." *Kitāb al-Ansāb*, fol. 21, 50 of the printed edition.
26. *Histoire des Berbères*, 1: 178. See also René Basset "Les généalogistes berbères," *Archives Berbers*, 1(1915), 2: 3-11. *Kitāb al-Ansāb*, fols. 21, 25, printed text, 27 et sq.
27. *Histoire des Berbères*, 1: 232.

28. *Histoire des Berbères,* 3: 187, 201, 207.
29. *Histoire des Berbères*, 3: 207.
30. *Histoire des Berbères,* 3: 291. About the genealogist Kehlan b. Abī Luwā, Ibn Khaldūn said that he crossed over to Spain as well finding refuge with ʿAlī al-Nāṣir, the Ḥammūdī ruler of Malaga. *Histoire des Berbères*, 1: 169, 3: 187.
31. "Jāna, the father of all the Zanāta, was the son of Dharīs or Jālūt who was killed by David. Dharīs was the son of Luwā...son of Berr, son of Qays, son of Elyan, son of Moḍar. As a result the Zanāta were Arabs of pure race, but because of the alliances which they contracted with their neighbors, the Maṣmuda, they became Berbers as well." Al-Idrisi, *Description de l'Afrique et de l'Espagne*, eds. R. Dozy and de Goeje (Leiden, 1866), 63, tr. 75.
32. When speaking about the genealogy of the Marīnid tribes, the author reproduced poems quoted by several Zanāta scholars who lived in al-Andalus, and described the circumstances under which this collection of poems was assembled, *Dhakhīra*, 13, 15. *L'historiographie méridine*, 120. On the events known as the *al-fitna al-barbariyya* see the detailed study by Peter C. Scales, *The Fall of the Caliphate of Córdoba*, 38-109.
33. *L'historiographie mérinide*, 119.
34. *Beni ʿAbd el-Wād*, 119. *Histoire des Berbères*, 1: 120-21, 180.
35. "Except for several insignificant exceptions, these Berbers descended from Goliath...The specialists of their genealogies, of their histories, and of their traditions, have disappeared,". Ibn Ḥawqal, *Configuration de la Terre*, trans. Gaston Wiet (Beirut, 1965), 105. See also T. Lewicki, "A propos d'une liste de tribus berbères d'Ibn Ḥawqal, " *Folia Orientalia* 1(1959): 128-35.
36. David Solomon Sassoon, *Diwan of Shemuel Hannaghid*, published for the first time in its entirety according to a unique manuscript (Ms. Sassoon 589) with an introduction and index of poems (Oxford, 1934), 21, 65, 94.
37. See *Megillat ahimaaz*, the chronicle of Ahimaaz, with collection of poems from Byzantine Southern Italy and additions, ed. and annot. Benjamin Klar (Jerusalem, 1974), 34, 36. I thank Professor Joseph Shatzmiller for drawing my attention to this source.
38. Abraham Ibn Daud, *Sefer Ha-qabbalah*, ed. and trans. Gerson D. Cohen (Philadelphia, 1967), 53-55, 70, 71.
39. Unfortunately, the Palestine connection did not come through in the English translation of *Sefer ha-kabala*, since the translator, G. Cohen, preferred to render the expression by the word Berbers.
40. *Talmud Bavli/Sanhedrin*, 91a, speaks about the Canaanites coming from Ifrīqiya to insist on their rights to Palestine, also H. Y. Levy, "Meriva," 63-64.
41. Évariste Lévi-Provençal, "Les "Mémoires" de ʿAbd Allāh, dernier roi zīrīde de Grenade, Fragments publiés d'après le manuscrit de la Bibliothèque d'al-Qarawīyīn à Fès avec une introducton et traduction française," *Al-Andalus* 3(1935): 245. On the Zīrīds' myth of origin see also Lucien Golvin, *Le*

Maghrib central à l'époque des Zīrīdes (Paris, 1957), 24. Hady Roger Idris, "Les Afṭasides de Badajoz," *Al-Andalus* 30 (1965): 278.

42. Amin T. Tibi, trans., *The Tibyān: Memoirs of Abd Allāh B. Buluggin, Last Zīrīd Amir of Granada* (Leiden, 1986), 10.
43. Tibi, *Tibyān*, 27-29.
44. On this issue see James T. Monroe, *The shuʿūbiyya in al-Andalus, the Risāla of Ibn Garcia and Five Refutations* (Los Angeles, 1970), and the references mentioned.
45. *Histoire des Berbères*, 1: 183.
46. On this period see Hady Roger Idris, *La Berbérie orientale sous les Zīrīdes (X-XIIe siècles)* (Paris, 1962), 2 vol. Muḥammad Talbi, *L'émirat Aghladide* (184-296/800-909), (Paris, 1966).
47. "*Ibn al-Raqīq*" *EI*[2] (M. Talbi). Idris, *Berbérie*, xiv. He was the only historian among this group of historians whose work has partially survived, *Ta'rīkh Ifrīqiya wa'l-Maghrib*, ed. Monji al-Kaabi (Tunis, 1968). Hady Roger Idris, "L'Occident musulman à l'avénèment des Abbasides d'après le chroniqueur zīrīde al-Raqīq," *Revue des Etudes Islamiques* 39(1971): 209-91.
48. Quoted frequently in *Kitāb al-Ansāb*.
49. Another uncertain attribution. Compare "*Ibn Rashīḳ*" *EI2* (Ch. Bouyahya and J.F.P Hopkins).
50. Talbi, *L'émirat*, 12, quotes the title as "al-mu'rib fī aḥbār al-maghrib." *Kitāb al-Ansāb*, fol. 112, 256 of the printed edition.
51. *Kitāb al-Ansāb*, 112-113, 256-261 in the printed edition.
52. It is still not clear who the historian referred to by this name was; he was frequently confused with that of Ibn Ḥammād to be mentioned later. Idris, *Berbérie*, 1: xix and note 44.
53. Idris, *Berbérie*, 1: xix and note 43. He was also the author of another chronicle published as *L'Histoire des rois Obaidides* (Les caliphs fatimides), ed. and tr. M. Vonderheyden (Alger-Paris, 1927). According to R. Brunschvig "it should read as Hamado et non Ḥammād", see "Un aspect de la littérature historico-géographique de l'Islam," *Mélanges Gaudefroy-Demombynes* (Cairo, 1935-45): 60, note 2. He is quoted nonetheless by Ibn Khaldūn as Ibn Ḥammād, *Histoire des Berbères*, 2: 57, 3: 266.
54. Quoted in *Kitāb al-Ansāb* as Abū al-Ṣalat, fol. 86, 191 in the printed edition. Also Idris, *Berbérie*, 1: xvii and notes 29-32. Ibn ʿIdhāri, *Bayān al-Mughrib,* ed. G. S. Colin et E. Lévi-Provençal (Leiden, 1948), 2. Al-Ḥasan ibn Yaḥyā ibn Tamīm ibn al-Muʿiz ruled in Mahdia between 515-543/1121-1148.
55. Évariste Lévi-Provençal, *Documents inédits d'histoire almohade*, Fragments manuscrits du "Legajo" 1919 du fonds Arabe de l'Escurial (Paris, 1928), 32 et sq.
56. That the act of the usurpation of political power needed legitimation. Sectarian movements and political rebels all over the Islamic world have used this

method, including the head of the black slaves, *Zanj*, who revolted in Iraq in the 9th century. Alexandre Popovic, *La révolte des esclaves en Iraq au IIIe/IXe siècle* (Paris, 1976), 189 and Annexe II.

57. Ibn al-Athīr, *Annales du Maghreb et de l'Espagne*, trans. E. Fagnan (Alger, 1898), 8-9.
58. Al-ʿUmarī did not speak about the myth of the Berbers' origin, but quoted an Abī Ḥayyān, to whom the *Kitāb al-Ansāb* is attributed in manuscript K1275 of Rabat. Al-ʿUmarī could have met the grammarian Ibn Ḥayyān, his contemporary, in Egypt, see *Masalik el-abṣār,* 147.
59. *L'Historiographie mérinide*, 116-17.
60. Daniel Eustache, *Corpus des dirhams idrisites et contemporains* (Rabat, 1970-71). The only coin portraying an inscription which simulates the myth of origin is a double dinar of a Marīnid sultan, Abū Ziyān Muḥammad 788/1386, which reads "Muḥammad amīr al-muslimīn b. al-khulafā' al-rashīdīn." See Henry Hazard, *The Numismatic History of Late Medieval North Africa* (New York, 1952), 221. The use of this title appears in the work of the Marīnid poet al-Malzūzī, *Naẓm al-Sulūk*. See *L'historigraphie mérinide*, 12-13, 116.
61. Almoravid and Almohad inscriptions in Gaston Deverdun, *Inscriptions arabes de Marrakech* (Rabat, 1956). The funeral inscriptions of the Ḥafṣid rulers retain only the title "Mahdī" derived from the Almohad protocol to which this dynasty traced its origins. See S. M. Zbiss, *Inscriptions du Gorjani: Contribution à l'histoire des Almohades et des Ḥafṣides* (Tunis, 1962), 89, 92.

Chapter 3

1. This work is the most often quoted by the compiler of the *majmūʿa*, see for instance fols. 14, 20-24, 28, 32, 84, 99, 110 and 45, 52, 187, 192, 220, 237, 246 of the printed edition.
2. Robert Brunschvig, "Un aspect de la littérature historico-géographique de l'Islam," *Mélanges Gaudefroy-Demombynes*, (Cairo, 1935): 58-59.
3. Thanks to the Polish historian T. Lewicki, who studied the literature of this community, we are much better informed today about their historiography. See for example, "Les historiens biographes et traditionnistes ibāḍites-wahbites de l'Afrique du Nord du VIIIe au XVIe siècle," *Folia Orientalia* 3(1961): 1-134. Réné Basset, "Les généalogistes berbèrs," 4-5. Also Elizabeth Savage, *A Gateway to Hell, a Gateway to Paradise: The North African Response to the Arab Conquest* (Princeton, 1977).
4. E. Masqueray, *Chronique d'Abou Zakariya* (Alger, 1878), 11-18. E. Savage, *A Gateway to Hell*, 9.
5. Urvoy, "La pensée d'Ibn Tūmart," 29.
6. Fol. 6 in manuscript K1275, 22-23 of the printed edition.

7. *Histoire des Berbères*, 1: 198-206.
8. On al-Warrāq see R. Brunschvig, "Un aspect," 147-58.
9. Idris, *La Berbérie*, 1: XIV. Entry "*Ibn al-Raqīq*" *EI2*. *Kitāb al-Ansāb*, fol. 91, 201 of the printed edition.
10. Idris, *Berbérie*, 1: XVII and notes 29-32. Fol. 86, 190-92 of the printed edition. The title was attributed in the *Kitāb al-Ansāb* to Ibn Ḥammād. In the 13th century, we have two historians of similar name, Ibn Ḥammād and Ibn Ḥamadūh, which gives reason to confusion.
11. Idris, *Berbérie*, 1: XIX note 43. Also C. Brockelmann, *G.A.L.*, Supp. 1: 555, author of *Histoire des rois 'obaydides*, (Les califes fatimides), ed. et tr. M. Vonderheyden, (Alger-Paris, 1927). According to the *Kitāb al-Ansāb* he is the author of the *Dibāja fī Akhbār Ṣanhāja*. Fol. 93, 191 of the printed edition. The *Kitāb al-Ansāb* mentioned two Ibn Ḥamādu(h), the first, the 12th century al-Burnūsī al-Sabtī, is the author of *Kitāb al-muqtabas*. The other, al-Ṣanhājī, is the author of *al-nubadh*, and like Ibn Ḥammād, has the first name of Abū 'l-Ḥasan, see fols. 94, 100, and 191, 208, 222 of the printed edition. Ibn Khaldūn clearly stated that he used these chronicles: "here ends the text of Ibn al-Raqīq...the following information is provided from Ibn Ḥammād," *Histoire des Berberes*, 3: 266. E. Lévi-Provençal, *Mafākhir al-Barbar* (Rabat, 1934), 64-65.
12. Cl. Cahen's view was that dynastical history was a late bloomer in the Maghreb, and lagged behind the development of the genre in al-Andalus. See Cl. Cahen, "L'historiographie Arabe des origines au VIIe. H.," *Arabica*, 30(1986): 166 et sq.
13. Muḥammad Talbi explained that chronicles were written down but did not survive, mentioning a chronicle written by Muḥammad b. Saḥnūn, d. 256/870, and a *tārīkh* written by the ruler Ziyādat Allāh II, d. 283/896M. Talbi, *L'émirat Aghlabide,* (Paris, 1966), 9-10.
14. On the conversion story see Chapter One. Fols. 35-37, 73-76 of the printed edition. On this author see F. Pons Boigues, *Ensayo bio-bibliografico sobre los historiadores y geografos arabigo-espanoles* (Madrid, 1898), 391.
15. A 14th century historian, Abū Zakariya Yaḥya Ibn Khaldūn, brother of the more famous ʿAbd al-Raḥman, also referred to him as the source for this information, quoting him in his chronicle of the Banū ʿAbd al-Wād *History of the Banū ʿAbd al-Wād. Histoire des Beni ʿAbd el-Wād,* 1:10-11. The other source which this author quoted for similar traditions about the early conversion of the Berbers, was Obeid Allāh, identified by A. Bel as el-Bakrī, 9-10. The younger Ibn Khaldūn also agreed that the source of the above mentioned data was al-Abīlī, teacher and admired mentor of both brothers.
16. On the myth of Arab origin see Chapter Two.
17. E. García Gomez, *Andalucia contra Berberia*, (Barcelona, 1976). E. Lévi-Provençal, *Histoire de l'Espagne Musulmane*, (Paris, 1950-1953), 3: 74, 80-88.

18. Maya Shatzmiller, "Professions and ethnic origin of urban labourers in Muslim Spain: evidence from a Moroccan source," *Awraq* 5(1983): 149-159. Thomas F. Glick, *Islamic and Christian Spain in the Early Middle Ages, comparative perspectives on social and cultural formation* (Princeton, 1979), 165 et sq.
19. E. Lévi-Provençal, "Les Memoires," 247-48.
20. Quoted in H. R. Idris, "Les Zīrīdes d'Espagne," 43. See also, 50, "The berberophobia reached its peak in the capital, where the most heinous crimes were committed, crimes which the chronicler from Qairawān, al-Raqīq, described in the most sinister colours." E. Lévi-Provençal, "Les memoires" d'Abd Allāh dernier roi Zīrīde de Grenade, fragments publiés d'après le manuscrit de la Bibliothèque d'al-Qarawīyīn à Fès," intro. et tr., *Al Andalus* 3(1935): 233-344, 4(1936-39): 29-145.
21. *Tibyān*, 13.
22. H. R. Idris, "Les Zīrīdes d'Espagne," 51-52.
23. Ignaz Goldziher, "Die suʿubijja unter den Muhammedanern in Spanien," *Zeitschrift der Deutchen Morgenländischen Gesellschaft*, 53(1899): 601-20, in particular, 603, where the role of the Eastern genealogies in the *shuʿūbiyya* movement is pointed out. See also James Monroe, *The shuʿūbiyya in al-andalus* (Berkley, 1970).
24. A study of three segments written during the 14th century and pieced together by E. García Gomez under the non-equivocal title "Andalucia contra Berberia", display anti-Berber feelings. E. García Gomez, *Andalucia contra Berberia* (Barcelona, 1976), 51-52.
25. The denigration of everything "Berber", even land and city, continued to feature in Andalusian literature all the way to the end and was very much alive in Muslim Spain. García Gomez was correct in making the observation that the segments of the *majmūʿa*, to which he referred as *Mafākhir al-Barbar*, were the "anti-thesis" to the anti-Berber literature which he was translating. See *Andalucia*, 53.
26. E. Lévi-Provençal, *Histoire de l'Espagne Musulmane* (Paris-Leiden, 1950-53), 3 vols.
27. Guichard says: "Culturally speaking, the Berbers in al-Andalus arabized rapidly, and because of their social structures, structures shared by the Arabs, constituted one of the most effective orientalising agents of the Peninsula," in Pierre Guichard, *Structures sociales "orientales" et "occidentales" dans L'Espagne musulmane* (Paris, 1977), 276.
28. Thomas Glick, *Islamic and Christian Spain in the Early Middle Ages* (Princeton, 1979).
29. "By the early fifth/eleventh century all inhabitants of al-Andalus fused together in a common identity". David Wasserstein, *The Rise and Fall of the Party-Kings*, (Princeton, 1985), 163 et sq. Also, "The evidence suggests very strongly that a rapid linguistic acculturation took place among these old Berbers. On

the literary level they adopted Arabic and on the non-literary level, Arabic and Romance," 165. Also, "There is no evidence to suggest that Berber speech survived for very long after the establishment of these Berbers in the Peninsula," 167-68.

30. "Berbers in the Maghreb and al-Andalus," 59.
31. See Helena de Felipe, "Berbers in the Maghreb and Al-Andalus: Settlements and Toponymy," *The Maghreb Review*, 18(1993): 57-62.
32. H. de Felipe, "Berbers in the Maghreb and al-Andalus," 61.
33. On the correlation between social status, ethnic origin and trade, see M. Shatzmiller, *Labour in the Medieval Islamic World*, (Leiden, 1994), Chapter 6.
34. Hady Roger Idris, "Les Zīrīdes d'Espagne," *Al-Andalus*, 29(1964): 43.
35. Idris, "Les Zīrīdes d'Espagne," 39-147.
36. H. R. Idris, "Les Afṭasides de Bajadoz," *Al-Andalus*, 30(1965): 277-90.
37. *Histoire des Berbères*, 3: 291. H. R. Idris, "Les Birzālīdes de Carmona," *Al-Andalus*, 30(1965): 49-62.
38. *Histoire des Berbères*, 3: 288-29.
39. *Histoire des Berbères*, 3: 224.
40. Two such literary figures are the historians al-Warrāq and Ibn Sharāf. See Idris, *Berbérie*, 1: XVI.

Chapter 4

1. See Henri Terrasse, *Histoire du Maroc* (Casablanca, 1950), 2: 5-6. Ch.-A. Julien, *Histoire d'Afrique du Nord*, 2d ed. rev. by R. Le Tourneau (Paris, 1952), 162-65, 192. Jean Brignon et al., *Histoire du Maroc* (Paris, 1967), 138-40. J. M. Abun-Nasr, *History of the Maghrib* (Cambridge, 1971), 120-21. Rudolf Thoden, *Abū 'l-Ḥasan ʿAli: Merinidenpolitik zwischen Nordafrika und Spanien in den Jahren 710-752/1310-1351* (Freiburg im Breisgau, 1973), 43-44.
2. R. S. Lopez, "The Origin of the Merino Sheep," *Joshua Starr Memorial Volume: Studies in History and Philology*, Jewish Social Studies Publications 5, (New York, 1953): 171-168.
3. Évariste Lévi-Provençal ed. et trans., *Documents inédits d'histoire almohade: Les mémoires d'al-Baidak* (Paris, 1928), 75-224.
4. Ibn ʿIdhārī, *Kitāb al-Bayān al-Mughrib*, ed. G. S. Colin and E. Lévi-Provençal (Leiden, 1948), 1: 4-5.
5. M. I. al-Kattānī, "al-ʿuthūr ʿalā khams makhṭūṭāt min al-bayān al-mughrib bimaktabat al-qaṣr al-malakī biRabāṭ lam takūn maʿarūfa min qabl," *Taṭwān* 9(1964): 167-71. Idem., "al-ʿuthūr ʿalā 'l-waraqāt al-akhīra min al-bayān al-mughrib li-Ibn ʿIdhārī al-marrakūshī," *Taṭwān* 10(1965): 237-44.
6. A. Bel studied and commented on several of the events dealt with here in his

article, "Les premiers emirs mérinides et l'Islam," *Mélanges de Géographie et d'Orientalisme offerts à E.-F. Gautier* (Tours, 1937): 34-44. His interpretations of them differ from mine, however.

7. On the B. ʿAskar see *Masālik al-abṣār*, 141, note 6. M. Gaudefroy-Demombynes, who translated the text, traced the independent activity of the B. ʿAskar during the early years, following the year 614/1217, without recognizing its role in the rise of the Marīnids to power.
8. *Dhakhīra*, 18.
9. Ibid., 19.
10. Ibid., 20-21. *Histoire des Berbères,* 4: 27.
11. For one such episode see *Bayān*, 351.
12. *Dhakhīra*, 21.
13. Ibid.,"...Before he died ʿAbd al-Ḥaqq managed to see the promise kept and his rule established over all the Marīnids."
14. Ibid., 21-23. *Qirṭās,* 187. *Histoire des Berbères*, 4; 27. Compare also J. Brignon et al., *Histoire du Maroc*, 138.
15. *Dhakhīra*, 32-34.
16. *Bayān al-Mughrib*, 352-53.
17. Ibid., 355.
18. *Dhakhīra*, 69. *Histoire des Berbères*, 4: 33-34.
19. Ibid., 4: 122.
20. Ibid., 4: 186.
21. Ibid.
22. Bel, "Les premiers émirs mérinides et l'Islam," 34-44, especially 42.
23. *Dhakhīra*, 22.
24. Ibid., 29.
25. Vincent Crapanzano, *The Ḥamadsha: A Study in Moroccan Ethnopsychiatry* (Berkeley and Los Angeles, 1973), on the *baraka*, 73-74.
26. *Dhakhīra*, 32.
27. Ibid., 33.
28. In the description of the activities of ʿAbd al-Ḥaqq given by this chronicler we can see the difference between the *sheikh* and another Berber saintly figure, believed to be invested with the power of the *baraka*, which is the *anflous*. The latter has magic powers and applies them in the necessary cases, but he has no political power. ʿAbd al-Ḥaqq, on the other hand, was both a spiritual and a military leader. See Robert Montagne, *Les Berbèrs et le Makhzen dans le Sud du Maroc* (Paris, 1930), 221-24.
29. *Dhakhīra,* 35.
30. *Bayān al-mughrib*, 262-63.
31. "When he found out the great misery of the Muslims of his country he ordered all the wheat stores to open and distribute food gratis to the poor, but the rich had to pay. He gave abundantly to charity and improved the people's living conditions." Ibid., 245.

32. *Dhakhīra*, 35, 57. *Bayān al-mughrib*, 244. *Histoire des Berbères*, 4: 31.
33. *Dhakhīra*, 36.
34. For jurists and pious men as intermediaries between the city's residents and the central government during those years, see for Meknès, *Dhakhīra*, 77. *Histoire des Berbères*, 4: 35. For Fez, *Dhakhīra*, 79. The Arab tribes also utilized the pious men as intermediaries, *Dhakhīra*, 34.
35. Ibid., 36.
36. Ibid., 36.
37. *Bayān al-Mughrib*, 247.
38. *Dhakhīra*, 35.
39. Ibid. 57.
40. *Bayān al-mughrib*, 332.
41. Compare with *Dhakhīra*, 37. *Histoire des Berbères*, 4: 32.
42. *Bayān al-mughrib*, 351-53. Ibn ʿIdhārī explained: "It was Ibn Wanūdīn, who since being appointed governor of the Gharb had conceived the idea of becoming independent, and the master of this region, as the Ḥafṣids, for whom he served as aide de camp and friend, have done. For this reason, he consistently bothered the Marīnids, notwithstanding the caliph's clearly stated orders to handle their ruler well. Thus, he did not give either the presents or the robes of honor sent by the Almohads to the *amīr* Abū Saʿīd," 351.

Chapter 5

1. Ignaz Goldziher, "Usages Juifs d'après la littérature religieuse des Musulmans," *Revue des Études Juives*, 28(1894): 92-94. E. Fagnan, "Arabo-Judaica," *Mélanges Hartwig Derenburg* (Paris, 1909): 103-20. *Musnad*, 381, tr. 315. Corcos, "Jews of Morocco Under the Marīnids," 77-78, n. 108.
2. Ashtor, *Toldot*, 1: 279-91. On the Jews in Mamlūk Egypt, Ashtor (Straus), A *History of the Jews in Egypt and Syria*. In Granada the Jews' involvement in the collection of taxes contributed to the hostility towards them there and resulted in their massacre. The *qaṣīda* which the poet al-Ilbīrī wrote to incite the Muslims to rise against the *dhimmī* who was put in authority over them, is widely cited, but see also the circumstances surrounding the compilation of the polemical work against the Jews written in Spain in 1360, al-Rakilī, *Ta'yīd al-milla*, Saving the community. Asin Palacios, "Un Tratado Morisco de Polémica Contre Los Judios," *Mélanges Hartwig Derenbourg* (Paris, 1909): 343-66.
3. This paper focuses on the Marīnid period only. For a comprehensive history of Moroccan Jewry see Haim Zafrani, *Les Juifs du Maroc: Vie sociale, économique et religieuse* (Paris, 1972). For the Jews in Fez in the post Marīnid era, see Jane Gerber, *Jewish Society in Fez, 1450-1700* (Leiden, 1982).

4. Even though opinions vary as to the extent to which the successors of the Mahdi Ibn Tūmart actually applied discriminatory laws and forced conversion on the Jews. David Corcos, "The Attitude of the Almohads towards the Jews," *Zion* 32(1967): 137-60. Reprinted in D. Corcos, *Studies in the History of the Jews of Morocco* (Jerusalem, 197): 319-34. Hirschberg, *A History*, 1: 123-39.
5. The possibility that Judaized Berbers existed in North Africa fascinated historians. Even though it was only mentioned in some obscure remarks made by Ibn Khaldūn, it was adopted as an established historical fact by French and Jewish scholars alike, at the end of the 19th and beginning of the 20th centuries. For details and bibliography see Hirschberg, *Toldot*, 1: 106-108, 2: 9-36. For a list of Jewish and French historians who supported this idea, see page 327, note 1. For a sample of the period's research, see Nahum Slouschz, "Hébraeo-Phéniciens et Judéo-Berbères," *Archives Marocaines* 14(1908), a Kraus Reprint (1974). Also Corcos, "The Jews of Morocco under the Marīnids," 273-75.
6. David Corcos, "The Jews of Morocco under the Marīnids," *Jewish Quarterly Review* 54(1964-5): 271-78, 55: 55-81, 137-50. Reprinted in Corcos, *Studies*, 1-62. In particular, 279.
7. The benevolent Marīnid attitude towards the Jews was probably more of a myth, sustained by 20th-century Moroccan Jews, such as D. Corcos, who wanted to believe in the compassion of the contemporary Moroccan monarchy towards "their" Jews. On David Corcos and his family, see Michel Abitbol, *Temoins et acteurs: les Corcos et l'histoire du Maroc contemporain* (Jerusalem, 1977).
8. Muḥammad Talbi, "Hérésie, acculturation et nationalisme des Berbères Bargāwaṭa," *Proceedings of the First Congress on Mediterranean Studies of Arabo-Berber Influence*, ed. M. Galley in collaboration with D. R. Marshall (Alger, 1973): 217-34.
9. The late H. Z. Hirschberg, author of a comprehensive history of North African Jewry, had several answers The first was the mere fact that the Marīnids in Morocco succeeded the Almohads, a dynasty which had distinguished itself by subscribing to and carrying out an anti-Jewish policy, including forced conversions. See Haim Zeev Hirschberg, *Toldot ha-yehudim be-afrika ha-tsfonit* (Jerusalem, 1966) 1: 277-78. English trans., rev., and ed. Eliezer Bashan and Robert Attal, *A History of the Jews in North Africa* (Leiden, 1974-81), 2 vols. Since the studies that dealt with the religious tendency and policies enacted by the two dynasties have painted them as diametrically opposed, the demise of the one necessarily meant better conditions for the Jews under the other. The concept that a change in the dynastic family automatically meant an improvement in the conditions of the Jews received some support, Hirschberg also suggested that the division of the Maghreb into three independent states, of which Marīnid Morocco was only one, created a situation whereby rulers of the indi-

vidual units were generally less inclined to persecute Jews than the previous ones, who commanded a large consolidated empire. This vision could have been inspired by analogy: in al-Andalus, the division into small *taifa* kingdoms in the 11th century, favored the rise of Jews to positions of power there. This perception was largely inspired by Yaʿov Toledano, *Ner ha-maʿarav* (Jerusalem, 1989), 56-65.

10. *Qirṭās, 24.*
11. S. D. Goitein, *Mediterranean Society*, (Berkeley and Los-Angeles, 1967), 1: 587 n. 17.
12. I have dealt in detail with this *fatwā* in my article "Property Rights and the Public Good: The case of the *Waqf khayrī* in the Islamic West," forthcoming.
13. On the cultural activity of the Jews under the Marīnids see studies by Zafrani, Hirschberg, Corcos, Toledano.
14. See Georges Vajda, *Juda ben Nissim Ibn Malka, philosophe Juif Marocain* (Paris, 1954). Idem, *Kitsur ʿivri shel Kitāb uns al-gharīb wa-tafsīr Sefer Yetsirah le-Rabi Yehudah ben Nisim ibn Malkah* (Ramat-Gan, 1974).
15. The Marīnid failure to claim descent from a noble family, *sharīfi* or other, is also considered a factor in their low-key religious fervor, and therefore more tolerant attitude towards the Jews. Finally, Hirschberg attached importance to the fact that from this period onwards, there was a greater diversity of ethnic and religious elements in the Maghreb. Recent immigrants from Spain, both Muslim and Jewish, and Christian merchants from Italy, France and Spain, not to mention the Christian soldiers from Castilia serving in the Marīnid army, all contributed to the formation of a tolerant, broad-minded attitude towards the "other" Hirschberg, *Toldot*, 277-82.
16. Both the anonymous author of *al-Dhakhīra al-sanniyya*, written circa. 727/1326, and Ibn Khaldūn in his *Kitāb al-ʿIbar*, written in 782/1380, referred to the atmosphere of fear and suspicion prevalent in their own times as being an outcome of that event. "Up to this very moment two people do not converse in seclusion..." said the author of the *Dhakhīra*, 84. Ibn Khaldūn explained, "That punishment brought about the capitulation of the people of Fez to the Marīnid dynasty. Up to this very day they invoke its memory with terror, and never will they dare raise their voices, or resist the orders of the government, or conspire against it...", *Histoire des Berbères*, 4: 39-41.
17. This happened on the second day of *shawwāl* of this year (674/1276), 186.
18. For example Roger Le Tourneau, *Fès avant le protectorant* (Casablanca, 1949), 61-63. Le Tourneau made only a vague reference to the tension between the Marīnids and Fez residents.
19. *Dhakhīra*, 138-41.
20. *Musnad*, 116, tr. 102. About Ibn Marzūq see the introduction to the Spanish translation. Also Shatzmiller, "Les circonstances,".
21. Muḥammad Ben Cheneb, *Étude sur les personnages mentionnés dans l'Idjāza*

du cheikh' Abd al-Quadir el Fasy (Paris and Alger, 1907), biography no. 273.
22. *Histoire des Berbères*, 4: 185-86.
23. *Extraits inédits relatifs au Maghreb*, tr. E. Fagnan (Alger, 1924), 13.
24. *Description de l'Occident musulman au IVeġXe siècle*, ed. and tr. Charles Pellat (Alger, 1950), 27.
25. Abou Obeïd el-Bekri, *Description de l'Afrique septentrionale*, trans. M. Baron De Slane (Paris, 1965), 229-30, quoting a jurist from the Moroccan port Aṣīla and a *qāḍī* from the desert oasis of Tahert.
26. *Dhakhīra*, 81-84. *Qirṭās*, 196-197. *Bayān al-Mughrib*, 399. *Histoire des Berbères*, 4: 39-41.
27. See the detailed description in Auguste Cour, *La dynastie marocaine des Beni-Wattas, 1420-1554*, (Constantine, 1920). Terrasse, *Histoire*, 109-10. M. García-Arenal, "The Revolution in Fās," 43-66.
28. *Qirṭās*, 278.
29. *Qirṭās*, 315.
30. *Histoire des Berbères*, 4: 185-86.
31. *Zahra*, 11, tr. 34-35.
32. On this literary motif, which reflected the historical evolution of attitudes and social changes in Marīnid Morocco see *L'historiographie mérinide*. We now have a monograph devoted to the Idrissid cult issue in the history of Fez, Herman L. Beck, *L'image d'Idrīs II, ses descendants de Fās et la politique sharīfenne des sultans Marīnids (656-869/1258-1465)* (Leiden, 1989).
33. See E. Molina López, "Dos importantes privilegios a los emigrados andalusies en el Norte de Africa en el siglo XIII, contenidos en el *Kitāb Zawāhir al-Fikā* de Muḥammad b. al-Murābiṭ, *Cuadernos de Historia del Islam* 9(1978-79): 5-31.
34. *Dhakhīra*, 138-41.
35. Ibid., 138.
36. Évariste Lévi-Provençal, "Un historiographe et poète de cour mérinide: Abu Faris al-Malzuzi," in *AIEO* 1(1934-35): 189-92. Also Benchekroune, *La vie intellectuelle*, 133-40.
37. Ibid., 141-46
38. *Histoire des Berbèrs*, 4: 165.
39. See details in Chapter 7.
40. Here, we are following Ibn Khaldūn's text about the advent of the Jewish courtiers. *Histoire des Berbèrs*, 4: 167-68. Corcos translated Ibn Khaldūn's passage from the *Kitāb al-ʿibar* into English in his previously mentioned article, "The Jews of Morocco under the Marīnids," 2: 138-43.
41. *Histoire des Berbères*, 4: 180-83.
42. Corcos, "The Jews of Morocco under the Marīnids," 2: 139-40, note 118.
43. Ibn al-Aḥmar describes this event in his *al-Nafḥa al-nisrīniyya*, confirming the information provided by Ibn Khaldūn. Both depict the circumstances of the

events surrounding the rise and fall of Yehoseph ha-Nagid, his family and the Jewish community in 11th-century Zīrīd Granada. "The Jew Khalīfa b. Ibrāhīm was the one who aroused the sultan Abū Rabīʿ against the *ḥājib* ʿAbdallāh b. Madyan, until the latter was killed with a lance near the tomb of the jurist the *imām,* the pious Abū Bakr Muḥammad, son of the jurist, the *imām* ʿAbdallāh Ibn al-ʿArabī al-Ghāfirī. The one who killed him was Gonsalo, the commander of the Christian guard. The Jew was later killed, in his turn, by Abū Rabīʿ." See also *Histoire des Berbères*, 4: 180-83.

44. Not as incorrectly stated by D. Corcos, like his cousin, Khalīfa b. Ibrāhīm, who was also a *ḥājib* under Abū Yaʿqūb's grandson, Abū Rābiʿ. Ibid., 2: 138. The difference is of some significance, since the position of palace attendant was traditionally a role entrusted to an individual of foreign origin, frequently a recent convert to Islam, whose loyalty in matters of discretion could be taken for granted. Another point which D. Corcos made, and which is supported by an unedited manuscript of a Marīnid chronicle composed by Ibn al-Aḥmar that the name was unmistakably Roqāsa and not Waqasa, as others have suggested. Ismāʿīl Ibn al-Aḥmar, *al-Nafḥa al-Nisriniyya wa'l-Lamḥa al Marīnniya*, ms. Escorial 1773. On this work see Maya Shatzmiller, "Étude d'historiographie mérinide: la "Nafḥa al-Nisriniyya" et la "Rawḍat al-Nisrin" d'Ibn al-Aḥmar," *Arabica* 24(1977): 258-268.
45. *Bayān,* 372.
46. Ibid., 364.
47. The following is based on Abū 'l-Ḥasan ʿAl ī b. Yūsuf al-Ḥakīm, *al-Dawḥa al-mushtabika fī ḍawābiṭ dār al-sikka*, ed. Ḥusain Mu'nis (Madrid, 1960).
48. There are indications that the trades practiced by Andalusian Jews were held in contempt by the Arabs. Eliyahu Ashtor, *Korot ha-yehudim bi-sefard ha-muslemit*, (Jerusalem, 1960) 1: 180. Ashtor also found a large number of Jews in goldsmithery. For correlation between trades and ethnic and religious affiliation, see my article, "The Image and Social Status of Urban Labour in al-Andalus," in *La mujer en al-Andalus: Reflejos historicos de su actividad y categorias sociales*, ed. María J. Viguera (Madrid, 1989): 61-70. Idem, *Labour*, Chapter 6.
49. Ibn al-Ḥakīm, *al-Dawḥa*, 118.
50. Ibid., 78-79.
51. A similar pattern was revealed in Muslim Spain where the Jewish court physician, Ḥasdai ibn Shaprut was appointed as supervisor over the taxes collected from export and import in addition to his position as the court physician. Ashtor, *Korot,* 113. Louis Massignon noted the correlation between the way the Jews provided the State with precious metals and the capital needed for financial transactions. He associated the pattern with the appearance of Jewish banks and bankers in the East, while recognizing that the early capitalists were in fact Christians. According to his interpretation the Jews initially provided

the financial means needed by the State to ensure through *ghaziya*, raids, the manpower and the material needed for the economic prosperity of the early Islamic expansion. Massignon used the appearance of Jews in international trade in the East, documented in the Geniza, to theorize about the rise of the international banks controlled by Jewish capitalists under the ʿAbbāsids. Louis Massignon, "L'influence de l'Islam au Moyen Age sur la fondation et l'essor des banques Juives," *Bulletin d'Etudes Orientales de l'Institut Français de Damas* 1(1931). Reprinted in Massignon, *Opera Minora* (Beirut), 1: 241-50.

52. Ibn al-Ḥakīm, *al-Dawḥa,* 118-19.
53. Ibid., 120-21. Al-Ḥakīm must have had the document before him, since he could cite its precise date as being the fourth of *Dhū al-ḥija* 756/1355.
54. On this monarch, Thoden, *Abu al-Hasan Ali.* Thanks to his scholarly reputation, Ibn Marzūq became his councilor and personal *imām*, prayer leader, and accompanied him later. He wrote his memoirs entitled *al-Musnad al-ṣaḥīḥ,* in 772/1370, describing his benefactor's good deeds, administrative feats and military exploits and also his devotion to the Muslim faith.
55. *Musnad*, 381-82, tr. 314-15: "In Tlemcen," said Ibn Marzūq" there was a very famous Jewish physician whose reputation had reached Fez. The sultan, who had been suffering from pain in his left elbow, refused to call upon him while in Fez. However, when he conquered Tlemcen, he was reminded about the existence of this physician and invited him to come to the court in order to be consulted about the monarch's condition. The Jewish physician contacted by Ibn Marzūq, who was an old acquaintance, came to the court, examined the patient, expertly diagnosed the disease and recommended treatment, impressing all present with his deep knowledge. The sultan ordered that he be brought before him, and offered him the position as his trusted court physician, after he converted to Islam. The physician considered the offer but could not entertain conversion to Islam. The sultan asked Ibn Marzūq to try and convince him, but in vain. When informed of the refusal the sultan said, "Allāh makes it possible for us, and for the whole Islamic community, to dispense with the service of this physician". He also refused to use the special ointment prepared by the physician for his treatment unless the physician converted to Islam.
56. Hirschberg, *A History*, 1: 89-95, 282-87, 389-99. Charles-Emanuel Dufourcq, *L'Espagne Catalane et le Maghreb aux XIIIe et XIVe siècles* (Paris, 1966), 139-44. "Tlemcen" *Encyclopeadia Judaica* (1971), (David Corcos). M. Weinstein, "The Uninterrupted Existence of Jewish Population in North Africa," *Mizraḥ umaʿarav* (Ramat-Gan, 1974): 37-58.
57. There are opposing views regarding the rarity on the one hand and the benefit, on the other, of the Responsum for the history of the Jews in North Africa. See for instance Shimon Schwarzfuchs, "Les Responsa et l'histoire des Juifs d'Afrique du Nord," *Communautés Juives des Marges Sahariennes du Maghreb*, ed. Michel Abitbol (Jerusalem, 1982): 39-53. An opposing view,

Menahem Ben-Sasson, "The Jewish Community of Gabes in the 11th Century, Economic and Residential Patterns," *Communautés*: 265-84. For Tlemcen in the 15th century see the following, *Responsa* by Isaac bar Sheshet (Ribash) (Constantinople, 1547) and Shimon b. Tzemaḥ Duran (Rashbatz), *Sefer ha-tashbetz* (Amsterdam, 1738). Isidor Epstein, *The Responsa of Rabbi Simon b. Zemah Duran as a Source of the History of the Jews in North Africa* (London, 1939).

58. On the Banū ʿAbd al-Wād see *Beni ʿAbd al-Wād*. Hans Kurio, *Geschichte und Geschichteschreibers des ʿAbd al-Wadiden* (Fribourg, 1973).
59. *Musnad*, 285, tr. 236.
60. *Kitāb al-ʿibar*, 7: 200.
61. For Jewish physicians in Spain see I. F. Baer, *A History of the Jews in Christian Spain* (Tel-Aviv, 1959), 40,53,83, 108-9, 119, 215, 228, 231, 241, 249, 297, 325, 364, 378, 388. Ashtor, *Korot*, 1: 111 et sq. 2: 185. For the Eastern Islamic lands, S. D. Goitein, "The Medical Profession in the Light of the Cairo Geniza Documents," *HUCA* 34(1963): 177-94. Idem, *Mediterranean Society*, 2: 240-70. Eliyahu Ashtor (Straus), *Toldot ha-yehudim be-mitsrayim ve-suriya taḥat shilton ha-mamlukim (A History of the Jews in Egypt and Syria Under the Rule of the Mamluks)*, (Jerusalem, 1944-70), 3 vol.
62. *Kitāb al-ʿibar*, 9: 632.
63. August Cour, "Les derniers Mérinides," *Bulletin de la Société de Géographie d'Alger* 10(1905): 103-19. Idem, *L'établissement des dynasties des Chérifs au Maroc* (Paris, 1904).
64. Johannes Leo Africanus, *Description de l'Afrique*, trans. A. Epaulard (Paris,1956), 235 and 239.
65. Shatzmiller, "Etude," 267-68.
66. Hirschberg, *Toldot*, 1: 290-98. Mercedes García-Arenal, "The revolution of Fās in 869/1465 and the death of sultan ʿAbd al-Ḥaqq al-Marīnī," *BSOAS* 41(1978): 43-66.
67. See Meir Benayahu ed. *Divre ha-yamim shel Fas*: *History of Fez, Misfortunes and Events of Moroccan Jewry as Recorded by Ibn Danan's Family and Descendants* (Tel-Aviv, 1993), 47-49.

Chapter 6

1. *Zahra*, 49-52, tr. 112-15.
2. On this city and its importance in the Marīnid period see "al-Manṣūra" *EI*[2] (M. Shatzmiller).
3. According to the author of the *Zahra*, the sultan forgave him after reading a poem which al-Mazdaghī had composed. *Zahra*, 51, tr. 115.
4. This episode was briefly reported in a later version which appears in Ibn al-Qāḍī, *Jazwat al-Iqtibās* (Fez, n.d.), 36.

5. *Musnad*, 230-34, tr. 193-96.
6. ʿAlī b. ʿAbdallāh al-Nubāḥī, *Tārīkh quḍāt al-Andalus: Histoire des juges d'Andalousie intitulée Kitāb al-markaba al-ʿulya* (Beirut, 1966), 129. Abū Jaʿfar held the position of *qāḍī* for the sultan Abū Yūsuf. See *Dhakhīra*, 94.
7. For Muḥammad b. Aḥmad al-sharīf al-ḥasanī al-Mazdaghī see *Miʿyār* 3:96, 5:295-96, 7:307, for Abū al-Rabīʿ al-Mazdaghī, 4:269 and 431.
8. *Dhakhīra*, 46, tr. 89-90.
9. *Qirṭās*, 45.
10. *Zahra*, 47-49, tr. 110-12.
11. *Dhakhīra*, 46. *Zahra*, 47-48, tr. 110.
12. *Dhakhīra*, 89-90.
13. Ibid., 90. *Qirṭās*, 45. *Zahra*, 49, tr. 112.
14. See for names of *imāms* *Qirṭās*, 42-47. *Zahra*, 42-54, tr. 101-20. The Marīnid historian, Ibn al-Aḥmar, provided lists of names of *qāḍī*s, viziers, secretaries and other appointees by individual ruler in his *Rawḍat en-Nisrin*.
15. *Zahra*, 50, tr. 113.
16. It would seem that the question of the wealth or the revenue of the clergy has been a subject for public scrutiny. The author of the *Qirṭās*, 42, mentions another jurist in Fez, named Abū Muḥammad Yashkur, who inherited a large herd with a great number of animals.
17. *Zahra*, 52, tr. 115.
18. Alfred Bel, "Inscriptions arabes de Fes," *Journal Asiatique* 18, II série, 11-12, sept.-oct., 189-276. For the Arabic text of the inscription see 256-57.
19. *Zahra*, tr. 115-16, note 3.
20. See Chapter 8.
21. On the personal motives of Ibn Marzūq, Maya Shatzmiller, "Les circonstances de la composition du Musnad d'Ibn Marzūḳ," *Arabica* 22(1975): 292-99.
22. Marīnid historiographers were not court historians, in the sense that they were not attached to the court or paid by it, but they wrote history, nonetheless, in anticipation of material rewards of which they spoke openly. I have elaborated on this aspect in *L'histoiographie mérinide*. On the motives of Ibn al-Aḥmar, Idem, "Etude d'historiographie mérinide: la 'Nafḥa al-nisriniyya' et la 'Rawḍat al-nisrīn'd'Ibn al-Aḥmar," *Arabica* 24(1977): 258-67.
23. The status of individuals in the Marīnid court depended on the personal relationship they were able to develop with individual monarchs which included deleterious and injurious comments against competitors for the royal favor. Ibn Khaldūn had that to say about his colleague Ibn Marzūq: "He entered the service of Abū 'l-Ḥajjāj, the sultan of Granada and became the preacher of the court, honor which he managed to obtain thanks to unfounded reputation that he was the most capable individual to preach in the presence of royalty." *Histoire des Berbères*, 4:348.

24. *Tuḥfat al-nuẓẓār: Voyages d'Ibn Batoutah*, eds. and trans. G. Defrémery and B. R. Sanguinetti (Paris, 1879), 4:348 et sq.
25. Al-Jaznā'ī gives the amount of this pension as 150 dinars. See *Zahra*, 52, tr. 115.
26. This confirms what we already knew from the *Zahra*, that he was shunned at first, but forgiven later. *Zahra*, 51, tr. 115.
27. See Chapter 6 for details.
28. See Chapters 6, 7, 8 and 9, for details of the struggle between the state and public institutions.
29. A number of studies on hereditary positions in al-Andalus were published in a collection entitled *Saber Religioso y Poder Político en el-Islam*, eds. Manuela Marín and Mercedes García-Arenal (Madrid, 1994). See articles by María Luisa Ávila, "Cargos hereditarios en la administración judicial y Religiosa de al-Andalus," 27-39, and the bibilography provided there. On families and political power, Halima Farhat, "Le Pouvoir des *fuqahā'* dans la Cité: Sabta du XIIe au XIVe siècle," 53-71, and Maribel Fierro, "The *qāḍī* as Ruler," 71-117.
30. On the limitations imposed on municipal life by the *waqf* system see Maya Shatzmiller, "Property Rights and the Public Good: The Case of the Islamic *Waqf khayrī* in the Islamic West," forthcoming.

Chapter 7

1. On the Marīnid monuments in comparison with those of three contemporary dynasties see Bernard O'Kane, "Monumentality in Mamlūk and Mongol Art and Architecture," *Art History* 4/19(1996): 499-522.
2. Alfred Bel, *La religion musulmane en Berbérie* (Paris, 1938), 295-96. Terrasse, *Histoire*, 79-84. Le Tourneau, *Fès*, 68. Julien, *Histoire*, 188.
3. *Dhakhīra*, 84. *Histoire des Berbères*, 4: 41. See details in Chapter 5.
4. *Zahra*, 74, tr. 159-60.
5. "He undertook the judgeship after refusal, *tamannuʿ*, and turning it down, *ibāya*, but was forced to by the ruler, *Khalīfa*." *Al-markaba*, 129. As we have seen his appointment can be traced to Abū Yūsuf.
6. *Zahra*, 76, tr. 162-63.
7. *Qirṭās*, 42.
8. *Zahra*, 42-43, tr. 101.
9. Ibid., 44.
10. *Zahra*, 45, tr. 107, 47, tr. 109.
11. *Qirṭās*, 45.
12. *Zahra*, 48-49, tr. 111-12.
13. Ibid., 48-49, tr. 111-12.

14. *Qirṭās*, 42-47. *Zahra*, 42-49, tr. 99-109.
15. *Dhakhīra*, 188. *Zahra*, 66, tr. 143. See also the list of *qāḍī*s appointed to their job by the sultans Abū Yūsuf and Abū Yaʿqūb in Ibn al-Aḥmar, *Rawḍat en-Nisrin*, 14, 17, tr. 62, 68.
16. *Qirṭās*, 45. *Zahra*, 49-54, tr. 112-20.
17. *Qirṭās*, 32, 38, 39, 40, 46. *Zahra*, 59, 65, 66, 73, tr. 131-32, 142-44, 157.
18. *Qirṭās*, 38. *Zahra*, 66, tr. 144.
19. Ibn Khaldūn, *al-Taʿrīf*, 15-55.
20. The role of the *medresa*, and by association that of Islamic institutions was seen as impeding the progress of Islamic science, see Toby E. Huff, *The Rise of Early Modern Science, Islam, China and the West* (Cambridge, 1993), 71-90.
21. Robert Brunschvig, "Quelques remarques historiques sur les médersas de Tunisie," *Revue Tunisienne* (1931): 261-85.
22. *Zahra*, 75, tr. 160. *Dhakhīra*, 188. Brunschvig, "Quelques," 269.
23. See A. Péretié, "Les Medersas de Fès," *Archives Marocaines* 18(1912): 257-372. A. Bel, "Inscriptions arabes de Fès," *Journal Asiatique* (1917-19). Ch. Terrasse, *Médersas du Maroc*, (Paris, 1927).
24. This is the opinion of Ch. Terrasse.
25. Ibn Marzūq referred to what he termed the renaissance of the Marīnid *medresa*s, which dated from the time of Abū ʾl-Ḥasan and Abū-ʿInān, rather than from the first establishment of the institution, but, on the other hand, this remark could have indicated that not much teaching took place in the first *medresas*.
26. Bel rendered the Arabic *al-fuqahāʾ al-madhkūrīn fī ahl Zanāta* into French as *les docteurs reputés de l'époque*, which seems to be misrepresenting the historical implications. *Zahra*, 75 tr. 161.
27. For a similar outlook among Andalusi religious scholars during the Umayyad period see Manuela Marĭn, "Inqibāḍ ʿan al-sulṭān: ʿUlamāʾ and Political Power in al-Andalus," *Saber Religioso y Poder político en el Islam* (Madrid, 1994): 127-41, on wages in particular, 138.
28. *Zahra*, 75, tr. 160-61. It is also possible that the notion that this *medresa* has the most correctly oriented *miḥrab* has its origin in this episode. Péretié, *Medersas*, 265.
29. *Dhakhīra*, 188.
30. Lévi-Provençal, "Un historiographe et poète de cour mérinide,". Also ʿAbdallāh Gannuūn, *Dhikrayāt mashāhir rijāl al-Maghrib* (Tetuan, 1948), no 9, 1-2.
31. Bel, "Les premiers émirs mérinides et l'Islam".
32. *Zahra*, 48. tr. 112.
33. Benchekroune, *La vie intellectuelle au Maroc*, 133 et sq.
34. Quoted in A. Bel, *La religion musulmane*, 325-26. See also statements by Henri Terrasse, *Histoire*, 79 et sq.

Chapter 8

1. The recent surge of scholarly interest in the *waqf* only befits its magnitude as a historical institution. The literature dealing with the various aspects of the *waqf* is too extensive to be reviewed here in detail, and the *Encyclopedia of Islam*'s new entry has not been published yet. The old one, while informative, needs to be updated. For recent review and studies see the special number of the *Journal of the Economic and Social History of the Orient* 38.3 (1995) devoted entirely to *Waqf* and other institutions of similar religious/philanthropic nature in comparative perspectives. See also a special issue of *Islamic Law and Society*, 4:3 (1997).
2. David S. Powers studied the *fatwās* dealing with the family *waqf* in this period in "The Maliki Family Endowment: Legal Norms and Social Practices," *International Journal of Middle Eastern Studies*, 25(1993): 379-406.
3. On the Marīnid *waqf*, Muḥammad al-Manūnī, "Nuẓūm al-dawla al-marīniyya," *al-Baḥth al-ʿilmī* (Rabat, 1964), 1: 255-57, reprinted in his *Waraqāt ʿan ḥaḍāra al-maghribiyya fī ʿaṣr Banī Marīn*, 93-94. For *waqf ahlī* in Fez, J. Revault, L. Golvin, A. Amahan, *Palais et demeures de Fès. I. Epoques mérinide et saadienne* (XIV-XVII siècles), (Paris, 1985), 203-14.
4. Bel, "Inscriptions arabes de Fès", *Journal Asiatique* (1917, Juillet-Aout): 163.If *waqf* registers from the Marīnid period have survived, no detailed study of them has been undertaken.
5. Brunschvig, *Berbèrie*, 2: 67, 190-92.
6. Ma del Carmen Villanueva and A. Soria, "Fuentes toponímicas granadinas: Los libros de bienes habices," *Al-Andalus* 19(1954): 457-62. Ma del Carmen Villanueva Rico, *Habices de las mezquitas de la ciudad de Granada y sus alquerias* (Madrid, 1961). Idem, *Casas, Mezuitas y Tiendas de Los Habices de Las Iglesias de Granada* (Madrid, 1966).
7. Until now, the methodological approach to the study of the *waqf* has been to take one region at a time and study it as a selective legal or economic topic. The flood of recent publications only demonstrates that a comprehensive, comparative and inclusive study of this multi-faceted, rich subject remains in the distant future. It also indicates that while regular and common sources for the study of the *waqf* such as *waqfiyyas*, endowment acts, registers of properties endowed and revenue ledgers are not only largely available, but outnumber the chronicles. Some regions have fared better than others so far as documentation goes. Egypt for example, a region with an unusual amount of records, also has detailed *waqf* data for both the early and later medieval periods, Geniza documents for the high Middle Ages and archival deeds for the Mamlūk period. Moshe Gil, "Maintenance, Building Operations, and Repairs

in the Houses of the Qodesh in Fustat," *Journal of the Economic and Social History of the Orient* 14(1971): 136-95. Idem, *Documents of the Jewish Pious Foundations from the Cairo Geniza* (Leiden, 1976). For an inventory of *waqf* documents in Egypt see Muḥammad Amīn, *Catalogue des documents d'archives du Caire de 239/853 a 922/1516*, Institut Français d'Archéologie Orientale du Caire, Textes Arabes et Études Islamiques, 16 (Cairo, 1981). Amīn's statement, that the majority of the buildings standing in Cairo before the Ottoman occupation were *waqf*, is quite revealing of the dimensions of the endowments. He also makes the point that the scale of endowed property had a negative effect on the overall economy since endowed property was exempted from taxes. See Muḥammad Amīn, *The Waqf and Social Life in Egypt 648-923 A.H./1250-1517 A.D.* (Historical Document Study), 278-79. Also Mona Zakarya, *Deux palais du Caire médiéval: Waqf et architecture* (Paris, 1983).

8. A methodological-semantic note regarding the use of the term *waqf* in this paper, instead of the usual Maghrebi term *habous*, seems pertinent. Heffening, in "Waqf" *EI*, stated that, "Among Mālikīs and therefore in Morocco, Algiers and Tunis, the name *hubus* (pl. of *habīs*) or the syncopated form *ḥubs* (pl. *aḥbās*) predominates (hence in the French legal language *Habous*)." However, most Marīnid chroniclers use the verb *waqafa* exclusively, hence *waqf* and *awqāf* in this paper. Two use *waqafa* and *ḥabasa* interchangeably. Inscriptions and *fātwa*s, the two other main sources for this study, use the verb *waqafa*, in some places though, the use of *ḥabasa* seems to be more common. Modern historians in Morocco when writing about Marīnid *waqf* use the term *waqf* and habous interchangeably. According to Lévi-Provençal, the term ḥabūs" became of use only at the end of the Middle Ages," Lévi-Provençal, *Histoire de l'Espagne muslmane*, 3: 133. The use of the term *waqf* in this paper is, therefore, consistent with precedent.
9. *Dhakhīra*, 100. In Granada this tax was used for building the public bath near the Alhambra, which revenue was declared *waqf.* Rachel Arié, *L'Espagne musulmane au temps des Nasrides, 1232-1492* (Paris, 1973), 215.
10. See Chapter 7. Bel, "Inscriptions," (1917): 147, mentions the al-Ṣaffārīn *medresa*, but no inscription commemorating it and enumerating the endowed properties has survived.
11. Bel, "Inscriptions," (1917): 158-64.
12. On the *medresa* in al-ʿUbbād see Charles Brosselard, "Inscriptions Arabes de Tlemcen," *Revue Africaine* 3(1858-59), 18(1859): 410-19, Kraus Reprint, 1968.
13. Abū 'l-Ḥasan was particularly enthusiastic about the *medresa* institution. According to his chronicler Ibn Marzūq, who devoted a whole chapter to the subject of *medresa*s in Abū 'l-Ḥasan's life, he built *medresa*s in the cities of Fez, Meknes, Salé, Tanger, Anfa, Azemour, Safi, Aghmat, and Marrakech as well in al-ʿUbbād, in what is now Algeria, *Musnad*, 405, 407, tr. 335-36.

Brosselard, "Inscriptions," 19: 410-19. An inscription for a *medresa* in Qṣar al-Kabīr, which was founded and endowed by his son, Abū ʿInān, circa 752/1351, and later partly destroyed, remains unpublished and might illuminate this matter. Georges Salmon, "El-Qçar el-Kebir," *Archives Marocainces* (Paris), 2: 146. Also Max Van Berchem, "Titres Califiens d'Occident à propos de quelques monnaies mérinides et ziyanides," *Journal Asiatique*, Mars-Avril(1907): 255.

14. Joseph Schacht, "Sur quelque manuscrits de la bibliothèque d'al-Qarawīyīn," *Études d'Orientalisme dédiés à la mémoire de É. Lévi-Provençal* (Paris, 1962), 1: 272, 283.
15. Joseph Schacht, "On Some Manuscripts in the Libraries of Morocco," *Hespéris-Tamuda* 11(1968): 44.
16. Schacht, "Sur quelques manuscrits," 279. Bechekroune, *La vie*, 50-51, 53. Many copies of the *Bayān* attest to its popularity in medieval Morocco. For more surviving copies see *Majmuʿa mukhtār li-makhṭūṭāt ʿarabiyya nādira min maktabāt ʿāmma fī 'l-Maghrib* (Beirut, 1986), 1: 21, 43.
17. Benchekroun, *La vie*, 52.
18. *Majmūʿa*, 225. Benchekroun, *La vie*, 53.
19. Schacht, "Sur quelques manuscrits," 272.
20. Schacht, "Sur quelques manuscrits," 51. *Majmūʿa*, 16. Also Muḥammad al-ʿAbīd al-Fāsī, *Fihris makhṭūṭāt khizānat al-Qarawīyyīn* (Casablanca, 1983), 3: 16-17. The same book was also endowed by Abū ʿInān, today in the Abū Yūsuf collection in Marrakech, mss. s 559, *Majmūʿa*, 218.
21. Henri Terrasse, *La grande mosquée de Taza* (Paris, 1943), 12.
22. Bel, "Inscriptions," (1917): 125.
23. Benchekroun, *La vie*, 56.
24. Bel, "Inscriptions," (1917): 117-26.
25. Eche, *Les bibliothèques*, 246.
26. Brosselard, "Inscriptions," 3(1858-59): 90.
27. Évariste Lévi-Provençal, "Note sur un Qor'an royal du XIVe siècle," *Hespéris* 1 (1921): 83-86.
28. See Ignaz Goldziher, *Le livre de Mohammed Ibn Toumert, Mahdi des Almohads,* texte arabe accompagné de notices biographiques et d'une introduction, (Alger, 1903).
29. Schacht, "On Some Manuscripts," 32.
30. *Masālik al-abṣār*, 129.
31. Eche, *Les bibliothèques*, 160, and for other titles endowed in the East, 59, 211. For Mamlūk Egypt, Amīn, *al-Awqāf*, 244-45.
32. Ibn Khaldūn, *The Muqaddimah: An Introduction to History*, trans. Franz Rosenthal, Bollingen Series XLIII (Princeton, 1958), 1: xci-xciii.
33. Y. Eche dwelt at great length on this question in his study, but recorded only the legal debate about who could use the endowed books, and the fees which

should be charged for borrowing them. Eche, *Les bibliothéques*, 367-86.

34. *Mi'yār*, 7: 293 *fatwā* by Aḥmad al-Qabbāb and another *fatwā* dealing with borrowing Qur'āns for private use from libraries, 7: 37. On the legal aspects for constituting a book or a library as *waqf*, see Eche, *Les bibliothèques*, 201-313.
35. On Ibn Siwār see Eche, *Les bibliothèques*, 100-102. On Qur'āns, ibid., 68-74, 271-91.
36. B. Roy and P. Poinsot, *Inscriptions Arabes de Kairouan* (Paris, 1950), 2: 28-32.
37. Gaston Deverdun and Mhammed ben Abdeslam, "Deux taḥbīs almohades (milieux du XIIIe siècle)," *Hespéris* (1954): 411-23.
38. Marius Canard, "Les relations entre les Mérinides et les Mamelouks au XIVe siècle," *Annales de l'Institut des Etudes Orientales* 5(1939-41): 42.
39. *Zahra*, 68-69, tr. 148-51.
40. *Histoire des Berbères*, 4: 239-42. *Musnad*, 475, 59, tr. 392-95.
41. Canard, "Les relations," 42, 65.
42. *Histoire des Berbères*, 4: 394. *Musnad*, 475, 59, tr. 392-95.
43. Khader Salameh and Robert Schick, "The Qur'ān Manuscripts of the Islamic Museum, the Haram al-Sharif, Jerusalem," *Al-'Usur al-Wusta*: *The Bulletin of Middle East Medievalists* 10/1, (1998): 2.
44. The special attention which this Marīnid ruler gave to Qur'āns as objects of *waqf khayrī*, can be compared with, and even attributed to, influences from Egypt. The Mamlūk rulers of Cairo, contemporaries of Abū 'l-Ḥasan and Abū 'Inān, made important endowments to support, maintain, and read from the sumptuous copies which they commissioned. Marīnid society and rulers, who retained some cultural links with Mamlūk Egypt, could not have remained unimpressed. David James, *Qur'āns of the Mamlūks* (London, 1988).
45. Canard, "Les relations," 65.
46. Ibid., 67.
47. *Musnad*, 475. *Histoire des Berbères*, 4: 394-95.
48. In order to illustrate the small scale of royal *waqf* endowed for the city's mosques, it is useful to compare it to endowments by non-royals in Fez. The assets endowed by Abū Muḥammad 'Abd Allāh al-Ṭarīfī, a Marīnid notable, in 811/1408, for the Lalla Grība mosque in Fez Jdid, were considerably more than those endowed by the Marīnid rulers for the mosques in their capital. The Lalla Ġrība mosque was a small mosque in the new government quarters, built entirely by al-Ṭarīfī clearly not in imitation of the acts of the rulers, which was a pattern typical of the contemporary Mamlūk *amīr*s in Egypt imitating the sultan. The *amīr*s adopted many of the cultural pattern of their rulers, including one which consisted in commissioning the copying and illustrating of military manuals, which have survived in great numbers and became an important source for the study of Islamic warfare. See Maya Shatzmiller, "The Crusades and Islamic Warfare—A Re-evaluation," *Der Islam* 69(1992): 247-87.

49. This observation about the two main mosques of Fez, al-Qarawīyīn and al-Andalus, was confirmed by studies on additions made to them by previous rulers, Terrasse, *Andalous*, 7-13 and *Qaraouiyin*, 61-68.
50. *Zahra*, 125-26. This was most likely money of account.
51. *Qirṭās*, 33.
52. *Zahra*, tr. 120.
53. Henri Terrasse, *La mosquée al-Qaraouiyin à Fès* (Paris, 1968), 19.
54. *Zahra*, tr. 121.
55. *Zahra*, 100.
56. *Zahra*, 123.
57. Henri Terrasse, *La mosquée des Andalous à Fès* (Paris, 1942), 11.
58. *Qirṭās*, 32. *Zahra*, 57, tr. 126, 73, tr. 157 respectively.
59. *Zahra*, 108.
60. Bel, "Inscriptions," (1917): 117-26.
61. *Qirṭās s*, 42. *Zahra*, 141-42.
62. *Zahra*, 148. Terrasse, *Qaraouiyīn*, 66.
63. Terrase, *La Grande Mosquée de Taza*, plates 2 & 3 with translation by É. Lévi-Provençal, 178.
64. Henri Basset and Évariste Lévi-Provençal, "Chella, une nécropole mérinide," *Hespéris* 2(1922): 32-33. Henri Terrase later identified the *ḥamām* al-Alou mentioned in Abū ʿInān's inscription, as one of a group of 3 Marīnid baths. The similarity in building style between the one identified and the other two made it possible for him to date them to the same time period. Henri Terrasse, "Trois bains mérinides du Maroc," *Mélanges offerts à William Marcais* (Paris, 1950): 311-20.
65. Details in "Les premiers Merinides". For the cases mentioned here, *Zahra*, 38, 59, 65, 66, 72. For uses made of *waqf* revenue of the mosque see *Zahra*, 42, 54, 55, 57, 59, 61, 65, 66, 72.
66. *Miʿyār*, 7: 266.
67. Abū 'l-Qāsim al-ʿAbdūsī, a Fezī jurist, issued a *fatwā* that dealt with the rulers' custom of borrowing money from the *waqf*'s revenue. *Miʿyār*, 7: 298-99.
68. This was the case in Muslim Spain during the period following the 11th-century collapse of the Caliphate, see Lévi-Provençal, *Histoire*, 3: 134, citing the jurist Ibn ʿAbdūn.
69. *Miʿyār*, 7: 304-310, a lengthy *fatwā* incorporating the views of several contemporary jurists from Fez about the validity of rulers' endowments from *bayt al-māl*'s revenue.
70. Brunschvig, *Berbérie*, 2: 191.
71. Brosselard, "Inscriptions," 18: 410-12.
72. Bel, "Inscriptions," (1919): 80-83.
73. Arié, *L'Espagne*, 219-20.
74. *Musnad*, 477-79, tr. 396-98. On these circumstances see Shatzmiller, "Les circonstances de la composition du Musnad d'Ibn Marzūḳ,".

75. *Zahra*, 30-31, tr. 73-74.
76. *Zahra*, 20-21, tr. 56-57. Compare with the purchase documents analyzed by Mona Zakarya, *Deux palais du Caire medieval.*
77. *Zahra*, 57, tr. 125-26. *Qirṭās*, 42. For earlier Andalusi practice, Lévi-Provençal, *Histoire de L'Espagne Musulmane*, 3:301. For Ḥafṣid areas, Brunschvig, *Berbérie*, 2: 178-93.
78. *Zahra*, 73, tr. 156-58.
79. Lévi-Provençal, *Histoire*, 3: 132-34.
80. Brunschvig, *Berbérie*, 2: 69.
81. *Zahra*, 61, tr. 132.
82. *Qirṭās*, 24.
83. Deverdun, "Deux Taḥbīs," 412-13.
84. Marie-Madeleine Viré, "Notes d'épigraphie Magribine: Trois inscriptions des XIVe et XVe siècles," *Arabica* 4(1957): 250-61.
85. Gil, *Documents*, 62.
86. See *Miʿyār*, 7: 302, a *fatwā* by ʿAbd Allāh al-ʿAbdūsī on the calculation of the *aḥbās* revenue.
87. *Zahra*, 65, tr. 141.
88. *Zahra*, 141-42, 148.
89. Bel, Inscriptions," (1918): 365, tr. 369, where the supervisor is identified as Abū 'l-Ḥusayn b. Aḥmad b. Ashqar.
90. R. Brunschvig was doubtful, however, whether the Ḥafṣīd *nāzir* was not rather a later creation, but given its early appearance under the Marīnids, one can assume that it was the case in Ifrīqiya as well. See Brunschvig, *Berbérie*, 2:67.
91. For the *waqf* supervisor in Muslim Spain, Lévi-Provençal, *Histoire*, 2: 134-35. Arié, *L'Espagne*, 285.
92. Johannes Leo, *A Geographical Historie of Africa* (London, 1600). Reprint Theatrum Orbis Terrarium (Amsterdam, 1969), 126. Compared to 10% perceived in Egypt, Gil, *Documents*, 52.
93. *Masālik*, 138: "Many of their dignitaries show extreme generosity and cover themselves with glory, by distributing food, and sheltering those who come to them looking for help, yet, their *awqāf* are few, in comparison to those of the Almohads or Almoravids before them. It is not in their doctrine to endow, nor do they recognize the value of such act. They also do not recognize the true value of charity, *zakāt*, or the building of *medresa*s." The entire section devoted to Marīnid Morocco, 137-223. This text with some variations was used by M. al-Manūnī, "Waṣf al-Maghreb fī ayyām al-sulṭān Abī 'l-Ḥasan al-Marīnī," *Waraqāt*, 292-98.
94. Ibn al-Jaṭīb (713-776), *Miʿyār al-Ijtiyār fī dhikr al-maʿāhid wa 'l-diyār*, ed. Mohammed Kemal Chabana (1977), 79.
95. Bel, "Inscriptions," (1917): 119-23.
96. Brosselard, "Inscriptions," 15: 170-71.
97. *Zahra*, 32, tr. 78.

98. *Zahra*, 39, tr. 94.
99. On these issues, Dufourcq, *L'Espagne catalane et le Maghrib*, and Thoden, Abū 'l-Ḥasan 'Ali.
100. Its institutions and municipal life, which survived intact to the 20th century, were studied by R. Le Tourneau, and the Marīnid domestic architecture by Revault, Golvin and Amahan. Le Tourneau, *Fès avant le protecorat* and R. Le Tourneau, *Fez in the Age of the Marinids*. J. Revault, L. Govin & A. Amahan, *Palais et demeures de Fès*. Catherine Cambazard-Amahan, *Le décor sur bois dans l'architecture de Fès, Époques almoravide, almohade et début mérinide* (Paris, 1989).
101. For history of Fez see *Qirṭās*, especially 4-27. *Masālik al-abṣār*, 153-60. Al-Jaznā'ī's *Zahra*, is essential for understanding the importance of *waqf khayrī* to the maintenance of the mosques in Fez. For the special place Fez occupied in Marīnid historiography, *L'historiographie mérinide*, 136-53.

Chapter 9

1. For discussion of these and the related economic aspects of the state see my *Labour in the Medieval Islamic World* (Leiden, 1994).
2. Jonathan Riley-Smith observed how the Crusaders adopted the administrative machinery inherited from the Muslims after the conquest of Jerusalem saying "The Franks, coming from an area in which jurisdiction was usually linked to the raising of revenue, found it hard to cope with a machinery of government in which finance and jurisdiction functioned separately: in Palestine they seem to have incorporated many of the financial offices into the hierarchy of their courts, either by turning local *sekretas* or *dīwāns* into tribunals or by attaching them to one their own courts." Jonathan Riley-Smith, "The Survival in Latin Palestine of Muslim Administration," in *The Eastern Mediterranean Lands in the Period of the Crusades*, ed. P. M. Holt (Warminster, 1977): 10.
3. Gladys Frantz-Murphy, *The Agrarian Administration of Egypt From the Arabs to the Ottomans* (Cairo, 1986).
4. Uninterrupted and solid coverage of the region by historical sources, has facilitated investigation by modern scholars, and can be found in the monographs devoted to single dynasties in Ifrīqiya, such as R. Brunschvig, *La Berbèrie orientale sous les Ḥafṣides* and H. R. Idris, *La Berbèrie orientale sous les Zīrīdes*. Muḥammad Talbi hardly touched on social and economic issues in his *L'Emirat Aghlabide*, but contributed to the topic in an article, "The Law and Economy in Ifrīqiya (Tunisia) in the third Islamic Century: Agriculture and the Role of Slaves in the Country's Economy," in *The Islamic Middle East, 700-1900, Studies in Economic and Social History*, ed. Avram Udovitch (Princeton, 1981): 209-51.

5. The study of rural life in general in the Maghreb, has not fared very well so far. One looks in vain for information about peasants or the agrarian system in the general histories of the Maghreb, and even those written by historians with a known interest in social and economic issues, such as Charles-André Julien, have little to say on these issues. See Julien, *Histoire*, as well as the English trans. Abdallāh Laroui criticized Julien for his interpretation of Maghrebi history, but does not provide an analysis of the land tenure structures. See Laroui, *The History of the Maghrib*. The lack of evidence is particularly severe in the case of pre-Marīnid Morocco, see for instance Vincent Lagardère, *Les Almoravides* (Paris, 1989), 207-19.
6. Frede Lokegaard, *Islamic Taxation in the Classical Period* (Copenhagen, 1950), 22.
7. Michael Morony, "Landholding in Seventh-century Iraq: Late Sasanian and Early Islamic Patterns," in *The Islamic Middle East, 700-1900: Studies in Economic and Social History,* ed. Avram Udovitch (Princeton, 1981): 136.
8. The case of the Crusaders in Syria and Palestine in the 12th century comes to mind, where a legal debate took place between the Church and the feudal lords about the acquisition of land by right of conquest. The feudal lords, nobles of the Crusaders' states in Palestine, did not see their right to the land as something invested in them by the religion, The legal interpretation they offered for refusing to yield the right over the lands they conquered to the Church, since they themselves had become jurists in the process, was that the Crusade was a "mass migration, over which there had been no true leader," a strange turn of events for an enterprise which was undertaken under the banner of Christianity, preached by the Papacy, and led by papal legates. Jonathan Riley-Smith, *The Feudal Nobility and the Kingdom of Jerusalem, 1174-1277,* (London, 1973), 136 et sq. Riley-Smith observed that the Crusaders interpreted the conquest as the event from which "all else flowed", and that ideas of conquest and the political theories built upon it were of particular relevance to them, because of repeated loss and gain of territories to the Muslims in the 13th century, 137.
9. Hamilton A. R. Gibb, "The Fiscal Rescript of ʿUmar II," *Arabica* 2(1955): 10.
10. Ibid., 3.
11. For an authentic description of the process involving the army commander and Berber soldiers settling in Sicily, see al-Dawūdiī, *Kitāb al-amwāl*, 429-30.
12. Even though his immediate concern was the settling of Ifrīqiya and Sicily, and not Morocco, *Kitāb al-amwāl*, 405-409. Using questions and answers, this text provides a good historical insight into the process of land appropriation which took place in the Maghreb as a whole, as well as to the development of the juridical discourse about it.
13. *Kitāb al-amwāl*, 408. Richard W. Bulliet, *Conversion to Islam in the Medieval Period: An Essay in Quantitative History* (Cambridge, Mass., 1979), which

studies Egypt and Tunisia, but not Morocco, identifies the peak of conversion in Tunisia by the mid-10th century.

14. For Eastern patterns of land distribution see D. Dennett, *Conversion and the Poll Tax in Early Islam* (Cambridge, 1950).
15. For the 14th century Marīnid view, see *Zahra*, 5, tr. 20-21, where the three alternatives are presented, including al-Dawūdī's version.
16. *Zahra*, 21-23.
17. Idrīs, *Berbérie*, 2:609-10.
18. With the help of several manuals of *Kitāb al-kharāj*, the "Book of land tax", written in the East in the early days of the organization of the State's domain, historians have been able to reconstruct the status of the lands, cultivation and collection of taxes for the State's treasury during the first three centuries. The published Eastern models of *Kitāb al-kharāj* include texts by Yaḥya Ibn Adām, trans. A. Ben Shemesh (Leiden, 1958), Qudāma Ibn Ja'far, trans. A. Ben Shemesh (Leiden, 1965) and Abū Yūsuf, trans. A. Ben Shemesh (Leiden, 1969). For a Western model of a *Kitāb al-kharāj*, we have to wait for the 11th century to al-Dāwudī's *Kitāb al-amwāl* written sometime before 1011. See H. H. Abdul-Wahhāb and F. Dachraoui, "Le régime foncier en Sicile au Moyen Age (IXe et Xe siècles). Edition et traduction d'un chapitre du "Kitāb al-amwāl d'al-Dāwudī," *Etudes d'Orientalisme dédiée à la mémoire de Lévi-Provençal* (Paris, 1962): 401-44.
19. B. H. Warmington, *The North African Provinces*, 62-68.
20. Ibid., 66-68. F. Decret and M. Fantar, *L'Afrique du Nord dans l'antiquité* (Paris, 1981), 132-37.
21. Talbi, "Law and Economy," 219 et sq. M. Talbi's study also showed that the status of serfs attached to the land, reflected the ancient serf-slave pattern, which had survived into the Islamic period, 209. Can we hypothesize on the basis of this information, that not only the land holding patterns but also the peasant-soldier type, who settled on the land in Ifrīqiya, was a direct continuation from the Byzantine model? Claude Cahen, who suggested such a premise for the introduction of the *iqṭā'* in the East, advised that although the probability does exist, and is very tempting, the pattern could well have developed on its own. I have argued for the long term framework for the study of labor in the Islamic world in *Labour*, Chapter 2.
22. *Qirṭās*, 129. Ibn Abī Zar' recounted: "In the year 554/1159 'Abd al-Mu'min ordered that the lands of Ifrīqiya and the Maghreb from Barqa to the land of Nūn in the extreme edge of the Ṣus, *al-aqṣa*, be divided. He subtracted one third which accounted for the mountains, rivers, scrub country, swamps, roads, and burned lands, and imposed the land tax on the rest. He gave each tribe its fair share of grain and vegetables, the first one to have done so in the Maghreb."
23. *Musnad*, 282-85, tr. 233-38. Ibn Marzūq mostly provides details on the reform

dealing with taxation, but the connection made here between conquest and reform is unequivocally stated.

24. The evidence about landholding provided by Talbi for the 8th-9th centuries and by Brunschvig for the 13th-16th centuries. Brunchvig, *Berbérie*, 2:180.
25. The growing dimensions of *waqf* land endowments in the 14th-century Marīnid Morocco have emerged through the recent work of David Powers, "The Maliki Family Endowment: Legal Norms and Social Practices," *International Journal of Middle Eastern Studies* 25(1993): 379-406. Also, Maya Shatzmiller, "Property Rights,". See as well the study of the Marīnid royal *waqf* in Chapter 8 in this volume.
26. For this category, see Yvon Linant de Bellefonds, "Un problème de sociologie juridique, les terres "communes" en pays d'Islam," *Studia Islamica* 10(1958): 111-36. The *fatwa* was written by Abū ʿAbdallāh al-Sattī, *Miʿyār*, 5:115-16. Collective cultivation of arboriculture in swamps in Brunschvig, *Berbérie*, 2: 198.
27. Ibid., 2:194. The "dead lands" of the State's land category in the East have received much attention from historians, since the chroniclers provided enough information about the effort and encouragement deployed by the State to draw more and more land into cultivation. See for instance, Morony, "Landholding in Seventh-century Iraq," and Ira M. Lapidus, "Arab Settlement and Economic Development of Iraq and Iran in the Age of the Ummayad and Early Abbāsid Caliphs," *The Islamic Middle East*, 177-208.
28. Used by Idris in his, "Contribution à l'étude de la vie économique en Occident musulman médiéval: glanes de données chifrées," *Mélanges Le Tourneau: Revue de l'Occident Musulamn et de la Méditéranée* (1972), 2:86-87.
29. See for Ifrīqiya, Brunschvig, *Berbérie*, 2: 194.
30. We are currently seeing a revival in the study of the *fatwā*s as historical source, starting from 1966, when Claude Cahen alerted scholars to the advantages offered to historians by the legal documents. He also warned against the "bad press", to which this category fell prey. Claude Cahen, "Considérations sur l'utilisation des ouvrages de droit musulman par l'historien," *Atti del III Congresso de studi Arabi & Islamici, Ravello, 1966* (Napoli, 1967): 239-47. Entry "Fatwā" EI^2 (E. Tyan) no longer reflects the scope of the research which has recently taken place based on the Malīkī *fatwā*s of the Maghreb, especially those collected in the *Miʿyār* by al-Wansharīsī. Francisco Vidal Castro, "Aḥmad al-Wansharīsī (m. 914/1508). Principales aspectos de su vida," *Al-Qantara* 12(1991): 315-52. Idem, "Las obras de Aḥmad al-Wansharīsī (m. 914/1508). Inventario analítico," *Anaquel de Estudios Arabes* 3(1992): 73-112. Idem, "Economia y sociedad en al-Andalus y el-Maghreb a traves del Miʿyār de al-Wansharīsī. Breve introduction a su contenido," *Actas del II coloquio Hispano-Marroqui de ciencias historicas* (Madrid, 1992): 339-56. Vincent Lagardère, "Moulins d'Occident musulman au moyen age (IXe au XVe siè-

cles): al-Andalus," *Al-Qantara* 12(1991): 59-118. Idem, *Histoire et société en Occident Musulman au moyen âge: Analyse du Miʿyār d'al-Wansharīsī*, Collection de la casa de Velázquez, 35 (Madrid, 1995).

31. There is always a danger of mistaking the State's domain for that of the private ownership of rulers and we know that Marīnid rulers owned parts or entire villages, as demonstrated by the endowment made by Abū 'l-Ḥasan of 7/8 of a village, and two parts which were owned by his mother, towards the establishment and maintenance of a *medresa* in Fez in the 14th century. See infra Chapter 9.
32. Ibid., 5: 97.
33. Consulted about the status of another category of land, *qānūn* land, and asked whether or not the person who cultivated it could also sell and bequeath it, he responded that in the Maghreb it was the custom that *qānūn* land could be sold and inherited, and it was obvious from its condition that it was under private ownership, *mamlūka*. Brunschvig thought that in spite of a jurists' indication that most of the lands in the villages of Ḥafṣid Ifrīqiya were not in private hands, private owning of land was very much in use, created and perpetuated not only by the inheritance law, but also by certain transformations, *Berbérie*, 2: 180 et sq.
34. *Miʿyār*, 5: 98-99. It is not easy to establish the chronology of this *fatwā* since at least 4 muftis by that name were active in Tlemcen during the 15th century: Al-ʿUqbānī, 811/1408, Al-ʿUqbānī, Qāsim ibn Saʿīd, d. Tlemcen 854/1450, Al-ʿUqbānī, Muḥammad b. Aḥmad, d. Tlemcen 871/1467, Al-ʿUqbānī, Abū Sālim Ibrāhīm, d. Tlemcen, 880/1475/76.
35. The fate of a *jazā'* land which fell into private hands is discussed in a *fatwā* written in Marīnid Fez. *Miʿyār*, 5: 43-44.A village, *qarya*, which the sultan had given to a man in return for another *qarya* in another region, *biarḍa ukhrā*. In the *qarya* which the sultan gave there was land, *arḍ*, on which no one claimed ownership, *lam yataqaddam ʿalayha mulk liaḥadden*, but which belonged to the *makhzen*, since it was, *mundhu kānat*, in the condition which prevailed outside it, (presumably around it and presumably uncultivated). The man took the land and sold it as owners regularly did with their property. The buyer built on it and planted it with trees, and ownership passed from one generation to another. Then after 4 generations, the sultan removed it from the one who held it and gave it to an agent who rented it out and declared that whoever cultivated a garden, build a house or a store on this land, should share the profits with the *makhzen*. The writer indicated that each of the buyers confirmed that they had bought and planted the land in the assumption that the seller was the owner, and therefore that they were getting full ownership of the land and what they built and planted on it. Was it their right to withdraw the price they paid? Or, was it a disaster, *maṣībatan*, which hit them? If the *makhzen* is entitled to the land, what about the money paid by each of the candidates? The jurist Abū

'l-Ḥasan ʿAlī al-Ṣaghīr al-Zarwīlī, in his response, delivered in Fez sometime before 719/1319 said: "The nature of the contract signed by the person who was given the land, a *muʿawaḍāt*, should have alerted everyone that the land in question never ceased to belong to the *makhzen*, and if the sultan brings this contract to an end, no one should expose the buyers to suffer the consequences. If and when he gave the land back, they should recover their payments. Those who built on it or planted it retain possession of the income from their investment because they were ignorant of the nature of the transaction into which they entered. The contract cannot be invalidated except by the sultan or his representative but they cannot share, either, whether small or large, in the proceeds."

36. "ḍarība," *EI2* (J. F. Hopkins).
37. "Kānuūn," *EI2* (Cl. Cahen).
38. Talbi, "Law and Economy," 210.
39. Such is the opinion of Brunschvig, *Berbérie*, 303.
40. Évariste Lévi-Provençal, "Le traité d'Adab al-kātib d'Abu Bakr Ibn Khaldūn," *Arabica* 2(1955): 30-41. Brunschvig, *Berbérie,* 2:195 and note 3.
41. See the recent work by Lagardère and Vidal Castro, mentioned above. Idrīs provided a detailed amounts of crops in relationship to irrigation quotas in the Zīrīd Maghreb, according to two *fatwā*s by al-Suyūrī, d. 460/1067. Idrīs, *Berbérie*, 2:623. For conditions under the Ḥafṣids, Brunschvig, *Berbérie,* 2: 198.
42. In another *fatwā*, the existence of a *munāṣafa* arrangement, the 50/50 division was attested to have been contracted between the State and the cultivators. See Idrīs, *Berbérie*, 605.
43. Brunschvig, *Berbérie e*, 184.
44. Egypt is most known for its elaborate land register, the *qānūn al-zirāʿa*, which was in constant use from ancient times to the modern period. Before the harvest the land was visited by the State's agents who revisited it later and noted the anticipated crop. A similar register was established for the fruit trees, the expected amounts of fruit inspected and written down, as individual peasants were informed by the government agent of their share of taxes. See G. Frantz-Murphy, *The Agrarian system*, and Richard Cooper, *Ibn Mammatī's Rules for the Ministries*, Translation with Commentary of the "Qawānīn al-dawāwīn". Ph.D. Diss. (Berkeley, 1973), unpublished.
45. Cahen, "L'évolution," 239.
46. Aḥmad b. Muḥammad al-Maqqarī, *Nafḥ al-tībb*, ed. Ihsan Abbas (Beirut, 1968), 6: 6. *L'historiographie mérinide*, 76 et sq.
47. *Masālik el-absār*, 205-16.
48. Ibid., 206.
49. Ibid., 215-16.
50. The basic study of the Islamic *iqṭāʿ* remains that by Claude Cahen,

"L'évolution de l'iqṭā' du IXe au XIIIe siècle. Pour une histoire comparée des sociétés médiévales," *Annales E.S.C.* (1953): 25-52. See also H. Ben Abdallāh, *De l'Iqta étatique à l'Iqta militaire* (Upsala, 1986).

51. Charles-Emanuel Dufourcq, *L'Espagane Catalane et le Maghreb aux 13e et 14e siècles* (Paris, 1966), 160-61. Dufourcq noted that in the dealings of Aragon with the Maghreb the money of account was the silver besant, but gold dinars were most regularly used, see p. 170.
52. On several instances especially during the last quarter of the 13th century, see Dufourcq, *L'Espagne Catalane*, 208 et sq.
53. Ibid., 216, 383.
54. Ibid., 215-16.
55. Al-Manūnī translated the relevant passage from another ms. but this version is no different from the one used by M. Godefroy Demombynes. M. al-Manūnī, "Waṣf al-maghreb ayām al-sulṭān Abū 'l-Ḥasan al-marīnī," *Waraqāt 'an al-ḥadāra al-maghribiya* (Rabat, 1979): 291-92, 305-6. *Masālik al-abṣār*, 146-47.
56. Ibid., 359.
57. *Histoire des Berbères*, 3:52-53. Ibn Baṭūṭa, *Tuḥfat al-nuẓẓār*, 4:350-51. Ibn Baṭūṭa, reports that Abū 'Inān commented on that occasion, "Thank God for having delivered the city to us from the hands of the enemy for such a trifle."
58. There is no room here to enter into the details and implications of the Maghrebi gold exports to Europe. See Dufourcq, *L'Espagne Catalane*, 133-37, and idem, "La question de Ceuta au XIIIe siècle," *Hespéris* (1955): 67-124. On the cardinal importance of the occupation of Ceuta and al-Manṣūra for the Marīnids see Dufourcq, *L'Espagane Catalane*, 351-75.
59. See Shatzmiller, *Labour*, 178-92, on exploitation of natural resources and State's participation.
60. Robert Henri Bautier disagreed with Lopez's interpretation of the role played by the African gold in the relations between Ceuta and Genoa. See Robert Henri Bautier, "Les relations commerciales entre l'Europe et l'Afrique du Nord et l'Equilibre Économique Méditerranéen," *Bulletin Philologique et Historique* (1952-54): 399-416.
61. *Musnad*, 283-86, tr. 233-38.
62. The term *kharāj* would most commonly apply in all Eastern regions to tax on agricultural land, to distinguish it from the tax on grazing land, *marā'ī*. On variations in the usage of the term *kharāj*, see Cahen, "Impots," 267. On the *kharāj* in Egypt see Rabie, *The Financial*, 79.
63. *Musnad*, 284, tr. 235.
64. Brunschvig deliberated over the meaning of the term *qānūn* which he found quoted by the Ḥafṣid historian al-Tijānī, and concluded that it alluded to actual taxes and not to the principle, as assumed by the translator of the text M. De Slane. Brunschvig, *Berbérie*, 2: 195, note 3.

65. *Musnad*, 285, tr. 236.
66. Ibn Baṭūṭa, *Tuḥfat al-nuṭṭār,* 4:348.
67. See Roger Le Tourneau, *Fez in the Age of the Marīnids* (Norman, 1961),
68. *Qirṭās*, 26. *Zahra*, 33-34, translated in R. S. Lopez and I. W. Raymond, *Medieval Trade in the Mediterranean World* (N. Y., 1955), 74-75.
69. *Musnad*, 283, tr. 234.
70. Rabie, *The Financial*, 80-105, 82-86.
71. Brunschvig, *Berbérie*, 2: 240, 10.000, 5000, 500, 1500, 300 dinars respectively.
72. Ibn ʿArafa, a contemporary of Ibn Khaldūn and a great jurist himself, seemingly designated all such monopolies as *maks*, non-Qur'ānic tax. Brunschvig, *Berbérie*, 2:238.
73. On the legal aspect of property ownership in Fez, see Chapter 8.
74. Al-Bakrī provides detailed information about the organisation and collection of taxes on trade, agricultural products and manufacturing in the 10th-11th centuries Ifrīqiya. Abou Obeïd el-Bekrī, *Description de l'Afrique Septentrionale*, ed. and trans. M. Baron De Slane (Paris, 1913) Reprint 1965, 58, on merchandise, 65, on animals, 78, on entry dues, 102, on the city of Gafṣa's taxes, 103, taxes on water, 104, taxes of the region of Qashtiliya. Also, Idris, *Berbérie*, 2: 641.
75. Egypt, where monopolies covered many items sold and bought within its borders, had long-standing experience with them which was documented before and throughout the Faṭimid and Mamlūk periods. It began with the monopoly over the manufacture of papyrus, "as it was in pre-Islamic Egypt", Geoffrey Khan, "Arabic Papyri," in *The Codicology of Islamic Manuscripts*, ed. Yasin Dutton (London, 1995): 14. Dr. Khan explained that the "the function of the protocol texts was to certify that a roll was produced by the state papyrus mill and so protect the monopoly." The practice continued with the *matjar*, the State's agency, selling and buying vital products such as metals, wood and food items from Europe, and culminated with the monopoly of the chicken industry, forcing the breeders to buy their chicks only from the State's incubators. Hassanein Rabie, *The Financial System of Egypt* A. H. 564-741/ A. H. 1169-1341 (Oxford, 1972), 117.
76. Eliyahu Ashtor, "Levantine Sugar Industry in the Late Middle Ages: A Case of Technological Decline," in *The Islamic Middle East 700-1900: Studies in Economic and Social History*, ed. Avram Udovitch, (Princeton, 1981): 91-133.
77. Wine arrived in jars in Tunis and Bijāya, but its sale was taken away from the Christian funduqs, when it was monopolised by the Tunisian revenue office according to a treaty signed in Barcelona on May 1st, 1323. Dufourcq, *L'Espagne Catalane*, 549.
78. The geographer al-Idrīsī wrote that under the Murābiṭūn the residents of Marrakesh ate locust, 30 loads of which came to the city and were sold every-

day; it was subject to the *qabāla* tax, as were other fabricated and imported items such as soap, perfume, copper. When the Maṣmūda, namely the Muwaḥḥidūn, conquered the land, they abolished these taxes on trade and threatened any governor who claimed them with death. "So far, in our time, no one has mentionned the *qabāla* tax in the provinces under their rule," said the author. Edrisi, tr. 80, quoted in Largardère, *Les Almoravides*, 215.

79. See Chapter 5.
80. At the end of the 13th century and the beginning of the 14th a *qafīz* of wheat was bought for 3 dinars from the Marīnid *makhzen*, while the merchants paid double this price in Tunis in addition to few dirhems tax. Dufourcq, *L'Espagne Catalane*, 551. Brunschvig, *Berbérie*, 2: 238-40.
81. Two documents quoted by Dufourcq, *L'Espagne Catalane*, 166, note 1. On the grain trade between Catalunia and Marīnid Morocco, 359, 551.
82. Ibn Ḥawqal, *Kitāb ṣūrat al-arḍ,* 95.
83. Ibid., 239.

Chapter 10

1. Ibn Khaldun, *Kitāb al-ʿIbar*, tr. Le Baron De Slane under the title *Histoire de Berbères*, (Paris, Geuthner, 1978) 4 vols. On this episode, see vol. 4: 259-68.
2. *Histoire*, 4:219-24.
3. See the description of the court workings while residing in newly constructed administrative capital of al-Mansūra near Tlemcen, supra 69-82. Entry "al-Mansūra" EI^2 (M. Shatzmiller)
4. On the Black Death see below.
5. Human ecology may suggest a reason: the nomads traveling on camels or driving their herds ahead of them, do not hoard grain and do not regularly transport stocks of stored grains in significant amounts and therefore do not expose themselves to black rats or house rats, to the same degree as town dwellers. See Ole J. Benedictow, *The Black Death 1346-1353. The Complete History* (Woodbridge, Boydell Press, 2004), 67.
6. On Morocco and the Atlantic Ocean in historical perspective, see Christophe Picard, *L'Océan atlantique musulman: de la conquête arabe à l'époque almohade*, (Paris, Maisonneuve & Larose, 1997) and Ch. Picard, *La mer et les Musulmans d'Occident at Moyen-Âge VIIIe-XIIIe siècle* (Paris, 1997)
7. Pedro Chalmeta, "al-Murabitun" EI^2
8. Maya Shatzmiller, "al-Muwahhidun" EI^2
9. *Histoire*, 4:224.
10. On this episode see J. A. Robson, "The Catalan Fleet and Moorish Sea-Power (1337-1344)" *The English Historical Review*, 74(1959): 386-408.
11. On Abū Inān and his attempts to re-conquer the lost territories, *Histoire*, 4:292-317.

12. On the Black Death in Egypt, Michael W. Dols, *The Black Death in the Middle East*, (Princeton, Princeton University press, 1977) and Stuart J. Borsch, *The Black Death in Egypt and England. A Comparative Study*, (Austin, University of Texas Press, 2005)
13. Benedictow, *The Black Death1346-1353*, 383.
14. Benedictow, *The Black Death 1346-1353, 383*. "...presumably this was also the case where plague appeared elsewhere according to the same pattern, for instance in North Africa, the Middle East and the Near East for which there are no usable mortality data". While true for North Africa, we now have good grasp of the plague in Egypt thanks to the studies of M. Dols and S. Borsch.
15. General considerations in Maya Shatzmiller, *Labour in the Medieval Islamic World*, (Leiden, E. J. Brill, 1994), 55-68.
16. M. Talbi, "Effondrement démographique au Maghreb du XIe au XVe siècle," *Les cahiers de Tunisie* 7(1977):51-60.
17. Al-ᶜOmarī, *Masālik el Absār*, 126-28.
18. *Histoire,* 4:234.
19. Charles Issawi, "The Area and Population of the Arab Empire: An Essay in Speculation," *The Islamic Middle East 700-1900. Studies in Economic and Social History*, A. L. Udovitch, ed. (Princeton, Darwin Press, 1981): 375-96.
20. Ralph Austen, *African Economic History. Internal Development and External Dependency,* (James Curry, London, 1987), and John Wright, *The Trans-Saharan Slave Trade*, (Routledge, London and New York, 2007)
21. See the conclusions reached by B. Musallam about the prevalence of birth control in medieval Islamic societies. B. Musallam, *Sex and Society in Islam*, (Cambridge, Cambridge University Press, 1983)
22. Andrew Ehrenkreutz, "Strategic Implications of the Slave Trade between Genoa and Mamluk Egypt in the Second half of the Thirteenth Century," *The Islamic Middle East 700-1900. Studies in Economic and Social History*, A. L. Udovitch, ed. (Princeton, Darwin Press, 1981): 335-45.
23. Austen, *African*, 59. The evidence may be found in R. Austen, "The Trans-Saharan Slave Trade: A Tentative Census," in H. Gemery and J. Hogendorn, (eds.) *The Uncommon Market. Essays in the Economic History of the Atlantic Slave Trade*, (San Francisco, Academic Press, 1979): 23-72.
24. Different estimates of the number of slaves shipped from the West Africa are recently offered but the numbers suggested by Austen remain valid. See discussion in Austen, "The Trans-Saharan", Ibid.
25. Elizabeth Savage*, A Gateway to Hell, a Gateway to Paradise,* (Princeton, The Darwin Press, 1997), 67-89.
26. Austen's table of Islamic armies using units of black slaves. Austen, "The Trans-Saharan," Table 2.6, p. 54-55.
27. Austen, "The Trans-Saharan", 57.
28. Austen, "The Trans-Saharan," 43.

29. Andrew M. Watson, "Back to Gold-and Silver," *The Economic History Review*, New Series, vol. 20, No. 1(Apr. 1967): 1-47. Maya Shatzmiller, "Islam and Europe: *Revisiting old theories in light of Prices." Prezzi delle cose nell'età preindustriale • The Prices of Things in Pre-industrial Times : selezione di ricerche = Selection of essays*. (Firenze: Firenze University Press, 2017). (Atti delle "Settimane di Studi" e altri Convegni, 48), pp. 387-391
30. Sture Bolin, "Mohammed, Charlemagne and Ruric," *The Scandinavian Economic History Review*, Vol. I/1(1953): 5-39, for a general introduction.
31. See A. Ehrenkreutz, "Money" in *Handbuch der Orientalistik,* (E. J. Brill, Leiden, 1977), 84-97.
32. Much of the literature dealing with the subject is concerned with this question. Michael Brett, "Ifriqiya as a market for Saharan trade from the tenth to the twelfth century A.D." *Journal of African History* 3(1960): 347-364.
33. Peter Spufford, *Money and its Use in Medieval Europe*, (Cambridge, Cambridge University Press, 1988), 7-26.
34. Pierre Bonassie, *From Slavery to Feudalism in South-Western Europe*, J. Birrell tr. (Cambridge, Cambridge University Press,1991), 183. Spufford, *Money*, 167.
35. According to Thomas Walker "It was not until well into the 14th century that a regular gold coinage began." Th. Walker, "The Italian Gold Revolution of 1252: Shifting Currents in the Pan-Mediterranean Flow of Gold," *Precious Metals in the Later Medieval and Early Modern World*, J. F. Richards, (ed.), (Durham, Carolina Academic Press, 1983): 45.
36. Bonnassie, *From Slavery*, 183.
37. Robert D. Leonard, "The effects of the Fourth Crusade on European Gold Coinage", in *The Fourth Crusade: Event, Aftermath, and Perceptions*, Th. Madden (ed.), (Ashgate, 2008): 84-84. R. Lopez's paper, "Back to gold," in the *Economic History Review*, 2nd series IX (1956): 219-240, is replete with factual errors in the part related to Islam.
38. Spufford, *Money*, 169.
39. Lopez, "Back to Gold,".
40. Spufford, *Money*, 177-78.
41. Spufford, *Money,* 180-186.
42. For the *millares* see Spufford, *Money*, 171-76.
43. Spufford, *Money,* 179.
44. See for example the monetary crisis in Egypt, Jere L. Bacharach, "Monetary Movements in Medieval Egypt, 1171-1517, in *Precious Metals*, 159-182.
45. Abū 'l-Hasan Alī b. Yūsuf al-Hakīm, *al- Dawha al-mushtabikka fī dawābit dār al-sikka*, ed. Husein Munis (Madrid, 1960)
46. Walker, "The Italian, 36. Shatzmiller entry "al-Muwahhidūn" *EI*².
47. See the discussion by Walker, "The Italian".
48. Spafford, *Money*, 163-186.

49. Spufford, *Money*, 180.
50. Walker, "The Italian, 31.
51. Ian Blanchard, "African Gold and European Specie Markets ca. 1300-1800" *Relazioni economiche tra Europa e mondo islamico. Secc. XIII-XVIII*, a cura di S. Cavaciocchi, (Firenze, Le Monnier / Istituto Internazionale di Storia Economica "F. Datini", Atti delle Settimane di Studi e altri convegni, 38. 2007) : 451-84.
52. See María Dolores López Pérez, *La corona de Aragón y el Maghreb en el siglo XIV*, (Consejo superior de investigaciones científicas, 1995). G. Jehel, *L'Italie et le Maghren au Moyen Age. Conflits et échanges du VIIe au XVe siècle,* (Paris, PUF, 2001)
53. On navigation and trade see Jehel, *L'Italie*, 143-156, 157-69. The two fundamental studies of the Catalan trade with Marīnid Morocco, are Ch.-E. Dufourcq, *L'Espagne catalane et le Maghreb aux 13 et 14 siècles*, (Paris, 1966), and M. D. López Pérez, *La corona de Aragón.*
54. Bruges imported low quality sugar from Morocco in the 13th century. Mohamed Ouerfelli, *Le sucre. Production, commercialization et usages dans la Méditerranée medievale*, (Brill, Leiden, 2008), 399.
55. J. H. Elliott, *Empires of the Atlantic. Britain and Spain in America 1492-1830,* (Yale University Press, 2006)
56. See the interesting case of the Golden Horde, D. De Weese, *Islamization and Native religion in the Golden Horde*, (University Park, 1994)
57. The economic history of the Merino wool is studied by Carla Rahn Phillips and W. D. Phillips, *Spain's Golden Fleece: Wool Production and the Wool Trade from the Middle Ages to the nineteenth Century*, (Baltimore, John Hopkins University Press, 1997)
58. Robert S. Lopez, "The Origin of the Merino Sheep", *The Joshua Starr Memorial Volume, Jewish Social Studies*, 5, (New York, 1953): 161. On the wool industry see John Munro, "Medieval Woolens: Textiles, Textile Tech-nology and Industrial Organisation, c. 800-1500," *The Cambridge History of Western Textiles*, ed. David Jenkins, (Cambridge, 2003), I: 181-386.
59. Lopez, "The Origin," 161.
60. G. Jehel reports an import of Maghribi sheep and goats to Sicily by Charles d'Anjou but does not think that these have any common traits with the Merino sheep. Regardless, this is additional indication about the existence of the practice. Jehel, *L'Italie*, 163, and note 40, p. 207.
61. Jehel, *L'Italie*, 164.
62. D. Acemoglu, S. Johnson, J. Robinson, "The Rise of Europe: Atlantic Trade, Institutional Change and Economic Growth, *The American Economic Review,* (June 2005): 546-79. Earlier explorations include papers in *The Political Economy of Merchant Empires*, J. D. Tracy ed. (Cambridge University Press, Cambridge, 1991)

63. See Douglass C. North, "Institutions, transactions costs, and the rise of merchant empires," in *The Political Economy,* 22-40.
64. D. Acemoglu, S. Johnson, J. Robinson, "The Rise of Europe: Atlantic Trade, Institutional Change and Economic Growth,"
65. Timur Kuran, "The Islamic Commercial Crisis: Institutional Roots of Economic Underdevelopment in the Middle East," *The Journal of Economic History*, 63(2003): 414-446. Idem., *The Long Divergence. How Islamic Law Held Back the Middle East.* (Princeton, Princeton University Press, 2011).
66. Maya Shatzmiller, *"Recent Trends in Middle East Economic History: Cultural Factors and Structural Change in The Medieval Period 650-1500," History Compass online. 2018e12504, 1251. DOI: 10.1111/hic3.12504 and DOI: 10. 1111/hic3.12511.*

Conclusion

1. This subject was examined in the literary and historiography of the modern Maghreb in a recent Princeton Ph.D. dissertation. Abdelmajid Hannoum, *The Legend of the Kahina: A Study in Historiography and Mythmaking in North Africa*, Dissertation presented to the Department of Near Eastern Studies (Princeton University, 1995), 134-36. On the *Kahina* see Charles-André Julien, *History of North Africa*, trans. John Petrie (London, 1970), 11-13. Abdāllah Laroui, *The History of the Maghrib*, trans. Ralph Manheim (Princeton, 1977), 82.
2. The writings of Tawfīq al-Madanī, (1899-1983), are one example of this interpretation. Hannoum, *The Legend of the Kahina*, 134-36, 145 et sq.

Bibliography

al-ʿAbbādī, A. M. *Dirāsāt f ī ta'rīkh al-Maghrib wa'l-Andalus*. Alexandria, 1967.

Abdul-Wahhāb, H. H. and F. Dachraoui. "Le régime foncier en Sicile au Moyen Age (IXe et Xe siècles). Édition et traduction d'un chapitre du "*Kitāb al-amwāl* d'al-Dāwudī." *Etudes d'Orientalisme dédiées à la mémoire de Lévi-Provençal*. (Paris, 1962): 401-45.

Abun-Nasr, J. M. *A History of the Maghrib*. 2nd ed. (Cambridge, 1975).

Abitbol, M. *Temoins et Acteurs: Les Corcos et L'histoire du Maroc*. Jerusalem, 1977.

Amīn, M. *Catalogue des documents d'archives du Caire de 239/853 a 922/1516*. Institut Français d'Archéologie Orientale du Caire. Textes Arabes et Études Islamiques 16. Cairo, 1981.

______. *The Waqf and Social Life in Egypt 648-923 A.H./1250-1517 A.D*.

Amrouche, F. A. M. *My Life Story: The Autobiography of a Berber Woman*. D. S. Blair trans. with an introduction. London, 1988.

Arié, R. *L'Espagne musulmane au temps des Naṣrides, 1232-1492*. Paris, 1973.

Ashtor, E. *A History of the Jews in Egypt and Syria under the rule of the Mamlūks*. Jerusalem, 1944-1970. 3 vol.

______. *Korot ha-yehudim bi sefarad ha-muslemit*. Jerusalem, 1960. 2 vol.

______. "Levantine Sugar Industry in the Late Middle Ages: A Case of Technological Decline." In *The Islamic Middle East 700-1900: Studies in Economic and Social History*, A. L. Udovitch ed. (Princeton,1981): 91-133.

Asin Palacios, M. "Un tratado morisco de polémica contre los judios." *Mélanges Hartwig Derenbourg* (Paris, 1909): 343-66.

Ávila, M. L. "Cargos hereditarios en la administración judicial y religiosa de al-Andalus." In *Saber Religioso y Poder Politico en el Islam*. (Madrid, 1994): 27-39.

Baer, I. F. *A History of the Jews in Christian Spain*. Tel Aviv, 1959.

Banani, A. and S. Vryonis eds. *Individualism and Conformity in Islam: 5th G. Levi de la Vida Biennial Conference*. Wiesbaden, 1977.

Bar Sheshet (Ribash), I. *Responsa*. Constantinople, 1547.

Basset, H. and É. Lévi-Provençal. "Chella, une nécropole mérinide." *Hespéris* 2 (1922): 1-92, 255-316.

Basset, R. "Les généalogistes berbères." *Archives Berbères* 1 (1915): 3-11.

Bautier, R.-H. "Les relations commerciales entre l'Europe et l'Afrique du Nord et l'équilibre économique Méditerranéen." *Bulletin Philologique et Historique* (1953-54): 399-416.

Beck, H. L. *L'image d'Idrīs II, ses descendants de Fās et la politique sharīfienne des sultans Marīnides (656-869/1258-1465)*. Leiden, 1989.

el-Bekri, Abou Obeïd. *Description de l'Afrique septentrionale*. W. M. Baron De Slane ed. and trans. Paris, 1965.

Bel, A. "Inscriptions arabes de Fès." *Journal Asiatique* (Mars-Avril, 1917): 303-29; (Juillet-Aout): 81-170; (Septembre-Octobre): 215-67; (Juillet-Aout, 1918): 189-276; (Novembre-Décembre): 237-399; (Janvier-Février, 1919): 5-87.

______. "Les premiers émirs mérinides et l'islam." *Mélanges de géographie et d'orientalisme offerts à E. F. Gautier.* (Tours, 1937): 34-44.

______. *La religion musulmane en Berbérie*. Paris, 1938.

Ben Abdallah, H. *De l'iqta étatique à l'iqta militaire*: *Transition économique et changements sociaux à Baghdad, 247-447 de l'Hégire/861-1055 ap. J.* Upsala, 1986.

Bénabou, M. *La résistance africaine à la romanisation*. Paris, 1976.

Benayahu, M., ed. *Divre ha-yamim shel Fas: History of Fez, Misfortunes and Events of Moroccan Jewry as Recorded by Ibn Danan's Family and Descendants*. Tel Aviv, 1993.

Ben Cheneb, M. "Étude sur les personnages mentionnés dans l'idjāza du cheikh 'Abd el-Qader el Fāsy." In *Actes du XIVe Congrès International des Orientalistes, Alger 1905*. (Paris,1908), 3: 512-15.

Ben-Sasson, M. "The Jewish Community of Gabes in the 11th Century, Economic and Residential Patterns." In *Communautés Juives des Marges Sahariennes du Maghreb*, M. Abitbol ed. (Jerusalem, 1982): 265-84.

Benchekroun, M. *La vie intellectuelle marocaine sous les Mérinides et les Wattāsides (XIIIe, XIVe, XVe, XVIe, siècles)*. Rabat, 1974.

Bencherifa, M. "Problems of Attribution in Historical and Geographical Works." In *The Codicology of Islamic Manuscripts,* Y. Dutton ed. (London, 1995): 103-21.

Bennison, A. *The Almoravid and Almohad Empires. Edinburgh, Edinburgh University Press, 2016.*

Blachère, R. "Quelqeus détails sur la vie privée du sultan mérinide Abū 'l-Ḥasan. In *Mémorial H. Basset: Nouvelles études nord-africaines et Orientales publiées par l'Institut des Hautes Études Marocaines* 17 (1928): 83-89.

Bonte, P. et al., eds. *La quête des origines. Anthropologie historique de la société tribale arabe*. Paris, 1991.

Bosch Vilà, J. "Pour une étude historico-sociologique sur les berbèrs d'Al-Andalus." In *Mélanges d'Islamologie dédiés à la mémoire de A. Abel* (Bruxelles, 1974), 2: 53-69.

______. "La ciencia de los linajes y los genealogistas en la Espana musulmana." *Miscelánea de Estudios dedicados al Profesor Antonio Marín Ocete*. (Granada, 1974): 63-77.

______. "A proposito de la berberizacion de Al-Andalus." *Les Cahiers de Tunisie* 26 (1978): 129-41.

Bouvat, L. "Notice bio-bibliographique sur Athīr ad-Dīn Moḥammad ibn Yousouf Aboû Ḥayyān al-Gharnati." *Revue Hispanique* 10 (1903): 5-18.

Bresc, H and Rāgib, Y.*Le Sultan mérinide Abū l-Hasan ʿAlì et Jacque III de Majorque: Du Traité de paix au pacte secret*. Cairo, Institut français d'archéologie orinetale, 2011.

Brett, M. "Ibn Khaldūn and the Dynastic Approach to Local History: The Case of Biskra." *Al-Qantara* 12 (1991): 157-80.

______. "Problems in the Interpretation of the History of the Maghrib in the Light of Some Recent Publications." *Journal of African History* 13 (1972): 489-506.

Brett, M. and E. Fentress. *The Berbers*. Oxford, 1996.

Brosselard, C. "Inscriptions Arabes de Tlemcen." *Revue Africain* 3 (Alger, 1858-1859); (Kraus Reprint, 1968): 14 (81-94), 15 (161-72), 16 (241-48), 17 (321-40), 18 (401-19), 4, (Alger, 1859-1860), 19 (1-17), 20 (81-93), 21 (161-74), 22 (241-58), 23 (321-31).

Brown, P. "Religious Dissent in the Later Roman Empire: The Case of North Africa." *History* 36 (1961): 83-101. Reprinted in *Religion and Society in the Age of Saint-Augustine*. (London, 1972): 237-99.

Brunschvig, R. "Quelques remarques historiques sur les médersas de Tunisie." *Revue Tunisienne* (1931): 261-85.

______. "Un aspect de la littérature historico-géographique de l'Islam." *Mélanges Gaudefroy-Demombynes* (Cairo, 1935-45): 147-58.

______. *La Berbèrie orientale sous les Ḥafṣides des origines à la fin du XVe siècle*. Paris, 1940-47, 2 vol.

Bulliet R. W. *Conversion to Islam in the Medieval Period: An Essay in Quantitative History*. Cambridge, Mass., 1979.

Cahen Cl. "L'évolution de l'iqtāʿ du IXe au XIIIe siècle. Pour une histoire comparée des sociétés médiévales." *Annales E.S.C.* (1953): 25-52.

______. "Douanes et commerce dans les ports méditeranéens de l'Egypte médiévale d'après le minhāj d'al-Makhzūmī." *Journal of the Economic and Social History of the Orient* 7 (1964): 217-314.

______. "Considérations sur l'utilisation des ouvrages de droit musulman par l'historien." *Atti del III Congresso de studi Arabi & Islamici, Ravello, 1966* (Napoli, 1967): 239-47.

______. "L'historiographie Arabe: des origines au VIIe.s. H." *Arabica* 33 (1986): 133-98.

Canard, M. "Les relations entre les Mérinides et les Mamelouks au XIVe siècle," *Annales de l'Institut des Etudes Orientales* 5(1939-41): 41-81.

Cooper, R. *Ibn Mammatī's Rules for the Ministries*. Translation with Commentary of the "Qawānīn al-dawāwīn". Ph.D. Diss. Berkeley, 1973. unpublished.

Corcos, D. "The Jews of Morocco under the Marīnids." *Jewish Quarterly Review* 54 (1964-5): 271-287, 55: 55-81, 137-50. Reprinted in *Studies in the History of the Jews of Morocco* (Jerusalem, 1976): 1-62.

______. "The attitude of the Almohads towards the Jews." *Zion* 32 (1967): 137-60. Reprinted in *Studies in the History of the Jews of Morocco* (Jerusalem, 1976): 319-42.

Cour, A. *L'établissement des dynasties des Cherifs au Maroc*. Paris, 1904.

______. "Les derniers Mérinids." *Bulletin de la Societé de Géographie d'Alger* 10 (1905): 103-19.

Crapanzo, V. *The Ḥamadsha: A Study in Moroccan Ethnopsychiatry*. Berkeley and los Angeles, 1973.

Decret, F. and M. Fantar. *L'Afrique du Nord dans l'antiquité*. Paris, 1981.

Dennett, D. *Conversion and the Poll Tax in Early Islam*. Cambridge, Mass., 1950.

Deverdun, G. *Inscriptions arabes de Marrakech*. Rabat, 1956.

Deverdun, G. and M. ben Abdeslem. "Deux taḥbīs almohades (milieu du XIIIe siècle J.-C)." *Hespéris* 41 (1954): 411-23.

Al-Dhakhīra al-Saniyya (le trésor magnifique): Chronique anonyme des Mérinides. M. ben Cheneb, ed. Alger, 1921.

Dinur, B. *Dorot u-reshumot*. Jerusalem, 1978.

Dufourcq, Ch.-E. *L'Espagne catalane et le Maghrib aux 13 et 14 siècles*. Paris, 1966.

Eche, Y. *Les bibliothèques Arabes publiques et semi-publiques en Mésopotamie, en Syrie et en Egypte au Moyen Age*. Damascus, 1967.

Ennahid, A and Maghraoui, D (eds). *Fez in World History*. Al-Akhawayn University, Ifrane. 2011.

Epstein, I. *The Responsa of Rabbi Simon b. Zemah Duran as a Source of the History of the Jews in North Africa*. London, 1939.

Eustache, D. *Corpus des dirhams idrisites et contemporains*. Rabat, 1970-71.

Fagnan, E. "Arabo-Judaica." *Mélanges Hartwig Derenburg*. (Paris, 1909): 103-20.

______. trans. *Extraits inédits relatifs au Maghreb*. Alger, 1924.

Farhat, H. "Le Pouvoir des fuqahā' dans la cité: Sabta du XIIe au XIVe siècle." In *Saber Religioso y Poder Politico en el Islam*. (Madrid, 1994): 53-71.

Al-Fāsī, M. *Fihris makhṭūṭāt khizānat al-Qarawīyīn*. Casablanca, 1983.

de Felipe, H. "Berbers in the Maghreb and al-Andalus: Settlements and Toponymy." *The Maghreb Review* 18 (1993): 57-62.

Fierro, M. "The qādī as ruler." In *Saber Religioso y Poder Polītico en el Islam*. (Madrid, 1994): 71-117.

Frantz-Murphy, G. *The Agrarian Administration of Egypt From the Arabs to the Ottomans*. Supplément aux annales islamologiques, 9. Cairo, 1986.

Frend, W. H. C. "The Revival of Berber Art." *Antiquity* (1942): 342-52.

Fromherz, A. *Ibn Khaldun: Life and Times*. Edinburgh University Press, 2011, second edition 2012.

Fromherz, A. *The Almohads: The Rise of an Islamic Empire*. London: I.B. Tauris, 2010. Paperback Edition 2012.

Gannūn, ʿA. *Dhikrayāt mashāhir rijāl al-Maghrib* (Tetuan, 1948), n° 9, 1-2.

García-Arenal, M. "The revolution of Fās in 869/1465 and the death of sultan ʿAbd al-Ḥaqq al-Marīnī." *Bulletin of the School Oriental and African Studies* 31 (1978): 43-66.

García-Gómez, E. *Andalucía contra Berbería*. Barcelona, 1976.

Garcin, J.-Cl. "Ibn Hawqal, l'Orient et le Maghreb." *Revue de l'Occident Musulman et de la Méditerranée* 35 (1983): 77-91.

Genicot, L. *Les généalogies*. Série typologie des sources du Moyen-Age occidental, 15. Louvain, 1975.

Gerber, J. *Jewish Society in Fez, 1450-1700: Studies in Communal and Economic Life*. Leiden, 1980.

Gernet, L. "De l'origine des Maures selon Procope." In *Mélanges de Géographie et d'Orientalisme offerts à E.-F. Gautier* (Tours, 1937): 234-44.

Gibb, H. A. R. "The Fiscal Rescript of ʿUmar II." *Arabica* 2(1955): 1-16.

Gill, M. "Maintenance, Building Operations, and Repairs in the Houses of the Qodesh in Fustat." *Journal of the Economic and Social History of the Orient* 14 (1971): 136-95.

Glick, T. F. *Islamic and Christian Spain in the Early Middle Ages: Comparative Perspectives on Social and Cultural Formation*. Princeton, 1979.

Goitein, S. D. "The Medical Profession in the Light of the Cairo Geniza Documents." *HUCA* 34 (1963): 177-94.

______. *A Mediterranean Society. The Jewish Communities of the Arab World as Portrayed in the Documents of the Cairo Geniza*. Berkeley and Los Angeles, 1967-1985. 5 vol.

Goldenberg, D. "The Curse of Ham, a Case of Rabbinic Racism?" *Struggles in the Promised Land*. J. Salzman and C. West eds. (Oxford, 1997): 21-51.

Goldziher, I. "Die suʿubijja unter den Muhammedanern in Spanien." *Zeitscrift der Deutchen Morgenlädischen Gesellschaft* 53 (1899): 601-620.

______. "Usages Juifs d'après la littérature religieuse des Musulmans." *Revue des Études Juives* 28(1894): 92-94.

Golvin, L. *Le Maghrib central à l'époque des Zīrīdes*. Paris, 1957.

Guichard, P. *Structures sociales "orientales" et "occidentales" dans l'Espagne musulmane*. Paris, 1977.

Guichard, P. and D. Menjot. "Les emprunts aux vaincus: les conséquences de la reconquête sur l'organisation institutionelle des Etats castillan et aragonais au Moyen Age." In *État et Colonisation au Moyen Age*. M. Balard ed. (Lyon, 1989): 379-96.

Al-Ḥakīm, Abū 'l-Ḥasan ʿAlī b. Yūsuf. *Al-dawḥa al-mushtabika f ī ḍawābiṭ dār al-sikka*. H. Muʿnis, ed. Madrid, 1960.

Hannoum, A. *The Legend of the Kahina: A Study in Historiography and Mythmaking in North Africa*. Ph.D. Diss. Princeton University, Dept. of Middle Eastern Studies. Princeton, 1995.

Hazard, H. *The Numismatic History of Late Medieval North Africa*. New York, 1952.

Hirschberg, H. Z. *Toldot ha-yehudim be-Afrika ha-tsfonit*. Jerusalem, 1965, 2 vols.

______. *A History of the Jews in North Africa*. E. Bashan and R. Attal, eds. Leiden, 1974-81. 2 vols.

Huff, T. *The Rise of Early Modern Science: Islam, China and the West*. Cambridge, 1993.

Ibn ʿAbd al-Ḥakam. *Conquête de l'Afrique du Nord et de l'Espagne*. A. Gateau trans. Paris, 1948.

Ibn Abi Zarʿ, Abū 'l-Ḥasan, *Kitāb al-anīs al-muṭrib bi-rawḍ al-Qirṭās*. C. J. Tornberg ed. Upsala, 1843.

Ibn al-Aḥmar, Abū 'l-Walīd. *Rawḍat en-Nisrīn*. G. Bouali and G. Marcais, eds. and trans. Paris, 1917.

Ibn al-Athīr. *Annales du Maghreb et de l'Espagne*. E. Fagnan trans. Alger, 1898.

Ib Baṭūṭah. *Tuḥfat al-Nuẓẓār: Voyages d'Ibn Batoutah*. G. Defrémery and B. R. Sanguinetti, eds. and trans. Paris, 1879. 4 vol.

Ibn Daud, A. *Sefer Ha-quabbalah*. G. D. Cohen ed. and trans. Philadelphia, 1967.

Ibn Ḥawqal. *Kitāb ṣūrat al-arḍ: Configuration de la Terre*. J. H. Kramers and G. Wiet trans. Paris, 1964.

Ibn ʿIdhārī. *Al-Bayān al-Mughrib*. G. S. Colin and E. Lévi-Provençal eds. Leiden, 1948-51. 2 vol.

_____. *Al-Bayān al-Mughrib*. 3rd part. A. Huici Miranda ed. Tétuan, 1960.

Ibn Khaldūn, ʿAbd al-Raḥman. *Al-Taʿrīf bi-Ibn Khaldūn wa-riḥlatuhu gharban wa-sharqan*. M. ben Tāwit al-Ṭanjī, ed., Cairo, 1951.

______. *Histoire des Berbères*. W. M. Baron De Slane, tr. Alger, 1852-56. Nouvelle édition publiée sous la direction de P. Casanova. Paris, 1925-56. 4 vols.

______. *The Muqaddimah: An Introduction to History*. F. Rosenthal, trans. Bollingen Series XLIII. Princeton, 1958.

Ibn al-Khaṭīb. *Miʿyār al-Ikhtiyār fī Dhikr al-Maʿahid wa 'l-Diyār*. M. K. Chabana, ed. 1977.

Ibn Khurradâhbih, Ibn al-Faqīh al-Ḥamadhānī et Ibn Rustih. *Description du Maghreb et de l'Europe aux IIIe-IXe sièles. (Extraits)* M. Hadj-Sadoq ed. and trans. Alger, 1949.

Ibn al-Qaṭṭān. *Kitāb Naẓm al-Jumān*. M. ʿAlī Makkī, ed., Tétuan, 1964.

Idris, H. R. *La Berbèrie orientale sous les Zirides (Xe-XIIe siècles)*. Paris, 1962. 2 vols.

______. "Les Zīrīdes d'Espagne." *Al-Andalus* 29 (1964): 39-147.

______. "Les Birzālides de Carmona." *Al-Andalus* 30 (1965): 49-63.

______. "Les Afṭasides de Bajadoz." *Al-Andalus* 30 (1965): 277-91.

______. "L'Occident musulman à l'avénèment des Abbasides d'après le chroniqueur zīrīde al-Raqīq." *Revue des Etudes Islamiques* 39 (1971): 209-291.

______. "Contribution à l'étude de la vie économique en Occident musulman médiéval: glanes de données chifrées." *Mélanges Le Tourneau: Revue de l'Occident Musulman et de la Méditerranée* (1972) 2: 75-87.

al-Idrīsī, Abū ʿAbd Allāh Muḥammad. *Description de l'Afrique et de l'Espagne*. R. Dozy and M. J. de Goeje eds. Leiden, 1866.

James, D. *Qur'āns of the Mamlūks*. London, 1988.

al-Jaznā'ī, Abū 'l-Ḥasan. *Zahrat el-As: La fleur du myrte*. A. Bel ed. and trans. Alger, 1923.

Johnson, M. A. *The Purpose of the Biblical Genealogies*. Cambridge, 1969.

Julien, Ch.-A. *Histoire d'Afrique du Nord*. 2nd éd. rev. R. Le Tourneau. Paris, 1952. English trans, *History of North Africa, Tunisia, Algeria, Morocco, from the Arab Conquest to 1830*. J. Petrie tr. and C. C. Stewart ed. London, 1970.

Kably, M. *Société, pouvoir et religion au Maroc à la fin du Moyen Age (XIVe-XVe siècle)*. Paris, 1986.

Kafadar, C. *Between Two Worlds: The Construction of the Ottoman State*. Berkeley, Los Angeles and London, 1995.

Khan, G. "Arabic Papyri." In *The Codicology of Islamic Manuscripts*. Y. Dutton ed. (London, 1995): 1-16.

Khaneboubi, A. *Les premiers sultans mérinides (1269-1331): Histoire politique et sociale*. Paris, 1987.

Kitāb al-ansāb li-Abī Ḥayyān. Ms. K1275 Bibliothèque Générale. Rabat, Morocco.

Klar, B. ed. *Megillat ahimaaz, the Chronicle of Ahimaaz, with collection of poems from Byzantine Southern Italy and additions*. Jerusalem, 1974.

Lacoste, Y. *Ibn Khaldun: naissance de l'histoire du tiers-monde*. Paris, 1966.

Lagardère, V. *Les Almoravides*. Paris, 1989.

______. "Moulins d'Occident musulman au moyen age (IXe au XVe siècles): al-Andalus." *Al-Qantara* 12(1991): 59-118.

______. *Histoire et société en Occident Musulman au moyen âge: Analyse du Miʿyār d'al-Wansharisi*. Collection de la casa de Velázquez 35. Madrid, 1995.

Lapidus, I. M. "Arab Settlement and Economic Development of Iraq and Iran in the Age of the Ummayad and Early Abbasid Caliphs." *The Islamic Middle East, 700-1900: Studies in Economic and Social History*. A. Udovitch, ed. (Princeton, 1981): 177-208.

Laroui, A. *The History of the Maghrib: An Interpretive Essay*. R. Manheim trans. Princeton, 1977.

Leo Africanus, J. *A Geographical Historie of Africa*. London, 1600.

______. *Description de l'Afrique*. A. Epaulard trans. Paris, 1956.

Le Tourneau, R. *Fès avant le protectorat*. Casablanca, 1949.

______. *Fez in the Age of the Marīnids*. Norman, 1961.

Lévi-Provençal, É. "Note sur un Qor'an royal du XIVe siècle." *Hespéris* 1 (1921): 83-86.

______. "Un nouveau texte d'histoire mérinide, le Musnad d'Ibn Marzūk." *Hespéris* 5 (1925): 1-82.

______. *Documents inédits d'histoire almohade: Fragments manuscrits du "legajo" 1919 du fonds Arabe de l'Escorial*. Paris, 1928.

______. *Fragments historiques sur les Berbères au Moyen-Age: Extraits inédits d'un receuil anonyme compilé en 712/1312 et intitulé Mafākhir al-Barbar*. Rabat, 1934.
______. "Un historiographe et poète de cour mérinide: Abū Fāris al-Malzūzī." *Annales des l'institut des études orientales* 1 (1934-35): 189-92.
______. "Les mémoires d'Abd Allāh dernier roi Zīrīde de Grenade: Fragments publiés d'après le manuscrit de la Bibliothèque d'al-Qarawīyīn à Fès." *Al-Andalus* 3 (1935): 233-344, 4 (1936-39): 29-145.
______., ed. *Trente-sept lettres officielles almohades*. Rabat, 1941.
______. *Un recueil de lettres officielles almohades*. Étude diplomatique, analyse et commentaire historique. *Extrait d'Hespéris 1941*. Paris, 1942.
______. *Histoire de l'Espagne Musulmane*. Paris, 1950-1953. 3 vol.
______. "Un nouveau récit de la conquête de l'Afrique du Nord par les Arabes." *Arabica* 1 (1954): 17-43.
______. "Le titre souverain des Almoravides et sa légitimation par le califat ʿabbāside." *Arabica* 2 (1955): 265-280.
______. "Le traité d'Adab al-kātib d'Abū Bakr Ibn Khaldūn." *Arabica* 2 (1955): 280-88.
Levy, H. J. "Meriva al Karka'a shel eretz-Yisrael baet ha'atika." *Studies in Jewish Hellenism*. (Jerusalem, 1960): 60-78.
Lewicki, T. "À propos d'une liste de tribus berbères d'Ibn Ḥawqal." *Folia Orientalia* 1 (1959): 128-35.
______. "Les historiens biographes et traditionnistes ibadites-wahbites de l'Afrique du Nord du VIIIe au XVIe siècle." *Folia Orientalia* 3 (1961): 1-134.
______. "Prophètes antimusulmans chez les Berbères mediévaux." *Atti del III Congresso di Studi Arabi e Islamici, Ravello, 1966*. (Napoli, 1967): 461-66.
______. "Les origines de l'Islam dans les tribus Berbères du Sahara occidental: Mūsa Ibn Nuṣayr et 'Ubayd Allāh Ibn Ḥabḥab." *Studia Islamica* 33 (1970): 203-14.
Linant de Bellefonds, Y. "Un problème de sociologie jurique. Les terres "communes" en pays d'Islam." *Studia Islamica* 10 (1959): 111-36.
Lopez, R. S. "The origin of the Merino sheep." *Joshua Starr Memorial volume: Studies in History and Philology*. Jewish Social Studies Publications 5 (New York, 1953): 168-71.
Lopez, R. S. and I. W. Raymond. *Medieval Trade in the Mediterranean World*. New York, 1955.
Makdisi, G. "On the Origin and Development of the College in Islam and the West." In *Islam and the Medieval West*. Kh. Semaan ed. (New York, 1980): 50-63.
al-Manūnī, M. "Nuẓūm al-dawla al-marīniyya." *Al-Baḥth al-ʿilmī 1* (Rabat, 1964): 97-127.
______. "Waṣf al-maghreb bī ayām al-sulṭān Abī 'l-Ḥasan al-marīnī." *Waraqāt ʿan al-ḥadāra al-maghribiya* (Rabat, 1979): 287-309.

al-Maqqarī, A. b. M. *Analectes sur l'histoire et la littérature des Arabes d'Espagne*. R. Dozy, G. Dugat, L. Krehl and W. Wright eds. Leiden, 1855-61.

______. *Nafḥ al-ṭibb*. I. Abbas, ed. Beirut, 1968.

Marín, M. "Inqibāḍ ʿan al-sulṭān: ʿUlamā' and Political Power in al-Andalus." In *Saber Religioso y Poder político en el Islam* (Madrid, 1994): 127-41.

Masqueray, E. *Chronique d'Abou Zakariya*. Alger, 1878.

Massignon, L. "L'influence de l'Islam au Moyen Age sur la fondation et l'essor des banques Juives." *Bulletin d'Etudes Orientales de l'Institut Français de Damas* 1 (1931). Reprinted in *Opera Minora* (Beirut) 1: 241-50.

Molina López, E. "Dos importantes privilegios a los emigrados andalusies en el Norte de Africa en el siglo XIII, contenidos en el Kitāb Zawāhir al-Fikār de Muḥammad b. al-Murābiṭ." *Cuadernos de Historia del Islam* 9 (1978-79): 5-31.

Monroe, J. *The shuʿūbiyya in al-andalus*. Berekely, 1970.

Montagne, R. *Les Berbèrs et le Makhzen dans le Sud du Maroc*. Paris, 1930.

Morony, M. "Landholding in Seventh-century Iraq: Late Sasanian and Early Islamic Patterns." *The Islamic Middle East 700-1900: Studies in Economic and Social History*. A. L. Udovitch ed. (Princeton,1981): 135-76.

Munson, H. Jr. *Religion and Power in Morocco*. New Haven, 1993.

al-Nābulusī, ʿUthmān b. Ibrāhīm. "Kitāb lumāʿ al-qawānīn." C. Becker and Cl. Cahen eds. *Bulletin des Etudes Orientales* 16 (1958-60): 119-29, Arabic text, 1-78.

Noriss, H. T. *The Berbers in Arabic Literature*. London and New York, 1982.

Al-Nubāhī, ʿAlī b. ʿAbdallāh. *Tārīkh quḍāt al-Andalus: Histoire des juges d'Andalousie intitulée Kitāb al-markaba al-ʿulya*. Beirut, 1966.

O'Kane, B. "Monumentality in Mamluk and Mongol Art and Architecture." *Art History* 4/19 (1996): 499-522.

O'mara, K. "The Kel Ahir Tuareg and the Problematic of Theories of the State." *The Maghreb Review* 19/1-2 (1994): 173-89.

al-Omari, Ibn Faḍl Allāh. *Masālik al-absār fī mamālik al-amsār*. Gaudefroy-Demombynes, trans. Paris, 1927.

Ouerdane, A. *La Question Berbère dans le mouvement national algérien, 1926-1980*. Québec, 1990.

Péretié, A. "Les Medersas de Fès." *Archives Marocaines* 18 (1912): 257-372.

Pons Boigues, F. *Los historiadores y géografos arábigo-españoles*. Madrid, 1898.

Popovic, A. *La révolte des esclaves en Iraq au IIIe/IXe siècle*. Bibl. d'études Islamiques 6. Paris, 1976.

Powers, D. "The Maliki Family Endowment: Legal Norms and Social Practices." *International Journal of Middle Eastern Studies* 25 (1993): 379-406.

Quandt, W. B. "The Berbers in the Algerian Political Elite." *Arabs and Berbers: From Tribe to Nation in North Africa*. E. Gellner and C. Micaud, eds. (London, 1972): 285-303.

Rabie, H. *The Financial System of Egypt A. H. 564-741/ A. H. 1169-1341*. Oxford, 1972.

Rachet, M. *Rome et les Berbères*. Collection Latomus 110. Bruxelles, 1970.

Revault, J., L. Golvin, and A. Amahan. *Palais et demeures de Fès: Vol. I. Époques mérinide et saadienne, XIV-XVII siècles*. Paris, 1985.

Riley-Smith, J. *The Feudal Nobility and the Kingdom of Jerusalem, 1174-1277*. London, 1973.

______. "The Survival in Latin Palestine of Muslim Administration." *The Eastern Mediterranean Lands in the Period of the Crusades*. P. M. Holt ed. (Warminster, 1977): 9-22.

Roy, B. and P. Poinsot. *Inscriptions Arabes de Kairouan*. Paris, 1950.

Salameh, Kh. and R. Schick, "The Qur'ān Manuscripts of the Islamic Museum, the Haram al-Sharīf, Jerusalem." *Al-ʿUsur al-Wusta: The Bulletin of Middle East Medievalists* 10/1, (1998): 1-3.

Salmon, G. "El-Qçar el-Kebir." *Archives Marocainces* 2 (Paris, 1905): 1-228.

Sassoon, D. S. *Diwan of Shemuel Hannaghid: Published for the first time in its entirety according to a unique manuscript (Ms. Sassoon 589) with an introduction and index of poems*. Oxford, 1934.

Savage, E. *A Gateway to Hell, a Gateway to Paradise: The North African Response to the Arab Conquest*. Princeton, 1997.

Scales, P. C. *The Fall of the Caliphate of Córdoba: Berbers and Andalusis in Conflict*. Leiden, 1994.

Schacht, J. "On Some Manuscripts in the Libraries of Morocco." *Hespéris-Tamuda* 9 (1968): 5-56.

______. "Sur quelques manuscrits de la bibliothèque d'al-Qarawīyyīn." *Études d'Orientalisme dédiés à la mémoire de É. Lévi-Provençal*. (Paris, 1962), 1: 271-284.

Schwartzfuchs, S. "Les Responsa et l'histoire des Juifs d'Afrique du Nord." *Communautés Juives des Marges Sahariennes du Maghreb*. M. Abitbol ed. (Jerusalem, 1982): 39-53.

Shatzmiller, M. "Les circonstances de la compostion du Musnad d'Ibn Marzūḳ." *Arabica* 22 (1975): 292-99.

______. "Etude d'historiographie mérinide: la "Nafḥa al-Nisrīniyya" et la "Rawḍat al-Nisrīn" d'Ibn al-Aḥmar." *Arabica* 24 (1977): 258-68.

______. *L'historiograhie Mérinide: Ibn Khaldūn et ses contemporains*. Leiden, 1982.

______. "Professions and Ethnic Origin of Urban Labourers in Muslim Spain: Evidence from a Moroccan Source." *Awraq* 5 (1983): 149-59.

______. "The Crusades and Islamic Warfare-A Re-evaluation." *Der Islam* 69 (1992): 247-87.

______. *Labour in the Medieval Islamic World*. Leiden, 1994.

Slouschz, N. "Hébraeo-Phéniciens et Judéo-Berbères." *Archives Marocaines* 14(1908). Kraus Reprint (1974)

Talbi, M. *L'Emirat Aghladide (184-296/800-909)*. Paris, 1966.

______. "Hérésie, acculturation et nationalisme des Berbères Bargawāṭa." *Proceedings of the First Congress on Mediterranean Studies of Arabo-Berber Influence*. M. Galley ed. with the collaboration of D. R. Marshall. (Algiers, 1973): 217-33.

______. "The Law and Economy in Ifrīqiya (Tunisia) in the third Islamic Century: Agriculture and the Role of Slaves in the Country's Economy." in *The Islamic Middle East, 700-1900, Studies in Economic and Social History*. A. Udovitch ed. (Princeton, 1981): 209-51.

Tibi, A. T., trans. *The Tibyān: Memoirs of ʿAbd Allāh B. Buluggin Last Zīrīd Amīr of Granada*. Leiden, 1986.

Terrase H. *La mosquée des Andalous à Fès: Avec une étude d'épigraphie historique de G. S. Colin*. Publications de l'Institut des Hautes Études Marocaines 38. Paris, 1942.

______. *La Grande Mosquée de Taza*. Paris, 1943.

______. *Histoire du Maroc des origines a l'établissement du protectorat français*. Casablanca, 1949-50. 2 vols.

______. "Trois bains mérinides du Maroc." *Mélanges offerts à William Marçais*. (Paris, 1950): 311-20.

______. *La mosquée al-Quaraouyin à Fès: Avec une étude de Gaston Deverdun sur les inscriptions historiques de la mosquée*. Archéologie Meditérranéene 4. Paris, 1968.

Thébert, Y. and J. L. Biget. "L'Afrique après la disparition de la cité classique: Cohérence et ruptures dans l'histoire maghrébine." *L'Afrique dans L'Occident romain*. (Rome, 1990): 575-602.

Thoden, R. *Abū 'l-Ḥasan ʿAli: Merinidenpolitik zwischen Nordafrika und Spanien in den Jahren 710-752/1310-1351*. Freiburg im Breisgau, 1973.

Tzemah Duran (Rashbatz), Shimon b. *Sefer ha-tashbetz*. Amsterdam, 1738.

Urvoy, D. "La pensée d'Ibn Tūmart." *Bulletin des Études Orientales* 27 (1974): 19-44.

Vajda, G. *Juda ben Nissim Ibn Malka, philosophe Juif Marocain*. Paris, 1954.

______. *Kitsur 'ivri shel Kitāb uns al-gharīb wa-tafsīr Sefer Yetsirah le-Rabi Yehudah ben Nisim ibn Malkah*. Ramat-Gan, 1974.

Van Berchem, M. "Titres califiens d'Occident, à propos de quelques monnaies mérinides et ziyanides." *Journal Asiatique* (Mars-Avril, 1907): 245-335.

Vidal Castro, F. "Aḥmad al-Wansharīsī (m. 914/1508). Principales aspectos de su vida." *Al-Qantara* 12(1991): 315-52.

______. "Las obras de Aḥmad al-Wansharīsī (m. 914/1508). Inventario analítico." *Anaquel de Estudios Árabes* 3(1992): 73-112.

______. "Economia y sociedad en al-Andalus y el-Maghreb a traves del Miʿyār de al-Wansharīsī. Breve introduction a su contenido." *Actas del II coloquio Hispano-Marroqui de ciencias historicas* (Madrid, 1992): 339-56.

Viguera, M. J. "Las cartas de al-Gazālī y al-Ṭurṭūshī al soberano almorávid Yūsuf B. Tashufīn." *Al-Andalus* 42 (1977): 341-74.

Villanueva Rico, M. del Carmen. *Habices de las mezquitas de la ciudad de Granada y sus alquerias*. Madrid, 1961-1966. 2 vols.

Villanueva Rico, M. del C. and A. Soria. "Fuentes toponímicas granadinas: Los libros de bienes habices." *Al-Andalus* 19 (1954): 457-62.

Viré, M.-M. "Notes d'épigraphie Magribine: Trois inscriptions des XIVe et XVe siècles." *Arabica* 4 (1957): 250-61.

Vonderheyden, M. *L'histoire des rois Obaidides (les caliphs fātimides)*. Alger-Paris, 1927.

Wansbrough, J. "The Decolonization of North African History." *Journal of African History* 4 (1968): 643-650.

al-Wathā'iq: majmū'āt dawriyya tuṣdiruha mudīriyyat al-wathā'iq al-malikiyya. Rabat, 1976.

Warmington, B. H. *The North African Provinces From Diocletian to the Vandal Conquest*. Cambridge, 1954. Reprinted Connecticut, 1971.

Wasserstein, D. *The Rise and Fall of the Party-Kings: Politics and Society in Islamic Spain, 1002-1086*. Princeton, 1985.

Weinstein, M. "The Uninterrupted Existence of Jewish Population in North Africa." *Mizrah uma'arav*. (Ramat-Gan, 1974): 37-58.

Witkam, J. J. "The Human Element Between Text and Reader: The Ijāza in Arabic Manuscripts." *The Codicology of islamic Manuscripts*. Y. Dutton ed. (London, 1995): 123-36.

Ya'là, M., ed. *Tres textos Árabes sobre Beréberes en el Occidente Islámico*. Fuentes Arábico-Hispanas, 20. Madrid, 1996.

Zafrani, H. *Les Juifs du Maroc: Vie social, economique et religieuse*. Paris, 1972.

Zakarya, M. *Deux palais du Caire médiéval: Waqf et architecture*. Paris, 1983.

Zbiss, M. *Inscriptions du Gorjani: Contribution à l'histoire des Almohades et des Ḥafṣides*. Tunis, 1962.

Index

www.ingramcontent.com/pod-product-compliance
Lightning Source LLC
Chambersburg PA
CBHW020700270326
41928CB00005B/210
9781558769519